No Longer the Same

NEW APPROACHES TO RELIGION AND POWER

Series editor: Joerg Rieger

While the relationship of religion and power is a perennial topic, it only continues to grow in importance and scope in our increasingly globalized and diverse world. Religion, on a global scale, has openly joined power struggles, often in support of the powers that be. But at the same time, religion has made major contributions to resistance movements. In this context, current methods in the study of religion and theology have created a deeper awareness of the issue of power: Critical theory, cultural studies, postcolonial theory, subaltern studies, feminist theory, critical race theory, and working class studies are contributing to a new quality of study in the field. This series is a place for both studies of particular problems in the relation of religion and power as well as for more general interpretations of this relation. It undergirds the growing recognition that religion can no longer be studied without the study of power.

Series editor:

Joerg Rieger is Wendland-Cook Professor of Constructive Theology in the Perkins School of Theology at Southern Methodist University.

Titles:

No Longer the Same: Religious Others and the Liberation of Christian Theology
David R. Brockman

The Subject, Capitalism, and Religion: Horizons of Hope in Complex Societies
Jung Mo Sung

Imaging Religion in Film: The Politics of Nostalgia
M. Gail Hamner

No Longer the Same

Religious Others and the
Liberation of Christian Theology

David R. Brockman

palgrave
macmillan

NO LONGER THE SAME
Copyright © David R. Brockman, 2011.

First published in hardcover in 2011 by PALGRAVE MACMILLAN® in the United States—a division of St. Martin's Press LLC, 175 Fifth Avenue, New York, NY 10010.

Where this book is distributed in the UK, Europe and the rest of the world, this is by Palgrave Macmillan, a division of Macmillan Publishers Limited, registered in England, company number 785998, of Houndmills, Basingstoke, Hampshire RG21 6XS.

Palgrave Macmillan is the global academic imprint of the above companies and has companies and representatives throughout the world.

Palgrave® and Macmillan® are registered trademarks in the United States, the United Kingdom, Europe and other countries.

ISBN: 978-0-230-10943-8

Library of Congress Cataloging-in-Publication Data

Brockman, David R.
    No longer the same: religious others and the liberation of Christian theology / David R. Brockman.
        p. cm.— (New approaches to religion and power)
    ISBN 978-0-230-10855-4 (alk. paper)
    1. Christianity and other religions. 2. Theology. I. Title.

BR127.B745 2011
261.2–dc22   2010028376

A catalogue record of the book is available from the British Library.

Design by Scribe Inc.

First PALGRAVE MACMILLAN paperback edition: March 2012

10 9 8 7 6 5 4 3 2 1

Transferred to Digital Printing in 2012

For Eleanor:

Inspiration, Collaborator, Spouse

Draco Dormiens Nunquam Titillandus

Also edited by David Brockman

The Gospel Among Religions, coeditor with Ruben L. F. Habito, 2010

Contents

a stranger, suddenly
showing up, makes the very thing you were doing no longer the same. That is[,] suddenly
what you thought, when you were alone, and
doing what you were doing, changes because someone else
shows up.

—Charles Olson, "COLE'S ISLAND"

Acknowledgments

It takes a village to raise a child—and to produce a book. Despite the solitary name on the title page, the present work has matured under the nurture and guidance of a number of "village elders" (in wisdom and experience, not in age). Charles M. Wood read and commented on an early version with a systematic theologian's eye for coherence and balance. Ruben L. F. Habito, whose own work embodies the principles I outline in the Conclusion, helped me to sharpen that chapter considerably. Catherine Keller has been an enthusiastic supporter of this project from its toddler stage; it was through her good offices that I was able to present a condensed version of parts of this book at a conference on Badiou, Deleuze, and Whitehead at Claremont in 2007.

Joerg Rieger deserves special thanks not only for laying the foundation for my work here (in his *God and the Excluded*), but also for his faith in the importance and viability of this project and his unstinting efforts to bring it to print. Joerg read through numerous drafts of this work; he pushed me to think more deeply about the issues and always to keep my eye on the larger social, political, and economic implications. It is an honor to help Joerg begin his new Religion and Power series for Palgrave Macmillan.

I should also mention two of my professors at Brite Divinity School, where I did my master's work in the 1990s. David Gouwens inspired my love of Christian theology and encouraged me to pursue a career as a theologian; he also introduced me to the theology of Karl Barth. Kenneth Cracknell awakened my interest in the theology of religions and encouraged my initial efforts to make theological sense of my experience as a Christian exploring the profound truths of the Buddhist tradition. Kenneth also took time to read and comment on the entire manuscript in its present form.

I would also like to thank my students, first at the Perkins School of Theology and now at Brite Divinity School, with whom I have discussed these issues over the past years. Their feedback and suggestions have helped to sharpen my thinking and spurred me to find ways to help nonspecialists grasp the Badiouan framework.

I am grateful to the anonymous reviewers who recommended this work for publication and made constructive suggestions for improving the work. My editors at Palgrave Macmillan, Burke Gerstenschlager and Samantha Hasey, deserve special thanks for helping me navigate the byways of the publication process.

I would be remiss if I did not also acknowledge the support of the staff at Panera Bread in Fort Worth, who provided the pleasant space where I did much of my work on this book, not to mention the coffee needed to keep my wits sharp.

This book began life as my doctoral dissertation, titled "Turning to Religious Others: Visions and Blindspots in Modern Christian Reflection about Non-Christians," and completed in December 2006. I owe an immense debt to the members of my dissertation committee, whose names I have already mentioned: Joerg Rieger (chair), Ruben L. F. Habito, Catherine Keller, and Charles M. Wood. For their wisdom, their probing questions, their perceptive suggestions, and their selfless assistance during the dissertation period and since, I remain deeply grateful.

Finally, words cannot express the depth of my debt to my spouse, Eleanor Forfang-Brockman. She made the turn to religious others many years before I, and she remains my principal source of inspiration. She has read and commented on every draft of this work, from the dissertation stage to the present form, which surely qualifies her for sainthood. For her support, patience, and love, I am truly grateful.

Needless to say, I am solely responsible for any errors, flaws, and infelicities.

Introduction

For much of its two thousand-year history, Christianity in the West has operated as if it were the only game in town, or at least the only game that mattered. While Christians were conscious of Jews as a minority in their midst and of Muslims at the borders of European Christendom, they engaged in surprisingly little dialogue with these two sister religions.[1] Christian theology—what Christians do whenever they think seriously about what they believe and what those beliefs mean for their own lives—tended to be a conversation in which Christians talked among themselves, as if the wider religious world did not exist, did not matter, or was simply a realm of the idolatrous and the damned.

As long as Christianity remained a major player in Western culture (as it was throughout the medieval and Renaissance periods), its insularity went largely unquestioned. Since at least the eighteenth century, however, European/neo-European Christianity (the Christianity of Europe and of those cultures transported by Europeans to other parts of the world[2]) has been shaken by two fundamental challenges: a crisis of authority that undermined the very foundations of Christian thought, and a growing awareness of religious diversity not only in the wider world but also in the West itself. Christians have been scrambling to deal with these challenges ever since.

A Crisis of Authority

The first challenge, which originated within Western culture itself, was a vigorous and sustained assault on the traditional sources of authority in Christianity: the assumed universally valid truth of divine revelation in the Bible, either as interpreted by the church (for Catholics) or in its "plain sense" (for Protestants). Advances in science and technology undermined traditional Christian beliefs about the structure of the cosmos and the origins and development of life. Buoyed by these advances, prophets of modernity such as Voltaire, Immanuel Kant, and G. W. F. Hegel promoted human reason as the basis of knowledge and thought. Scholars applied new methods of historical research and critical analysis to the biblical texts, calling into question the unity and privileged status of scripture, and challenging traditional views of Jesus as universal savior. The rise of democratic political systems, a new emphasis on the individual, and secular confidence in human progress undercut the traditional doctrine of original sin and the belief in evil as a personified force (Satan).

In recent decades, the challenge of modernity has given way to the even more severe challenge of postmodernism, poststructuralism, and postcolonialism. By interrogating how meaning is constructed, and stressing the critical role of language (the so-called "linguistic turn" in philosophy), these "post-ist" movements assert the fundamental cultural and historical situatedness of all thought. The collective force of these movements has been to call into question principles previously taken for granted in Christian thought, such as the possibility of absolute truth claims or of a Gospel message valid for all times and all peoples.

Some Christians have responded to these challenges by rejecting them and attempting to take refuge in various forms of fundamentalism that hew to a literal reading of an inerrant Bible. Other Christian thinkers, however, have struggled to rebuild the foundations of Christian theology for the new era. They have done so in at least four major ways. Liberal Christianity seeks to connect Christian faith with the human situation by grounding theology in religious experience, such as Friedrich Schleiermacher's "feeling of absolute dependence." In opposition to this liberal "turn" to experience, neo-orthodox Christians argue that theology should be based on the revelation of the transcendent God, primarily in and through the texts of the Bible (though, unlike fundamentalists, they reject biblical inerrancy and take advantage of recent scholarship on the biblical texts). Other Christian thinkers, influenced by the "linguistic turn" of post-ist thought, seek to ground Christian theology in the language and symbols of the Christian community. Additionally, the various theologies of liberation ground Christian thought in the experience of the poor, the oppressed, and others who are marginalized or excluded by the dominant social, political, and economic structures. (We will take a closer look at each of these four approaches in subsequent chapters.)

The Challenge of Religious Others

European/neo-European Christian thinkers have been much slower to come to grips with the second major challenge of the modern period: the growing realization of the vast religious diversity of the world. Throughout the last two centuries, it has become increasingly clear that Christianity is not the only game in town or even the only game that matters. Not only are most of the world's inhabitants not Christians, but there exist venerable and sophisticated religious systems that envision the Ultimate, the cosmos, and humanity in ways that differ radically from Christianity. Just as important, the West itself is growing religiously more diverse.[3] For many Europeans and neo-Europeans today, Christianity is merely one religious option among many.

Generally, European/neo-European Christian thinkers have relegated the task of coping with the challenge of religious others to a subdiscipline of Christian theology called the *theology of religions*.[4] This subdiscipline I have characterized elsewhere as "Christian theological reflection about the existence and significance of religious others, and about their relation to Christianity and that which it proclaims (e.g., salvation, knowledge of God)."[5] Until very recently, Christian theologies of religions have been characterized by three basic approaches, each based on a particular view of the place of religious others in salvation. *Exclusivist* approaches claim that salvation is available exclusively through faith in Jesus Christ. *Inclusivists* generally agree with their exclusivist counterparts that salvation is only through Jesus Christ, but argue that Christ's saving activity extends beyond the bounds of the explicitly Christian community. *Pluralist* theologies cast the net of salvific efficacy as widely as possible: there are many religious paths to salvation, Christianity being one.[6]

While much interesting and important work has been done in the Christian theology of religions, it has not altered the shape of Christian thought generally. In particular, it has yet to prompt Christian theologians to rethink their choice of *sources* and *norms* for theology. A theological *source* is any element that one uses in doing theology: for example, a religious text like the Bible, or the experience of particular groups of people. Theological *norms* are criteria the theologian uses to evaluate the sources she uses and to structure the theological claims she makes. Some of the norms that have been used in traditional Christian theology include the Bible, the tradition of the Church, and human reason.[7] Both sources and norms are necessary to any theology.

It is still rare—even recently—to find a Western Christian theologian making use of non-Christian texts, beliefs, or practices as sources or norms for theological reflection. Though there are a few notable exceptions, in the main Christian theology continues either to ignore or, in some cases, to dismiss the perspectives, texts, practices, and experiences of religious others as outside the bounds of the relevant, let alone the normative.[8] Christian theology in the West still tends to operate as if Christianity were the only game in town.

A Question of Power—and More

The stubborn insularity of Christian theology has come under fire in recent years. A number of Christian thinkers have called on their fellow Christians to engage in dialogue with religious others, on various grounds. Some thinkers, like Kenneth Cracknell and David Lochhead, find a "dialogical imperative" (as Lochhead calls it) within Christian teaching itself. Lochhead contends that Christ's command to love one's neighbor translates into an "imperative to seek dialogue and to be open to dialogue wherever and from whomever it is offered."[9] Similarly, Cracknell contends that dialogue with religious others constitutes truly authentic witness to the Christian gospel.[10] Other Christian thinkers promote dialogue on practical grounds. For instance, Paul Knitter argues that Christians must seek common ground with religious others in order to tackle the "suffering that is draining the life and imperiling the future of humankind and the planet."[11] The global situation of human and ecological suffering, Knitter contends, transcends religious differences and makes interreligious encounter both necessary and possible.[12] Religions are uniquely equipped to respond to this situation, both because they all offer a vision of hope that people and the world "can be different, transformed, better," and because "All religion, in infinitely varied forms, brings about *metanoia*, internal change, enlightenment."[13] Thus Knitter advocates a salvation-centered ("soteriocentric") approach to interreligious dialogue, an approach in which "a concern for *soteria* (salvation) or eco-human well-being and justice can and must provide the 'common ground' for interreligious dialogue in our global village."[14]

The arguments of Lochhead, Cracknell, Knitter, and other advocates of interreligious dialogue are important and worth serious consideration. This book, however, takes a different approach. First, it deals with theology as *discourse*. More than just talk, discourse actively *constructs* the objects about which it speaks. And it exerts power, by including some voices and excluding others, and by shaping what its practitioners accept as "real," "true," or "given."[15] Christian discourse constructs the Christian "thing"—what I will call "the Christian."

Unlike most arguments for interreligious dialogue, this book does not take the boundaries between Christians and religious others as simply a given. Instead, it treats the categories "Christian" and "not-Christian" in Christian theology as *discursively constructed*. The boundaries that set off Christians from religious others are not merely a fact of life, nor are they part and parcel of some mythical "essence of Christianity." Rather, the boundaries between the "Christian" and the "not-Christian" are actively created by Christian theological discourse, especially through the theologian's (and by extension, the Christian community's) inclusion of some elements and exclusion of others. The process of discursive construction in theology will be discussed in some detail in Chapter 1.

Furthermore, this book focuses on how those basic boundary-drawing processes are an exercise of *power*, and how the exercise of power affects Christian theology itself. The phrase "exercise of power" perhaps brings to mind a manager's power to hire and fire employees or a police officer's power to make arrests. While a theologian doesn't exercise that kind of power, she may exercise a kind of power that is ultimately even more important: the power to determine what can be said about Ultimate Reality and about our relation to it. As we've seen, when a theologian does theology, she chooses certain sources and norms—for example, the Bible, works by other Christian thinkers, passages from denominational liturgies, or perhaps findings from contemporary scientific or historical research. It is precisely in making those choices that the theologian exercises power. She determines who's "in" and who's "out"; whose voices will be heard prominently in the theological conversation, whose voices will be marginalized, and whose voices will be absent altogether. In other words, by choosing sources and norms, she exercises the power to set the boundaries between what's "Christian" and what's not.

Despite their far-reaching consequences, these acts of boundary drawing—of inclusion, marginalization, and exclusion—are frequently not conscious; they may be hidden beneath the surface of the theological arguments. Furthermore, they may have subtle connections with other dynamics of power in the theologian's social, political, or economic context; for example, the exclusion of certain voices from the Christian theological conversation may link with the mindset of Eurocentricism and colonialism (as we will see in later chapters).

Similarly, the theological exercise of power can even work against the content of theological reflection, the kinds of claims the theologian makes about God or about Christianity. To use a very simple illustration: if the theologian declares that God reaches out to all people and yet does not bother to listen to how religious others experience God, one has reason to wonder whether the theologian really means what she says about God.

A Personal Encounter

This book is not inspired merely by theoretical considerations. The approach I take here grows out of my own experience in awakening from a relatively narrow view of Christianity, in response to personal challenges that parallel those facing Western Christianity as a whole.

When I began theological studies in the mid-1990s, I was a fairly conservative Protestant. My personal theology was something of a muddle, mingling poorly digested bits of Anglo-Catholicism (to which I had recently converted) with the *sola scriptura, sola fide* perspective of the Lutheran church where I had initially learned my Christianity. Like many Christian seminarians, I had felt the transforming power of God's love in Christ, and I sought to share that good news with others (and still do today). Religious others were not really on my radar screen. Certainly I knew that Christianity was not the only game in town. In my youth I had had some informal exposure to Buddhism through the works of Beat writers such as Allen Ginsberg and Gary Snyder; they in turn led me to read the Zen scholar D. T. Suzuki, though without much real comprehension at the time. Although my experience of a loving God did not predispose me to believe that salvation would be unavailable to non-Christians, I really didn't

6 • No Longer the Same

have the conceptual categories to make sense of that problem. Thus other religions hovered as a vaguely troubling, ghostlike presence, just beyond my firmly Christian-centered consciousness.

This changed a few years into my seminary studies, when, initially for entirely therapeutic reasons, I began to practice Zen meditation (*zazen*). At first I practiced under the guidance of my spouse Eleanor, who had participated in Zen *sesshins* (extended meditation sessions) in past years; later, Eleanor and I sat with a local Zen group. To my great surprise, not only did I find that *zazen* calmed the mind, but I began to have fleeting glimpses of nonduality, the "dropping away of self," the fundamental breakdown of separation between subject and object, self and other. As those familiar with Buddhist teaching know, this meditative experience—I will call it "the Zen experience," without claiming either that it is authoritative or that my experience is duplicated by all practitioners—is not escape to some placid, disembodied, other-worldly transcendence. Rather, it is an immersion in immanence, in "interbeing" or interdependent arising (*pratītya samutpāda*). It is the realization of radical *non*separation from the living, breathing, buzzing, spinning world.

The Buddhists, I began to realize, were definitely on to something—and something that was largely ignored within the Christian community as I knew it. In order to understand what I was experiencing, I began a serious study of Buddhism generally. This continued and deepened in the following decade, as one component of my PhD work at Southern Methodist University, where I studied with another Christian practitioner of Zen, Ruben L. F. Habito.

Though the Zen experience has had a powerful impact on my life and work, it has not challenged my belief in the fundamental authority of Christ. Yet having undergone something of the Zen experience, I faced a special problem as a Christian: to "articulate [that] experience in a way that issues from and resonates with the Biblical worldview upon which [one] bases her own self-understanding as a Christian."[16] The Zen experience raised some sticky theological questions, which have been the focus of my work ever since.[17] How does an authentically Christian theology account for the existence of deep, powerful, life-changing truth outside the Christian tradition? If the Church is, as the Episcopal *Book of Common Prayer* puts it, "the pillar and ground of truth," how are we to account for and understand the existence of truth outside the Church?[18] Furthermore, if Christians have missed out on the important truths revealed in Zen, what else have we missed by excluding religious others from the theological conversation? What are we doing to ourselves—to our theology—when we fail to listen to what religious others have to say?

The Aim of This Book

Those questions are at the heart of this book. It seeks to bring to light the often-hidden dynamics of inclusion, marginalization, and exclusion that are at work in four major forms of contemporary Christian thought. It links these theological power dynamics with the exercise of social, political, and economic power in the context in which each form of Christian theology arose.

The central argument of this book is that excluding non-Christian voices from the theological conversation blinds Christian thought to aspects of its own character and of the God to whom it seeks to be faithful. If Christians do not attend to these blind spots, all the interreligious dialogue in the world will change nothing.

To see why this is so, we need to dig down to the very foundations of Christian thought, to the level where theology establishes itself as Christian rather than as something else. We need to investigate some very basic questions. How does the split between "Christian" and "not-Christian" occur in the first place, and what power dynamics are at work in that division? How do these dynamics link with processes of marginalization and exclusion already at work in the social, political, and economic spheres? How do these dynamics affect basic decisions about which voices "count" in Christian theology and which do not? Most important, what are the consequences of these most basic of choices? How do dynamics of marginalization and exclusion affect the theology that results—the kinds of things Christians say about God, humanity, salvation, and Christianity itself?

Chapter 1 tackles the question of why and how the witness of non-Christians is relevant to an authentically Christian theology. It does so by drawing on the example of Jesus and considering factors in the contemporary world. It also describes in more detail the process of discursive construction, the process by which Christian theology constructs the "Christian" and the "not-Christian." In this chapter, I argue that the fundamental insight of liberation theology—that Christian theologians must learn to see the world through the eyes of the marginalized—should be applied to those who are marginalized and excluded by Christian discourse itself. To further this effort, Chapter 2 offers conceptual tools for thinking about how power operates in Christian theology's construction of religious others, and how the exercise of power introduces blind spots in the resulting theological formulations.

Using these conceptual tools, Chapters 3 through 6 investigate power dynamics and blind spots toward religious others in the work of four theologians who represent the major modes of Christian theological discourse, which developed in response to the modern-postmodern crisis of authority discussed earlier: liberalism, neo-orthodoxy, postliberalism, and liberation theology. The investigation into each mode addresses four questions: How does it construct the Christian and religious others? What is the theologian's attitude toward religious others, and how does this attitude follow from the nature of the discourse? In what ways does this approach contribute to meaningful encounter with religious others, and in what ways does it fall short? How does the exclusion of religious others limit or distort the Christian theological vision?

Finally, Chapter 7 offers a constructive proposal for meaningful encounter between Christian theology and religious others. It calls for several substantial changes in the way Christians do theology: a more fluid sense of Christian inside-outside boundaries; a renewed emphasis on Christian theology as self-critical inquiry, focusing on theological blind spots toward the religious other; and the incorporation of the witness of religious others by widening the range of theological sources and norms beyond those traditionally considered "Christian."

CHAPTER 1

Outsiders and Insiders
Why Religious Others Matter
to Christian Theology

In the previous chapter, I criticized Christian theology for failing to listen to what religious others have to say. Yet why should Christians care about what non-Christians think? What's wrong with a sharp separation between the Christian "inside" and the non-Christian "outside"? Isn't Christian theology an inherently intra-Christian conversation, a discourse carried on *by* Christians *about* Christian belief *for* Christian purposes? If so, why should it include non-Christian voices?

These are good questions. In a sense, this book as a whole constitutes one large-scale response to them. Several rationales for rethinking the boundaries of the Christian "thing" will be discussed later in this chapter. For a preliminary answer, however, we need look no further than the ministry of Jesus himself.

Jesus, Religious Others, and the Divine Other

As the powerful of his time recognized all too well, Jesus was a troublemaker. He made a habit of unsettling insiders, especially religious insiders—a fact too often neglected by many Christian insiders after Jesus' time. The Gospel accounts speak of a Jesus concerned with breaking down religious, ethnic, and social barriers between people—particularly those barriers by which some persons exalt themselves and exclude and oppress those who are different. Jesus' eschatological community, which he called the "Reign of God," was made up of the poor, women, heretics, the sick—in short, people who were "othered" (marginalized or excluded) by the dominant social and religious structures of his society and his time. One scholar describes Jesus' Reign of God as composed of "nuisances and nobodies."[1]

Indeed, Jesus even intimated that religious outsiders have much to teach religious insiders. The paradigmatic text is the parable of the compassionate Samaritan (Lk 10:29–37), addressed to a religious insider, a scholar in the Jewish law. In this story, love of neighbor is personified not by religious insiders but by a despised outsider. A traveler is assaulted by bandits and left for dead by the side of the road. A priest and a Levite, two religious insiders in the Temple cult of Judaism of the first century CE, do not stop to help the victim; if he turns out to be dead, touching his body would make them ritually unclean. However, a Samaritan does stop to help, and ends up nursing the victim back to life. The story takes on an added "edge" when one considers the enmity that prevailed between Jews and Samaritans at that time—not to mention the fact that only a few verses earlier, the evangelist tells us that Jesus and his disciples had recently been rejected by a Samaritan village (Lk 9:51–56).[2]

Having told the story, Jesus asks the scholar which of the three characters displayed neighbor love, and the latter has no choice but to answer, "The one who showed him mercy," meaning the Samaritan. (It is perhaps symptomatic of the first-century Jewish community's contempt for Samaritans that the scholar cannot bring himself to say "the Samaritan.") Jesus replies, "Go and do likewise" (Lk 10:37); in other words, follow the example of the religious outsider, not the priest or the Levite.

In this tale, when the stranger—the religious outsider—shows up, things are no longer the same. No longer does the hegemonic purity code prevail, dividing clean from unclean. One who lives outside that code (at least from the priestly perspective) turns out to be more faithful to the spirit of the divine law than those who scrupulously follow what they have always assumed to be God's teaching. This story is not an indictment of the Jewish Law itself; rather, it serves as a reminder that God always transcends religious structures and practices, even those of people who seek to follow God.

What Jesus does here, and in other instances in which he contrasts the faith of religious outsiders with that of insiders, is indicate that the dominant religious, ethnic, and social conceptions of "inside" and "outside" have no part in the Reign of God. In short, insider status conveys no assurance of righteousness or truth.[3]

The result is (or should be) a revolutionary transformation of the understanding of inside and outside, and of the processes that establish the boundaries of the Christian "thing." The "inside" Jesus proclaims is constituted by faithfulness to the fundamental truth that God exceeds the systems and structures erected by humans—those that establish the dominance of some persons over others, and even those that appear to have divine authority behind them. As Joerg Rieger puts it, "We will not find God where God can be controlled."[4]

This divine excess points to another key Christian concept, which will be crucially important to the argument in this book: the concept of God as *divine Other*. As the transcendent source of all being, God is qualitatively different from humans and other beings. (In philosophical terms, God is "ontically" other.) While Christians hold that God can be known through the divine self-revelation in Jesus Christ, God nevertheless remains beyond whatever finite humans can conceive or imagine. (Philosophers would say that God is "noetically" or "epistemologically" other.) As fundamentally other, God can never be fully represented or explained, let alone controlled, by mere human systems or constructions—even those of Christianity itself.

The otherness and excess of God have two crucial implications. First, God is always capable of surprising us—not least by self-emptying, "taking the form of a slave, being born in human likeness," and becoming "obedient to the point of death—even death on a cross" (Phil 2:7–8).[5] Second, just as the omnipotent God becomes slave and victim in Jesus, God may also speak and act through those who are enslaved, victimized, repressed, or othered by the dominant social, political, economic, and religious structures—the stranger, the poor, the oppressed, the religious other. The "Judgment of the Nations" in Matthew (25:31–46) illustrates this. In this passage, the Son of Man identifies himself with the hungry, the stranger, the sick, and the prisoner; he rewards those who cared for these marginalized persons, and punishes those who did not. Here, Jesus engages in some inside-outside discourse but of a very unusual sort. He insists that devotion to him must be lived out in compassionate service to those who are on the underside of society—the poor, the stranger, even the prisoner. He explicitly aligns the "king" and "judge" with those on the underside. In this astonishing reversal of the status quo, as in many similar passages, Jesus' "insiders" are those who remain open to the God who cannot be controlled.

Liberating Christian Theology

Sadly, traditional Western Christian theology has failed to grasp this fundamental lesson of Christ's teaching. Instead, it has itself engaged in marginalization and exclusion, often linked to similar processes in the wider culture, such as patriarchy, heterosexism, classism, racism, colonialism, Eurocentrism, and other forms of sociopolitical-economic oppression. For centuries, Christian theology has sided with the powers that be, either explicitly, by providing them with religious justification, or implicitly, by systematically excluding the voices and experience of those who were also excluded by the dominant social, political, and economic structures. Women, people of color, gay and lesbian persons, the poor, and others have been largely shut out of the theological conversation.

To date, only one strand of Christian theology has fully taken to heart Jesus' boundary-shattering command to embrace as full partners in the theological conversation those estranged by social, political, and economic structures. I have in mind the various theologies of liberation, which include not only the liberation theology associated with Latin America but also a host of other theological concerns, including feminist, womanist, *mujerista*, and black theologies. These diverse liberation approaches share a common focus on the marginalized and the excluded, and a common critique of the structures that marginalize and exclude. Indeed, theologies of liberation explicitly name those structures as *sinful*: sin is no longer just a personal problem; it is also systemic, embodied in social, political, and economic structures.

Liberation's focus on the marginalized and the excluded stems in turn from a realization of the long-neglected connection between God and the excluded, between the divine Other and marginalized human others. Roberto Goizueta states the connection succinctly: "Unless we place ourselves alongside the poor, unless we look at reality through their eyes, we are unable to see, recognize, or worship the God who walks with the poor."[6] Joerg Rieger makes the link in terms of the divine Other: "Without respect for the [human] other, respect for the [divine] Other is in trouble." In short, "no Other without others."[7]

Yet liberation theology is not concerned solely with promoting the liberation of marginalized peoples from structures of sin (crucial though that process continues to be). It also works to liberate *Christian theology itself* from its own structures and processes of marginalization and exclusion. In the wake of liberation theology, Christian theological discourse can no longer be just more of the same. It can no longer be limited to a conversation among white, male, straight, economically privileged, First World theologians (such as myself). Liberation theology teaches us that insofar as we wish to do theology in fidelity to the Christ event, we must learn to listen to those with whom Christ chooses to walk, those who have been made strangers by structures of sin—both within the Church and without.

As Rieger argues, the concerns of mainstream Christian theology in the modern-postmodern era have grown increasingly disconnected from those of the vast majority of the world's population. He contends that theology has failed to address, let alone resist, the widening gap between rich and poor, the rise in hunger and infant mortality, and the emergence of a new slavery, in which between 27 and 200 million persons worldwide live in slavelike conditions of exploitation.[8] Worse yet, the mechanisms of exclusion in global society today are actually mirrored in contemporary Christian theology. Contemporary Christian theology lacks the critical tools that would enable it to resist "the powers of exclusion in the global market" or "that would be able to deal with the suffering of people who are excluded" by the powers of the global economy. As a result, as Rieger writes, "theology itself is, by default, drawn into exclusivist relationships and the widening gap between those who are 'in' and those who are 'out.'"[9]

If Rieger is right, as I believe he is, the liberation of Christian theology requires that theologians rethink how they do theology. To date, this has meant opening theology to the experience and perspective of women, African Americans, Latina/os, the poor, gays and lesbians, and other marginalized groups, as both source and norm for theological reflection. What motivates this expansion of sources and norms is not just a perceived need to do justice to those traditionally excluded by social structures of sin. It also arises out of the recognition that exclusion of the voices of the marginalized has structurally distorted Christian theology itself. Pamela Dickey Young expresses the problem in terms of the marginalization of women's voices: "Traditional theology . . . has been written, almost totally, *by* men. It has been formulated, despite claims to universality, as though maleness were the normative form of humanity, and thus, it has been *about* men. When theology is specifically 'about' women, it is about them in negative ways, not as part of the category 'human,' but as negative exceptions to that category, as deviant."[10] In other words, processes that exclude the experience and perspectives of women have distorted Christian theology. The same goes, *mutatis mutandis*, for African Americans, Latina/os, the poor and oppressed, and other marginalized people.

To correct this pervasive distortion of the Christian message, liberation theologians argue, Christians must learn to listen to all those estranged by traditional Christian discourse. Insofar as it is transformed by the witness of these "strangers," Christian theology moves toward liberation from its own structures of sin and is freed to follow more closely the Christ to whom it seeks to be faithful.

More Work to Be Done

Yet even in much liberation theology, other strangers have yet to be heard in the Christian theological conversation. Religious others have been excluded at a very basic level, by the very processes that mark the conversation as "Christian": in the choice of sources and norms for theological reflection. Indeed, if theology today is truly as disconnected from the world's excluded as Rieger claims, it may very well be because Christians still fail to listen to religious others. We might rephrase Young's quote accordingly: "Traditional Christian theology has been written by Christians. It has been formulated, despite claims to universality, as though Christians were the normative form of humanity, and thus, it has been *about* Christians. When theology is specifically 'about' religious others, it is about them in negative ways, not as part of the category 'human,' but as negative exceptions to that category, as deviant." The liberation of Christian theology from its own structures of sin will be incomplete so long as religious others are excluded from the theological conversation. In other words, if there is no divine Other without human others, there is also no divine Other without *religious* others. Marjorie Hewitt Suchocki makes a similar point:

> Liberation theology has pointed to the invidious effects that follow when one mode of humanity is made normative for others. Such normativeness, combined with power, allows and invites exploitation of all those falling outside the norm. Furthermore, it distorts the perspective of those counted as falling within the norm, leading to problems in adequately knowing either self or others. . . . [This] principle holds for religion as well: universalizing one religion such that it is taken as the norm whereby all other religions are judged and valued leads to oppression, and hence falls short of the norm that liberationists consider ultimate—the normative justice that creates well-being in the world community.[11]

There is a growing realization of this problem in the liberation community. For example, Juan José Tamayo Acosta speaks of a "new *interreligious* horizon" that "implies a step from a single or privileged theology to religious pluralism, which will lead to the elaboration of a theology of religions from an intercultural and interreligious dialogue, beginning from the victims and with a liberating praxis. The theology of liberation is not a matter of only one religion, rather of all."[12] While Tamayo does not explain in detail what he has in mind, he does at least suggest the outlines of a broader liberation discourse in which both Christian and non-Christian voices can be heard.

Yet for many in the Christian community, it is by no means self-evident that non-Christians should play any more than an incidental part—if that—in the Christian theological conversation. Some fear that an opening to religious others would cause a slide into a syncretism in which the inclusion of non-Christian voices dilutes or distorts key elements of the Christian message and perhaps results in the loss of a distinctive Christian identity. Such fears are by no means groundless. After all, what differentiates the Christian witness from the witness of non-Christians is precisely the fact that the latter arises *outside* the Christian community and its traditions. For example, whereas the poor of Latin America may interpret their own struggles for liberation in terms of the deliverance of the Israelites from bondage, or in terms of the Kingdom of God proclaimed by Jesus, religious others will see their own liberatory struggles in a very different light—for instance, in terms of Arjuna's search for truth in the *Bhagavad Gita*, or Shinran's teaching about the power of the vow of Amida, or as the work of the *orixás* of Afro-Brazilian religions. In addition, religious others may experience Ultimate Reality not as one personal God, but as impersonal (e.g., Brahman, the Dharmakaya) or as manifest in many supernatural personages (e.g., the various Hindu deities and *avataras*, or the Afro-Brazilian *orixás*).

Indeed, even the fundamental Christian category *liberation* may be understood quite differently by religious others.

Why Care about Religious Others?

Why, then, should Christians believe, with Tamayo, that the theology of liberation is not a matter of Christianity alone but of all religions? Why should religious others have any part to play in the Christian theological conversation? There are at least three major reasons for including religious others in the Christian theological conversation. Two of these will be discussed in the following subsections; the third, which deserves extended treatment, will be discussed in the next section.

Contextual Reasons

The first rationale can be found among Christian theologians working in contexts that have been shaped by, and are often still dominated by, other religious traditions: Africa, Asia, the Pacific, and indigenous communities in the Americas. In these contexts, Christians cannot afford to ignore the texts, traditions, and perspectives of religious others; they are part of the cultural air these Christian theologians breathe. To speak the gospel in such contexts is necessarily to speak in terms and categories shaped by non-Christian religious life and practice. To be authentic to their own cultural heritage, contextualist theologians find it not only necessary but desirable to incorporate non-Christian insights and concepts into Christian theology.[13]

For instance, South Korean theologians Choi Man Ja, Heup Young Kim, and Jung Young Lee unashamedly declare not only their Christian faith but also the fact that they have been shaped by the other religions of Korea— Confucianism, Daoism, Buddhism, and shamanism. As Kim writes, these religious traditions "are important parts of our own identity, functioning as native religious languages or spiritual DNA."[14] Lee draws on yin-yang thought to develop a theology of the Trinity, while Kim draws on the concept of the Dao ("Way") to retrieve ancient Christian insights about God and the world, insights that have been suppressed by Western dualistic thinking.[15] Choi borrows god-goddess metaphors from Korean shamanism as a theological resource for rethinking patriarchal notions of God.[16] Similar developments can be found in the work of Christian theologians in dialogue with the religions of the Indian subcontinent, such as Wesley Ariarajah, Lynn de Silva, Raimundo Panikkar, Aloysius Pieris, and M. Thomas Thangaraj.[17]

Another form of contextualization can be found in the African American and Latina/o Christian communities in North America, communities that maintain strong connections to non-Christian religious traditions as a legacy of slavery and European conquest. Theologians working in these contexts find that their own non-Christian roots are relevant to Christian theological reflection. Dwight N. Hopkins, for example, notes the contribution of African traditional religions to African American notions of God and salvation.[18] Ada Maria Isasi-Díaz refers to Latinas' *cotidiano* ("everyday") as a theological source, which includes the *orixás* and the deities of American Indian religions.[19]

Given the growing religious diversity in the West today, religious others are likely to have a greater influence in shaping Western society and culture. If so, these arguments for contextualization become ever more relevant to Western Christian thinkers.

Globalization

Another reason for welcoming religious others into the Christian theological conversation involves applying liberation theology's key insight—that because God walks with the marginalized, we must learn to see reality through their eyes—to the increasingly globalized context in which Christianity finds itself today. Sociologist Malcolm Waters defines globalization as "a social process in which the constraints of geography on economic, political, social and cultural arrangements recede, in which people become increasingly aware that they are receding and in which people act accordingly."[20]

One area where the constraints of geography are receding is economic. In the interconnected global market, the cross-border flow of goods, services, and capital is increasingly beyond the effective control of nation-states. Global capitalism and its associated ideology, neoliberalism, have been widely hailed not only as a solution to the world's economic problems but also as supremely "natural"—as if capitalism were somehow God's plan for all creation.[21] Far from initiating a global democratic free-market utopia, however, economic globalization has instead created a new global class structure of haves and have-nots, one that is largely beyond the control of governments and is indeed often imposed upon them (for instance, through the economic "restructuring" regimes imposed by the International Monetary Fund and the World Bank).[22] Globalization means that the structures of sin are no longer confined within geographical boundaries of nation-states. It is with good reason that Peter McLaren calls this latest stage of capitalism "the globalization of misery."[23]

In terms of locating the marginalized, therefore, we must think globally as well as locally. We must look beyond geographical and national boundaries, for the structures and processes that marginalize are global in nature and extent. In this new context, the marginalized are mostly non-Christian. Pui-lan Kwok notes that while liberation theology originally argued that the poor were in the Church, today "we have become sensitive to the fact that the majority of the world's poor are outside the church, and many do not want to join its ranks for good reasons."[24] A 1985 study shows that in the countries with very low per capita incomes, the predominant religions are Islam, Buddhism, Hinduism, and African primal religions.[25] In this context, a Christian theology that seeks to see reality through the eyes of the marginalized must learn to *look through non-Christian eyes.*

How Christian Discourse Constructs Religious Others

Important though the foregoing reasons for listening to religious others are, a third may be most important of all, and certainly is critical to liberating Christian theology from its own structures of sin. This involves attending to power dynamics within the most fundamental processes of Christian theology: its processes of boundary-drawing and identity formation, the ways by which it marks itself as *Christian* theology. These dynamics and this rationale for including religious others in the Christian theological conversation become evident when we consider the *discursive* nature of Christian theology.

Whatever else it may be, Christianity is a community of discourse. As we saw in the introduction, discourse actively *constructs* the objects about which it speaks. It exerts power by including some voices and excluding others, and also by shaping what its practitioners accept as "real," "true," or "given." Christian discourse constructs "the Christian" by marking the *boundaries* of the Christian community. Within the rich diversity of human religious life, some people self-identify as Christians and mark off certain elements (beliefs, practices, texts, traditions, perspectives, behaviors, communities, institutions, and so on) as Christian.[26] In so doing, they explicitly or implicitly exclude other elements. Whatever lies inside the boundaries is labeled "Christian"; whatever lies outside, "not-Christian." In drawing these boundaries and defining what is "Christian," theological discourse constructs, explicitly or implicitly, the domain of the not-Christian—religious others.

In other words, *Christians and religious others do not exist* as such *apart from the discourse of Christians themselves.* Both come into being through Christian discourse.

An Example: Discursive Construction in Christian Worship

Consider the discourse of a typical Sunday morning worship service in an Episcopal church in the United States.[27] The congregation will gather in a space decorated with images illustrating scenes from the life of Jesus or certain saints. The parishioners will sing hymns, chosen from a collection authorized by the denomination. One or more passages from the Bible (in a translation authorized by the denomination) will be read. A clergyperson will give a sermon or homily, usually focusing on one or more of the Bible readings. The congregation will say the Nicene Creed. After the celebrant relates the story of the Last Supper, the congregation will recite the Lord's Prayer and then gather at the altar to receive the consecrated bread and wine.

For the participants, these discursive practices serve to construct and to reinforce a sense of what is Christian.[28] Although the participants are probably aware that other understandings of the Christian are in circulation, the discourse of Sunday worship draws boundaries around certain perspectives and behaviors as being the "correct" way in which one expresses and lives out a relationship to God through Jesus Christ. In sociological terms, Sunday worship is a form of ongoing socialization: the participant learns the community's sense of "reality" and internalizes it, making it her own.[29] What is Christian will appear to participants to be a given—"the way it's always been."

At the same time, participants also internalize a sense of what is *not* Christian. In the discourse of Sunday Christian worship, much is repressed or excluded. For example, it is highly unlikely that passages from religious texts such as the Qur'an or the *Bhagavad Gita* will be read. The congregation will not chant the *Nembutsu*. There will be no *zazen* or *prasad*. No images of Shiva Nataraja or Kuanyin will be displayed. The implicit message is that what is absent does not belong in a Christian context, and is therefore of little or no significance to the Christian life.

Why are these and other religious elements excluded from the worship service? No doubt some Christians assume that such elements are excluded because they are somehow "wrong," contrary to Christian faith and practice. For most worshippers, however, the exclusion is not, strictly speaking, intentional or even conscious. While the participants may well be aware that there is a diversity of religious belief and practice among humans, most (at least in the First World) will have little or no acquaintance with the actual beliefs and practices of religious others, or any in-depth understanding of why those beliefs and practices are excluded from the Christian. Many Christians likely assume that excluded beliefs and practices have developed outside the Christian tradition and therefore do not witness to the revelation of God in Jesus Christ. However, without an understanding of these beliefs and practices, how can the participants *know* that they do not witness to God?

Indeed, the discursive construction of "the Christian" often occurs without any in-depth understanding (and in too many cases, no understanding at all) of what is being excluded. If my own experience in teaching college-level religion courses as well as parish catechetical classes is representative, most Christians in the United States self-identify as such without any in-depth knowledge of other religious traditions. Nor do the churches seem to think such familiarity necessary or even desirable. To my knowledge, no mainline Christian denominations require their initiates to undergo training in other religions or one-on-one dialogue with religious others, before baptism or confirmation.[30] As a result, Christians operate as if the boundaries around the Christian were simply given. Such an attitude might be excusable in a heterogeneous society, but not in the religiously plural society that we find in Western Europe and North America today.

Discursive Construction in Christian Theology

As the Episcopal worshipper participates in practices that originated in the distant past, so the Christian theologian enters a theological conversation that began in the ministry of Jesus and stretches forward more than two thousand years. And the theologian engages in similar processes of discursive construction. Here again, it is the choice of theological sources and norms that matters: some things will be included, others will be excluded.

As for what is included, theologians tend to rely on four main resources: the biblical texts; the tradition of theological and spiritual reflection; reason; and experience.[31] There are certain broad patterns. In Protestant theology, the biblical texts will likely be given a place of prominence; Catholic theologians will likely draw on magisterial texts as well. Historically, however, Christian theology has ranged freely over a wide variety of topics, from the being of God to the ethics of in vitro fertilization. Basically, almost anything is in bounds and may come under the consideration of Christian theologians.

If that is the case, what do Christian theologians exclude? The voices of religious others, if past practice is any indicator. Historically, the voices of religious others have been conspicuous by their absence from the Christian theological conversation. A Buddhist's experience of *satori* or a Vodounist's experience of possession by a *loa*, for example, has rarely been a factor in European/neo-European Christian theological reflection. On those rare occasions when religious others *do* show up in Christian theology, they tend to serve as the "other" against which the theologian defines what is characteristically or essentially Christian. Sadly, this has frequently involved making claims (and often quite misguided ones) about the beliefs and practices of religious others without listening to what religious others themselves have to say.[32]

When a Christian theologian excludes the beliefs and perspectives of religious others as theological sources and norms, she constructs a sense of what is Christian and what is not. Even when the theologian does not explicitly rule out the beliefs and perspectives of religious others as inappropriate or irrelevant to Christian theology, the lack of any reference to those beliefs and perspectives in Christian theological reflection draws a de facto boundary between resources that are deemed appropriate for Christian reflection and those that are not.

Certainly there is nothing intrinsically wrong with the discursive drawing of boundaries around the Christian. Quite the contrary: boundary drawing is as necessary to theology as it is to other forms of conceptual thought. As Cressida Heyes observes (following the philosopher Ludwig Wittgenstein), we draw lines around certain concepts in order to use them, and it is through use that they become meaningful.[33] This is true of the elements that make up the Christian: they take on meaning through their use in a Christian context and their relation to other elements that make up the Christian "thing." To cite what may be an obvious example, bread and wine only become *eucharist* by their relation to the story of Jesus' last supper, which in turn gains its significance in light of his death, resurrection, and ascension, as well as the larger narrative of God's work in the world. Similarly, there can be no properly *Christian* theology (the present work included) without at least some provisional sense of what constitutes the Christian and what does not.

Necessary though such boundary drawing is, it also manifests dynamics of power and domination. Christian boundary drawing attempts to control, to impose order upon, the mind-boggling diversity of human religious life, including the diversity within the Christian community itself. By defining the Christian against the witness of religious others, Christian theologians seek to give unity and coherence to their theological reflections. However, this is frequently achieved by repressing religious differences, by treating them as nonnormative or irrelevant to Christian belief and practice. While necessary, boundary drawing can easily become a way to stop thinking about the true complexity of reality. Christian theology can blind itself by creating an illusion of internal consistency, giving the impression that it has thereby attained truth. Truth, however, always lies beyond our merely human constructions.

All too often, Christians overlook the constructed nature of the boundaries —the fact that they are not given but are formed by the discourse of Christian individuals and communities. Instead, the boundaries are either taken for granted or regarded as essential, immutable, or worse, divinely appointed. The result is a strong dualism between inside and outside, between Christian and not-Christian. This dualism can take several forms, including the explicit exclusion of non-Christian voices as either corrupt or merely irrelevant to Christian theological reflection; the misrepresentation of religious others in order to support claims of Christian superiority; or the mere absence of non-Christian voices in Christian theological discourse. This is true even of some of the leading lights in recent Christian theology, as we will see in Chapters 3 through 6.

The Need for Radical Theological Self-Critique

We can now address questions raised at the beginning of this chapter. Isn't Christian theology inherently a conversation by Christians about Christian belief for Christian purposes? If so, why should it include non-Christian voices?

Theological discourse is *not* purely intra-Christian, for it constructs social relations, and it has social effects. It constitutes a community, and its processes of inclusion, marginalization, and exclusion define the boundaries of that community—who is in, who is out. Insofar as Christian theological discourse marginalizes or excludes, it fails to emulate Christ's own radical shattering of boundaries, social and religious.

One might object that since Christian discourse doesn't concern religious others, they will have no desire to take part in it. Perhaps. Yet even were this the case, Christian processes of marginalization and exclusion still affect *Christians*. As with the traditional exclusion of the witness of women, the poor, and people of color, the exclusion of religious others from the Christian theological conversation has distorted the resulting theology. Furthermore, Christian thought will be challenged and enriched by including the witness of religious others. This book seeks to demonstrate that by excluding religious others, Christian discourse makes unavailable to itself potential truths and insights about Christianity itself and the God to whom it seeks to witness. It remains trapped in its own circular self-affirmation, mistaking its own constructs for divine truth.

The repressed witness of religious others both haunts and motivates Christian theological discourse. Its stubborn presence beyond the bounds of the Christian serves as a nagging reminder that there are other, different—even radically different—ways of thinking about and relating to the Ultimate, the human condition, and the world, and that the unity and wholeness of the Christian (or the illusion thereof) are constructed upon the repression of a rich variety of religious differences. Furthermore, as will be discussed in Chapter 2, these power dynamics in theological discourse link up with wider social, political, and economic processes of marginalization and exclusion.

To counter its own sinful tendencies to marginalize and to exclude, then, Christian theology must engage in a project of *radical theological self-critique*. Here we might call to mind George Santayana's insight that we must learn from the mistakes of the past so as not to repeat them. Christian theology needs to take a hard look at where it has been: how major forms of theological discourse have constructed the Christian and religious others through boundary drawing and the selection of theological sources and norms; and how these processes have distorted the resulting content of the theological formulations.

To do this, new tools are needed, new ways of thinking about the power dynamics in Christian theology's discursive construction of religious others and the ways in which those dynamics introduce blind spots in the resulting theological formulations. That will be the subject of the next chapter.

CHAPTER 2

Discourse, Power, Exclusion
How Christian Theology
Constructs Religious Others

A radical theological critique of Christian reflection about religious others should begin with the root question: what is the relation between the Christian and religious others? There is no one "right" answer. Indeed, as we will see in subsequent chapters, different Christian theologians conceive of this relationship in different ways, based on different assumptions.

Why begin by establishing the relation between the Christian and religious others? Why not, as comparative theologians contend, dispense with such theological prolegomena and instead get on with the process of interreligious dialogue?[1] I begin here because the way in which a given theologian conceives of the Christian's relation to religious others not only shapes the resulting theological reflection but also limits the kind of dialogue that is possible. This can be seen in the work of two theologians who will be the focus of later chapters. Karl Barth opposes divine "revelation" to human "religion," the latter of which he equates with unbelief (*Unglaube*). Since Barth holds that Christianity is the only religion that arises in faithfulness to revelation, it follows that other religions are species of unbelief. George Lindbeck, in contrast, conceives of Christianity and other religions as languagelike entities, each with its own "grammatical rules" which are essentially incommensurable with the "grammatical rules" of other religions. In this way, Lindbeck treats relations between religions as purely external: Christianity, for instance, in no way depends on other religions for its existence and self-understanding.

Although Barth's and Lindbeck's starting assumptions differ, both have the effect of minimizing the need for Christians to be in dialogue with religious others. If other religions are species of unbelief, they have nothing of value to contribute to Christian reflection. If religions are mutually incommensurable, they have no basis for comparing and contrasting their beliefs, practices, perspectives, and so on, and it is difficult to see what value dialogue would have. Furthermore, the project of comparative theology, though founded on a call for dialogue without a priori theologizing, makes its own theological assumptions about religious others before dialogue begins. Its very raison d'être is the *possibility* that other religions have something true to say to Christians; indeed, one of the foremost comparative theologians, James Fredericks, seems to see it as more likelihood than mere possibility.[2] To take the position that religious truth may be present, at least potentially, outside the Christian community—and why bother with dialogue if that potential is absent?—is to take a *theological* position regarding the relation between Christianity and religious others. It is, in other words, to theologize *before* dialogue. This is by no means a fatal flaw in the comparative theology project, which I consider to be one of the most promising developments in recent Christian theology. It is, however, to point out that theological prolegomena, particularly concerning Christianity's relation to religious others, may very well be at least a necessary evil and perhaps a necessary good.

In this chapter, I lay out a new way of thinking about the Christian and its relations to religious others. This conceptual framework builds on the notion (discussed in Chapter 1) that both the Christian and religious others are constructs, that is, that they are constructed by discursive processes. This framework, unlike Barth's approach, does not privilege the Christian a priori. Unlike Lindbeck's approach, it highlights the intrinsically relational nature of the Christian. Perhaps most important, it brings to light the often hidden dynamics of power—inclusion, marginalization, and exclusion—in the discursive construction of the Christian and the ways in which those dynamics introduce blind spots in the resulting theological formulations. It allows us to explore how the exercise of this power limits and distorts Christian theology, and how encounter with religious others can reveal wider and deeper truths not only about religious others, but about Christianity itself and about the divine Other to which it seeks to witness.

The conceptual framework I lay out here has two parts—a psychosocial component and a structural component. The first gets at the dynamics of power in the four major modes of theological discourse that will be the focus of this book: liberalism, neo-orthodoxy, postliberalism, and liberation theology. It draws upon the work of Joerg Rieger to uncover how repression is built into each of these discourses and to link these discourses with wider processes of "othering" on the social, political, and economic levels.

The second, or structural, component draws on concepts from the philosophy of Alain Badiou to uncover ways that religious othering is structured. It allows us to analyze the structures of exclusion in theological discourse, their epistemological consequences, and the possibilities for transformative encounter with those who are excluded.

The Psychosocial Dynamics of Theological Discourse

The search for dynamics of power and exclusion in theology is not new. Numerous theologies of liberation, such as feminist and Black theologies, have pointed out various ways in which social hegemonies (e.g., patriarchy, White racism) distort traditional Christian theology. These liberation theologies have advocated a turn to the voices traditionally excluded from the Christian conversation. Standing firmly in this critical tradition, the work of Joerg Rieger offers a particularly thoroughgoing analysis of power dynamics in recent Christian theology. Two of his books, *Remember the Poor* and *God and the Excluded*, set the stage for the work I undertake in the rest of this book.³

In *God and the Excluded*, Rieger analyzes the four theological discourses that have, as mentioned in the introduction, dominated Christian theological discussion in the wake of the crisis of authority in the modern-postmodern period. These are the liberal turn to the experience of the self; the neo-orthodox turn to the divine Other; the postliberal turn to the tradition and texts of the Church; and the turn to those traditionally excluded from mainline theological discourse, found in the various theologies of liberation, including feminist, womanist, Black, and similar theologies.

Although these four theological approaches appear quite different, Rieger shows that they are deeply interconnected. Drawing upon the work of French psychoanalyst Jacques Lacan, Rieger uncovers the ways in which each theological discourse participates, often unconsciously, in the dominant structures of power and repression at work in the wider social, political, and economic spheres.

The setting in which these discourses arise is what, following Lacan, Rieger calls "the era of the ego," the modern-postmodern period. In this era "the modern self has finally won most of its battles for autonomy and fortified its positions of power, authority, and control."⁴

What is meant by the "modern self"? It is not the unified and autonomous agent assumed by modern individualism; indeed, individual autonomy turns out to be a fantasy, a symptom of the modern self's own narcissism and alienation. Rather, Lacan holds that the modern self is "essentially bound up with the existence of others."⁵ Though it comes into being in relation to the other, the self *misrecognizes* the other; that is, it turns the other into an object, a prop to support the self's own desires and its illusions of autonomy.⁶ In misrecognizing the other, the subject also misrecognizes, and thus is alienated from, itself. This failure to come to grips with its real relation to the other constitutes what Rieger calls the "blind spot" in the discourse of the modern self.

Far from a purely personal problem, the psychosocial dynamics of the modern self have global implications. In the ego's era, the modern self creates "narcissistic structures that manifest themselves not only in personal relationships but also in the economic and political realms where this self has managed aggressively to draw everything into its force field and to exclude the rest of humanity."[7] Rieger writes, "The modern self is controlled by dreams of fixation and objectification as well as control and power. . . . Today this self is increasingly able to make the world over in its own image, as a result of technological advances and the international expansion of capitalism. . . . The continuing drive to appropriate new worlds, itself symptomatic of the rise of modernity and the ego's era, has exported the power structures of modernity to other places."[8] To get a sense of what Rieger has in mind here, consider the rampant spread of global capital and the European/neo-European consumerist lifestyle that accompanies it, remaking the world in its own image and, in so doing, suppressing difference, excluding other ways of life.

What has all this to do with theology? Quite a lot, as it turns out. Rieger argues that for the past two centuries, this expansive modern self has also co-opted Christian theology. With the advent of the liberal turn of Schleiermacher and his successors, the locus of theological authority shifted decisively to the allegedly universal experience of the self. However, as Rieger shows (and as we shall see in Chapter 3), this new locus of authority turns out not to be universal at all; indeed, the fantasy of universality is a function of the self's blindness to difference. The new locus of theological authority is instead the expansive, self-confident, European/neo-European middle-class—and Christian—self whose interests are embodied in laissez faire capitalism, colonialism, and globalization.

One might think that a remedy to this self-centered fantasy would be found in one of the other three dominant discourses—neo-orthodoxy, postliberalism, and liberation theologies—since they seek to ground theology not in the experience of the self, but in (respectively) the divine Other, the tradition of the Church, or the witness of those traditionally excluded by mainstream theology.

However, Rieger's Lacanian analysis in *God and the Excluded* demonstrates that no single one of these alternatives offers a full solution. Each discourse has its own blind spots. Each is in its own way constructed upon repression. In the case of neo-orthodoxy, the repressed element is the experience of the self; in postliberalism, the divine Other; in theologies of liberation, the tradition of the church. More importantly, each discourse fails in its own way to come to grips with the power of the modern self in the ego's era. In promoting a single element—divine Other, tradition, or the excluded—to the locus of authority, each alternative merely represses the modern self. As a result, all three turns are susceptible to being shaped unconsciously by the modern self "and its dreams of being in control."[9] Each form of theological discourse is in danger of "becoming a self-serving monologue," "a discourse of like-minded individuals talking primarily to each other (the danger of the liberal modes of theology), a discourse about the divine Other that never really connects to God's and other people's otherness (the danger of the neo-orthodox modes), a turn to language and the texts of the church that shuts out differing readings (the danger of the post-liberal modes), or a turn to others that ends up in identity politics or special-interest deals (the danger of liberation modes)."[10]

Rieger's analysis warns us that theological discourse is a complex interrelationship of psychosocial factors and, consequently, that problems in contemporary theology cannot be solved simply by nominating a new candidate for locus of theological authority. Even those discourses that ostensibly reject the authority of the modern self do not fully escape its force field.

Rieger's analysis also reveals that repression is in fact part of the *structure* of the dominant modes of contemporary Christian theological discourse; it is constitutive of each mode. Rieger shifts the focus from debates about the selection of theological authority to an examination of the discursive structures that manifest authority. He shows that relations of authority and power in theological discourse are not preordained but are products of repression, and that these relations are bound up with relations of authority, power, and repression in the wider social-economic-political context (e.g., capitalism, colonialism, globalization).

The Structural Dynamics of Theological Discourse

Important though it is in shifting theological attention to discursive structures of repression, Rieger's work to date has not discussed the ways in which the very drawing of the boundary "Christian" marginalizes and represses others, and how that boundary drawing also supports existing structures of power. To address those questions, I turn to the philosophy of Alain Badiou, one of the most interesting thinkers to emerge since the days of poststructuralists such as Foucault and Derrida.[11] Although Badiou is not a theologian, his notions of *situation, void,* and *event* are particularly helpful in thinking about the relationship of "the Christian" to religious others, as I hope will be borne out by the following discussion. (For those interested in a basic overview of Badiou's philosophy, see the Appendix to this volume, "A Crash Course in Alain Badiou's Philosophy."[12])

The Christian Situation

Humans exhibit a bewildering variety of religious communities, beliefs, perspectives, and practices. This multiplicity is the ontological ground for the Christian. Within this richly plural context, some religious practitioners self-identify as Christians, and mark off certain entities (beliefs, practices, texts, traditions, perspectives, behaviors, communities, institutions, and so on) as Christian, through discursive practices such as those discussed in Chapter 1.[13] I call this construct "the Christian."

The Christian thus functions as a *situation*, Badiou's term for a structured collection of elements selected out of the wider multiplicity;[14] it is roughly equivalent to the mathematical concept of a set. The Christian situation stands on the distinction between inside and outside: some things that are counted as "belonging" to the situation, in contradistinction to those things that are not.[15] Those things that are not counted as Christian are "othered" by the criteria that define the Christian situation—thus my choice of the term "religious others" for the non-Christian.

Granted, Christian self-definition is a complex process. The criteria used to answer the question "What is Christian?"—that is, to establish the Christian situation—vary from community to community and from person to person. And, as we will see in subsequent chapters, they vary from one Christian theologian to another. However, the complexity and variations should not distract us from the common theme. We use the category "Christian" to present certain entities as belonging together and, explicitly or implicitly, to exclude other entities as "not-Christian" or "other." Insofar as it is meaningful to speak of the *Christian* tradition or a *Christian* theology or the *Christian* community, we can also speak of a *Christian* situation.

The Void of the Christian Situation

That which is excluded by a situation Badiou calls the *void*; it comprises whatever literally "does not count" according to the criteria that construct the situation.[16] As mentioned earlier, the void of the Christian situation is the not-Christian, the domain of religious otherness. This includes all aspects of non-Christian religious life: beliefs, practices, sacred texts, traditions, perspectives, behaviors, communities, institutions, and so on.

Yet the void is more than merely what a situation excludes: it is also the situation's ground of being.[17] The void *constitutes* the situation as much as the elements included therein (as the null set is a member of any set). It is with good reason that Badiou speaks of the void as that which "haunts" the situation.[18]

Religious others haunt the Christian situation in the same way, for the latter exists only in contradistinction to what is deemed not-Christian. If there were nothing with which to contrast it, the category "Christian" would be meaningless. Without the not-Christian, there can be no Christian. Thus religious others are constitutive of the Christian situation as a kind of absent presence or present absence. And, as we will see in later chapters, while religious others may be excluded from the spotlight of Christian theological reflection, they remain just off stage, a nagging truth that cannot be entirely ignored. This dimension of the Christian has largely been overlooked by theologians to date.

The Governing Order of the Christian Situation

Since a situation is constituted as much by what it excludes (its void) as what it includes, its integrity is continually threatened by the possibility that what is excluded will call the boundaries of the situation into question and disrupt it. This is especially true at points of inconsistency in the situation—elements that do not fit well together or even contradict one another. As human constructs, all situations contain such imperfections.

In order to protect the situation's integrity, what I'll call the *governing order* arranges the elements: it establishes their relation to one another.[19] The governing order attempts to establish coherence among the various elements of the situation by marginalizing or suppressing elements that are inconsistent or that call into question other relations within the situation. The governing order, in other words, attempts to suppress inconsistency and block encounter with that which is excluded.

As we will see in later chapters, some theologians arrange elements in a situation hierarchically; they treat some elements as inferior to others, often due to their being tainted by "alien" influences (i.e., the void). By marginalizing those elements that (allegedly) resemble the excluded, the governing order works to reinforce the boundaries of the Christian situation and keep the void at bay.

Christian Knowledge, Truth, and the Event

The inclusion-exclusion process that constructs the situation and its void has important epistemological implications, which Badiou presents in terms of a distinction between "knowledge" (*savoir*) and "truth" (*vérité*). Knowledge is a function of the elements included in the situation; it is what can be "known" within it. For those operating within the Christian situation, what lies outside the Christian situation can only be designated from a Christian perspective and usually in Christian terms. For example, as we've seen, traditional Christian theologies of religions were principally concerned with the salvific status of religious others; this is reflected in the threefold categorization, exclusivism, inclusivism, pluralism. While salvation is a major concern in Christianity, it is arguably far less important in other religions, for whom wisdom, balance, or right practice assume the centrality salvation holds for Christians. By "reading" religious others in terms of salvation, Christians miss important aspects of other religions.

While knowledge is limited by the perspective of the situation, truth is universal and thus exceeds the situation. It is, from the perspective of a situation, always something new, something extra.[20] As excess, a truth is "foreign" and cannot be grasped from within a situation. Rather, truth is revealed through encounter with that which the situation excludes, that is, the void. Picturesquely, Badiou says that a truth "punches a 'hole'" in knowledge.[21]

This in-breaking of truth into a situation Badiou calls an *event.* Encounter with truth calls into question what is "known" within a situation and can provoke a revolutionary rethinking of the situation, its rationale, and its construction.[22] The point in a situation at which such an encounter can happen is what Badiou calls the *evental site.*[23]

Evental Sites in the Christian Situation

I suggest that the Christian situation includes at least two evental sites, points within the situation at which encounter with the void is possible. These operate (so to speak) as windows that open out onto the excluded; they open the Christian situation to the influence of the excluded, potentially calling into question the criteria that excluded it in the first place. I have already discussed one site in the introduction: the scriptural accounts attesting to Jesus' own teaching and practice regarding religious others. The implications of these accounts militate against the very processes of exclusion upon which the Christian situation is (often) founded. Jesus' teaching and example thus open the Christian situation to the irruption of the void, to religious others.

A second evental site is the Christian doctrine of divine transcendence, which holds that God and God's revelation infinitely surpass any merely human reckonings, including those of the Church. Though this doctrine often functions as a warrant for the authority of the particular revelation that the Church proclaims, it also calls Christians not to mistake human understandings of God for divine truth. As we have seen, Badiou claims that truth always exceeds any situation; similarly, Christianity teaches (or should teach) that divine truth always exceeds the historical forms proclaiming that truth. Like Jesus' teaching and example, the doctrine of divine transcendence opens the situation to the irruption of the void, of that which exceeds the Christian situation.

Truth and Encounter

A frequently cited benefit of Christian dialogue with religious others is that through it, Christians come to understand themselves and their faith more deeply. Raimundo Panikkar notes that *intra*religious dialogue flows naturally from *inter*religious dialogue: "Dialogue serves the useful purpose of laying bare our own assumptions and those of others, thereby giving us a more critically grounded conviction of what we hold true."[24] James Fredericks notes that such encounter is fruitful for Christians precisely *because* it is destabilizing: "An encounter in depth with a religion not our own can be frightening and confusing. . . . But such encounters can be life giving as well. The truths of non-Christian religions can stimulate Christians to look into their own religious tradition with new questions and emerge, perhaps, with new insights."[25]

The situation-void-event framework helps us to understand why this is so. As long as Christians operate solely within the Christian situation, what they can "know" is limited to the elements collected in it. Since the governing order of the Christian situation works to keep the void (religious others) off the radar, Christians can have no sense of either the wider realm of human religiosity or the ways Christian elements relate to it. Encounter with religious others, on the other hand, brings the void of the Christian situation into consciousness, relativizing the situation's content and disrupting the relations imposed by its governing order.

Encounter with religious others, in other words, is an *event*. It calls into question the "taken-for-granted-ness" of "the Christian" and transforms the understanding—and self-understanding—of those operating within it. It reveals the limitations of knowledge available within the Christian situation and opens Christians to the in-breaking of a transcendent truth.[26]

What, then, is the truth revealed by the event of encounter with religious others? Let me address this question by first establishing what does *not* constitute that truth. Truth cannot necessarily be identified with any particular beliefs (or traditions, practices, etc.) of any particular religious others (e.g., the Four Noble Truths of Buddhism, the Qur'anic revelation). As discussed earlier, each such belief (or tradition, practice, etc.) has meaning only in the historical and cultural context in which it arises; it cannot be arbitrarily wrenched from its context and inserted into the Christian context without significant loss of meaning. Just as (for instance) the bread and wine of the Christian eucharist have significance only in the context of the life and ministry of Christ, so, for instance, the Four Noble Truths take on meaning only in light of the Buddha's corpus of teachings and the *sangha* that preserves and honors them.

Nor can this truth be wholly identified with the "knowledge" available within any *non-Christian* religious situation. Other religious communities engage in their own processes of situational boundary drawing, and create structures of authority, power, and repression-exclusion similar to those of Christians. My comments on the Christian situation apply equally to the Hindu situation, or the Jewish situation, or the Candomblé situation. Non-Christians may also need transformative encounter with their own religious others—including, in this case, Christians.

Particular religious situations, Christian and non-Christian alike, stand in need of encounter with truth because truth always exceeds them. The truth of transformative encounter with religious others cannot be captured by any predicate of the language of the Christian situation (or of that of any other situation) and, unlike the knowledge available within the Christian (or other) situation, truth is infinite. Furthermore, like the truth Badiou's Saint Paul proclaims, it is "offered to all, or addressed to everyone, without a condition of belonging being able to limit this offer, or this address."[27] As Paul's truth exceeds both Jewish and Greek regimes of discourse,[28] so this truth exceeds the *Christian* regime of discourse as well.

As a Christian theologian, I am able—indeed, compelled—to make a claim that Badiou the atheist philosopher cannot make: the ground of this disruptive truth is the divine Other to which the Christian faith witnesses. The divine Other is, so to speak, the Void of all voids. Precisely because it is that divine Other, it exceeds the merely Christian situation. As Joerg Rieger writes, "We will not find God where God can be controlled."[29] By setting the parameters for what is and is not included as "Christian," Christian discourse does indeed attempt the impossible task of controlling God. All too often the boundaries of the Christian situation declare that God speaks and is present through *these* elements, not *those*, or that God is to be understood through *these* categories, not *those*. Furthermore, religious others are all too often understood solely in these (Christian) terms and not in their own terms.

Yet God—indeed, the very God revealed in and by Jesus Christ—cannot be so circumscribed. This God transcends mere human expectations, even mere *Christian* expectations. "God's Otherness," Rieger writes, "has to do with the fact that God is different from what we expect."[30] Theology needs to recognize that the God defined (in Badiouan terms) by the knowledge of the Christian situation is not God in truth. The true God is free to be revealed anywhere—in the beliefs and experiences of religious others just as much as in those included within the Christian situation.

By disrupting the logic of the Christian situation and thereby revealing its finitude, encounter with religious others witnesses to the sublime excess, the utter freedom, and the universality of the divine Other. It is for this reason that the event of encounter with religious others also helps Christians come to a deeper understanding of themselves and their faith. Such encounter reveals that the God they worship cannot be circumscribed by the Christian situation any more than God can be identified with a particular nation, class, ethnic group, or cause. Furthermore, such encounter reminds Christians that there is no encounter with the divine Other without respect for human others—including *religious* others. The event of encounter with religious others can call forth a radical transformation of Christian belief and practice, a revolutionary new way of relating and witnessing to the divine Other.

The Next Move

Badiou's situation-void-event framework provides the conceptual grid for a radical critique of Christian theological reflection about religious others. Yet Badiou's set-situation paradigm does not capture the whole picture. Behind the dynamics of theological situations lie psychosocial processes and structures of authority, power, and repression, manifested in discourse. Rieger's Lacanian framework gives us a way of identifying those aspects, linking them to wider social-political-economic structures of repression and uncovering "blind spots" that result from repression.

In the following four chapters, we will put this grid to work in an analysis of actual Christian theologies. We will examine theological reflection about "the Christian" and religious others in the work of representatives of the four major discourses in modern-postmodern Western Christian theology: liberal Protestantism (Schleiermacher), neo-orthodoxy (Barth), postliberalism (Lindbeck), and liberation theology (Gutiérrez). For each theological discourse (via its representative theologian), we will examine three major questions. First, how does the discourse construct religious others? Second, how does the construction of religious others affect the resulting theological formulations, and particularly those concerning the Divine? Third, what are possible evental sites and blind spots in the discourse?

CHAPTER 3

Schleiermacher

"Religion" in Service to "the Christian"

Friedrich Schleiermacher is widely acknowledged to be the father of modern liberal Protestant theology and perhaps of modern theology generally. Karl Barth, though vigorously opposed to key aspects of Schleiermacher's theology, admitted, "The first place in a history of the theology of the most recent times belongs and will always belong to Schleiermacher, and he has no rival."[1] Keith Clements notes that "Schleiermacher's ascription of religion to the realm of *feeling* marked the start of modern Protestantism's habitual emphasis on the knowledge of God as inward and experiential."[2]

More relevant to our concerns here, Schleiermacher is one of the first major modern Western Christian theologians to recognize the existence and significance of religions other than Christianity—indeed, to speak, in the contemporary sense, of Christianity *as* religion, as one religion among many.[3] Although he never developed a full-blown theology of religions, his work sparked a tradition of thought about religion that emphasizes its experiential dimension. We can hear echoes of Schleiermacher in Rudolf Otto's *mysterium tremendens et fascinans*, in Paul Tillich's "questings" in human experience, and in David Tracy's appeals to limit experience.

Rejecting both the Enlightenment elevation of human reason and premodern views of Christian doctrine, Schleiermacher makes two key theological moves. First, he grounds Christian theological reflection in immediate interior experience, in what he calls the "feeling of absolute dependence." Second, he claims that this experience is a universal feature of human consciousness and is the essence of all "religion," a category of which Christianity is the most developed instance.

For some contemporary scholars, Schleiermacher's approach points the way to greater openness to religious others. Jacqueline Marina holds that his affirmation of a single universal core experience opens the door to true dialogue.[4]

Thomas Reynolds argues that Schleiermacher exemplifies "dialectical plural-ism," a stance characterized by "tensional interplay between the universal and the particular."[5] This is "a pluralism of particular differences in relation, of con-trasts in connection. . . . [It] is nothing other than a robust and dynamic sharing of differences."[6] For Reynolds, Schleiermacher exemplifies both the possibility of encounter with difference without falling into relativism, and the possibility of perspectivism without falling into "religious narcissism and ethnocentrism."[7]

Yet, as this chapter will demonstrate, Schleiermacher's theology is less open to religious others than it appears. The structure of his theological discourse—his discursive construction of "religion," "the Christian," and religious others—manifests toward religious others the narcissism and aggression that Rieger and Lacan recognize in the modern self. Schleiermacher's theological discourse both represses religious others and blocks meaningful encounter with them.

This chapter will focus on Schleiermacher's discourse on religious others in his magnum opus, *The Christian Faith* (or the *Glaubenslehre*, as Schleiermacher referred to it), with occasional glances at his earlier work, *On Religion: Speeches to Its Cultured Despisers*.[8] As will be the case for the following three chapters, the investigation will focus on three questions:

1. How does the discourse construct religious others?
2. How does the construction of religious others affect the resulting theo-logical formulations and particularly those concerning the Divine?
3. What are possible evental sites and blind spots in the discourse?

Schleiermacher's Construction of Religious Others

Schleiermacher reflects the growing European Christian awareness of religious diversity, an awareness that Christianity qua religion shares something in com-mon with religious others. Accordingly, Schleiermacher defines "the Christian" in the context of religious diversity, as one religion among many.

In the *Glaubenslehre* Schleiermacher constructs two situations: one for "religion," the other for "the Christian," the latter being a subset of the for-mer. While the earlier *On Religion* is concerned with religion generally, the *Glaubenslehre* presents religion not for its own sake, but only insofar as it serves to support the presentation of the Christian faith.[9] Schleiermacher's goal in this later work is to isolate Christianity's "peculiar essence," by distinguishing Chris-tianity "from religions co-ordinate with it."[10] To do so, he lays out criteria by which to define "religion" and then shows how Christianity alone satisfies them. In other words, he constructs the religion situation so as to serve the interests of the Christian situation.

The Religion Situation

For Schleiermacher, five characteristics constitute the defining criteria for religion. (The sources for these criteria will be discussed later.) First, Schleiermacher holds that religion is fundamentally—and universally—an interior and personal phenomenon. Religion, he writes in *On Religion*, "springs necessarily and by itself from the interior of every soul" and only later takes social forms.[11] In the *Glaubenslehre*, Schleiermacher discusses religion in terms of "self-consciousness," which he describes as having three levels. The lowest, the "animal" self-consciousness, perceives no "antithesis" (i.e., cannot discriminate) between self and others. The middle, or "sensible" self-consciousness rests wholly on that discrimination, and combines a feeling of dependence with a feeling of freedom. The highest is the religious self-consciousness (the feeling of absolute dependence, discussed later), in which the self-other antithesis disappears.[12] In any given religious communion, Schleiermacher claims, there is "uniformity of religious consciousness."[13]

Nonetheless, the religious self-consciousness varies in intensity and is never found on its own; it is always mediated by the sensible self-consciousness.[14] The influence of the sensible self-consciousness introduces distortions into religious expression, including doctrinal formulations. For instance, Schleiermacher attributes the recurrence of anthropomorphic descriptions of God to the continuing influence of the sensible upon the religious self-consciousness.[15]

Schleiermacher's second defining characteristic for religion is that it is fundamentally affective. Religion is piety (*Frömmigkeit*), which in turn is fundamentally a matter of "feeling" (*Gefühl*).[16] In the *Glaubenslehre*, he defines religion as "the totality of the religious affections" (*frommen Gemützstände*) forming the foundation of a communion.[17] He also insists that piety (i.e., religion) is fundamentally feeling, and not either knowing (*Wissen*) or doing (*Tun*), or a state composed of all three.[18]

Third, religion involves not feeling generally, but a specific type of feeling, the "feeling of absolute dependence." Schleiermacher posits this feeling, and the piety that arises from it, to be a universal element of human life; it is also the hallmark of religion: "The more a subject takes the attitude of absolute dependence, the more religious is he."[19]

Fourth, the feeling of absolute dependence is fundamentally monotheistic. While it is by definition present in all religions, Schleiermacher holds that it can be explained only as an awareness of the Divine "as the absolute undivided unity."[20] Only in monotheism do "all religious affections express the dependence of everything finite upon one Supreme and Infinite Being."[21] Belief in multiple divinities is therefore an inadequate manifestation of the feeling of absolute dependence.

Fifth, all religions recognize both the condition of God-forgetfulness and the human need for redemption.[22] Additionally, Christianity is not the only religion concerned with redemption; other religions attest to a similar concern by instituting "penances and purifications."[23]

These five criteria, then, establish for Schleiermacher what counts as religion. They mark off the boundaries of the religion situation.

The Governing Order of the Religion Situation

As we saw in Chapter 2, the governing order organizes a situation's elements in relation both to one another and to the situation as a whole. In the *Glaubenslehre*, Schleiermacher arranges the elements of his religion situation according to development from "lower" to "higher" forms of religiosity. Like other European thinkers before and after him (e.g., David Hume, Emile Durkheim, E. B. Tylor), Schleiermacher holds that religion can progress from an inferior state to a superior state.[24] Although he holds that all religions in some way involve a feeling of absolute dependence, Schleiermacher ranks them according to their level of progress toward monotheism, the highest state, in which all "religious affections" express dependence upon the "highest totality," upon "one Supreme and Infinite Being."[25] At the lowest level of development is "idol-worship" or "Fetichism," which "ascribes to the idol an influence over only a limited field of objects or processes." Consequently, it is "based upon a confused state of self-consciousness which marks the lowest condition of man."[26] Polytheism occupies an intermediate stage of development. Here, Schleiermacher argues, there is a greater sense of dependence of the finite on the "highest totality"; however, since this totality is understood as a multiple (many deities), the feeling of absolute dependence "cannot appear in its complete unity."[27]

Only the highest stage, monotheism, reflects the full development of the higher self-consciousness, the feeling of absolute dependence. Indeed, whenever the feeling of absolute dependence is fully developed, monotheism results. At this level Schleiermacher places Judaism, Christianity, and Islam.[28]

Yet Schleiermacher finds degrees of development even at this highest stage. "Judaism," he writes, "by its limitation of the love of Jehovah to the race of Abraham, betrays a lingering affinity with Fetichism."[29] Islam, on the other hand, exhibits "that influence of the sensible upon the character of the religious emotions which elsewhere keeps men on the level of Polytheism."[30] Only Christianity remains free from these weaknesses, and therefore is "the purest form of Monotheism"—that is, the most highly developed religion.[31]

In short, this governing order marginalizes all religions other than Christianity as lower forms of expression of the religious consciousness. Further aggravating their marginalized status in the religion situation, Schleiermacher devotes very little space to any of these religions; they are introduced, summarized, and dismissed with sweeping and unsubstantiated generalizations.

It should be noted that in the *Glaubenslehre*'s stress on the superiority of Christianity, we see a marked divergence from the position Schleiermacher takes in *On Religion*. In that earlier work, Schleiermacher rejects any order of superiority among religions. When he takes up the question of whether Christianity is destined to "rule humanity as the only form of religion," he answers in the negative: "Just as nothing is more irreligious than to demand uniformity in humanity generally, so nothing is more unchristian than to seek uniformity in religion."[32] He then declares, "Let the universe be intuited and worshiped in all ways. Innumerable forms of religions are possible, and . . . it would at least be desirable that one could have an intimation of many at all times."[33]

A far less irenic picture emerges in the *Glaubenslehre*. There Schleiermacher makes the clearly supersessionist claim that "all other fellowships of faith are destined to pass into the Christian fellowship."[34]

Schleiermacher's Christian Situation and Its Governing Order

Schleiermacher's religion situation is merely the opening act for the main show, the Christian situation. It functions merely as a way of setting up his argument on the essence of Christianity.

Schleiermacher recognizes the difficulties of defining that essence (i.e., of establishing the boundaries of "the Christian"). He notes that Christianity is highly fragmented and is characterized by a variety of doctrinal positions. Consequently, Christians disagree among themselves about what separates them from religious others.[35] Despite the diversity, Schleiermacher does think it possible to establish the essence of Christianity.

Significantly, Schleiermacher does not differentiate between the Christian and the not-Christian in terms of truth versus error (as we will see Karl Barth do, in the following chapter). He takes it as axiomatic that "error never exists in and for itself, but always along with some truth."[36] Consequently, no religion can be entirely false. This is bound up with Schleiermacher's notion of religious development: movement from a lower to a higher state of development is only possible if the lower state contains something of the higher.

Instead, Schleiermacher draws the boundaries of the Christian situation in terms of its focus on redemption. While all religions recognize the condition of God-forgetfulness and the need for redemption, Schleiermacher contends that Christianity alone makes these fundamental, the focus of "all religious emotions."[37] Additionally, while other religions seek to accomplish redemption through "penances and purifications," only in Christianity is redemption accomplished by Jesus of Nazareth; while Judaism and Islam are also concerned with redemption, it is "only through Jesus, and thus only in Christianity, [that] redemption [has] become the central point of religion."[38]

Accordingly, "the Christian" is the exclusive realm of salvation. Although Christ's mission (and that of Christ alone) "is . . . gradually to quicken the whole human race into life," connection with Christ is now (i.e., now that Christ no longer lives among us in human form) only available within the Church.[39] Schleiermacher asserts that the "true essence" of "the Christian" consists "only of the totality of the sanctified elements of all who are assumed into living fellowship with Christ."[40] Membership in the Christian common life means being in Christ's "sphere of operation," and it is only through fellowship with other Christians that one has a share of the Holy Spirit.[41] Christ redeems by assuming believers (Christians) "into the power of His God-consciousness."[42] It is only through Christ "that the human God-consciousness becomes an existence of God in human nature."[43] For Schleiermacher, this clearly means membership in the Christian Church: "Only that part of the world which is united to the Christian Church is for us the place of attained perfection, or of the good, and—relatively to quiescent self-consciousness—the place of blessedness."[44]

As that quote shows, while some parts of Schleiermacher's discourse suggest a fundamental continuity between Christianity and religious others, other parts of his discourse suggest a sharp discontinuity between them. This can be seen most prominently in the way Schleiermacher describes the relationship between Christianity and Judaism. Although he acknowledges Christianity's "special historical connexion with Judaism," he holds that Christian piety is not by any means "a remodelling or a renewal and continuation of Judaism."[45] Judaism prior to the ministry of Jesus did not contain the germ of Christianity; nor was Jesus merely a reformer of Jewish law.[46] Consequently, Schleiermacher claims that the Old Testament "is, for our Christian usage, but the husk or wrapping of its prophecy, and that whatever is most definitely Jewish has least value."[47]

Indeed, Schleiermacher speaks of "the whole non-Christian world" as hovering "between idolatry and godlessness."[48] He sets forth his own version of *extra ecclesiam nulla salus* (no salvation outside the church): "The world, so far as it is outside this fellowship of Christ, is always, in spite of that original perfection, the place of evil and sin. No one, therefore, can be surprised to find at this point the proposition that salvation or blessedness is in the Church alone, and that, since blessedness cannot enter from without, but can be found within the Church only by being brought into existence there, the Church alone saves."[49]

Thus for Schleiermacher, the regeneration essential to redemption is bound up with conversion to Christianity. Before conversion, the stirrings of the God-consciousness are "never determinative of the will, being but casual and fleeting."[50] Accordingly, "it is by the very same act that the individual is regenerated and that he becomes a spontaneously active member of the Christian Church."[51]

As for the governing order of the Christian situation, Schleiermacher's hierarchy of development obtains within it as well as without. For Schleiermacher, Protestantism is a higher stage than Roman Catholicism or Eastern Orthodoxy. Since we are concerned here with non-Christians, we need not tarry on this point. However, what is pertinent to our discussion is the fact that he attributes the lower stage of development of some Christian groups to the continued influence of non-Christian elements. Schleiermacher ascribes the "errors" of Roman Catholicism, for example, to a persistence of elements from Judaism and "Heathenism."[52] Also, just as he holds to a sharp discontinuity between Christianity and Judaism, so he asserts that there is "no systematic connexion" between the doctrines of Protestantism and those of Catholicism.[53]

The Void of Schleiermacher's Situations

Despite the sharp distinction Schleiermacher draws between "the Christian" and religious others, he recognizes that Christianity does not exist in isolation. Indeed, religious others play a vital role in his theology: they constitute not only the context for his construction of "religion" but also the "other" against which he delineates "the Christian" and asserts its superiority. In this sense, religious others are as crucial to Schleiermacher's system as his criteria for the religion and the Christian situations or the theological sources he cites explicitly. Religious others make up the void that is both excluded by *and constitutive of* Schleiermacher's situations.

Despite Schleiermacher's recognition of the need to situate Christianity in terms of religious others, their voices are almost completely absent from *On Religion* and the *Glaubenslehre*. Schleiermacher makes sweeping statements about the character of "religion" and of particular religions, yet offers precious few examples demonstrating that he is actually familiar with the religions to which he refers. He occasionally refers to the polytheism of the ancient Greeks, and at one point mentions "the Norse and Indian [religious] systems," though without explaining what he means.[54] While he sometimes supports claims about the character of Judaism with citations from the Hebrew Bible and, in one case, to Philo, he demonstrates no familiarity with the rabbinical literature (e.g., Mishnah, Talmud), kabbalistic texts, near-contemporary Jewish thinkers such as Moses Mendelssohn, or the texts and traditions of Jewish worship.[55] As for Islam, the *Glaubenslehre* never cites the Qur'an, the *hadiths*, or any other sources recognized as authoritative by Muslims. Given the paucity of evidence from religious others, it is astonishing that Schleiermacher holds his propositions about religion to be self-evident and incontrovertible.[56]

Indeed, the only religion of which Schleiermacher demonstrates substantial knowledge is Christianity. This is ironic, since as Richard Crouter notes, in *On Religion* he criticizes the "cultured despisers" of religion for relying on deductive

concepts of religion "without having taken the trouble to justify this understanding inductively through knowledge of particular instances of actual religion."[57]
Schleiermacher's criteria for the religion situation also result in exclusion.
By insisting on the fundamentally interior character of religion, Schleiermacher
excludes aspects of those religious traditions that orient their adherents to the
Ultimate primarily in terms of communal praxis; Judaism and Confucianism
come to mind. Furthermore, by insisting on feeling as the fundamental defining characteristic of religion, he excludes religions (or aspects thereof), such as
Buddhism, with a strong cognitive and rational component. These exclusions
distort Schleiermacher's theological formulations, as we will see shortly.

Sources of Schleiermacher's Criteria for Religion

Now that we have identified how Schleiermacher constructs and organizes the
Religion and Christian situations, we are in a position to ask, Where do these
criteria come from? How is Schleiermacher able to posit these particular criteria
as universals without reference to the voices of religious others?

In both *On Religion* and the *Glaubenslehre*, Schleiermacher's primary source
is supposed to be "the religious self-consciousness present in [the] historic
Christianity [*sic*] community."[58] Schleiermacher claims to build his theology
from the "religious affections" common to all Christians: he famously holds
in the *Glaubenslehre* that "Christian doctrines are accounts of the Christian
religious affections set forth in speech."[59] In the *Glaubenslehre*, Schleiermacher
draws upon the Protestant confessions, the New Testament, and in some cases,
other Christian commentators.[60]

For all practical purposes, however, it is a particular subset of Christian religious experience that is the real source for his theology. It cannot be mere coin-
cidence that the criteria Schleiermacher universalizes as defining "religion" bear
a striking resemblance to the features of the religious tradition that formed him,
Pietist Protestant Christianity.[61] It is instructive to compare his thematic stress
on interiority and *Gefühl* with the theology of the founder of the Moravian
movement, Nikolaus von Zinzendorf. F. Ernst Stoeffler writes, "[Zinzendorf's]
theology revolves around the words *Empfindung* (feeling) or *Gemüt* (not trans-
latable). Personal religion, he held, is a matter of feeling, not of reasoning. Its
locus is not the head, but the 'heart.'"[62] Although Schleiermacher prefers the
term *Gefühl* to Zinzendorf's *Empfindung* and *Gemüt*, the common emphasis
on the affective dimension over other aspects of religious life is striking. This
similarity, combined with Schleiermacher's omission of evidence from religious
others, makes it reasonable to assume that he has taken what he considers the
most important features of Moravian pietism and elevated them to the status of
universal criteria for all religions.

By making the religious experience of his own tradition the norm for all religion, Schleiermacher manifests what Rieger calls "the discourse of the self," in which the human self assumes ultimate authority in theological reflection. Despite Schleiermacher's tendency to speak in universal terms, his locus of authority is in fact a very particular self—in fact, as Rieger demonstrates, the modern European/neo-European middle-class self. Schleiermacher's theological turn to the self partakes in a wider tendency in European/neo-European modernity, manifested in the related developments of bourgeois capitalism and colonialism. The subject of capitalism and colonialism is constructed on the subjugation of social, political, and economic others—people of color, the poor, the disenfranchised, the colonized. Rieger writes that "the modern [European] middle-class established itself by claiming access to the universal meaning of the universe and the right to reshape the key concepts and master signifiers of the modern world."[63] "While Schleiermacher does not buy into this development without reservation," Rieger observes, "his project could still be described in part as reconciling Christianity with the emerging middle-class claim to universality. The position of the modern self becomes normative for humanity in general and, in the process, also normative for matters related to God."[64] The result is the domination, marginalization, and repression of social, political, and economic others. In turning to the modern self as locus of authority, the liberal theology of Schleiermacher not only offers no critique of the modern self's narcissism and aggression but also helps to perpetuate the marginalization of others.[65]

The self that Schleiermacher promotes as the standard for all religions is not only European/neo-European and middle class; it is also Christian, Protestant, and predominantly Pietist. As Karl Barth puts it, Schleiermacher makes "the christianly pious person into the criterion and context of his theology."[66] Schleiermacher is able to universalize these particular criteria without reference to the voices of religious others because the authority and power of the modern self are rooted in the conquest of others; a mark of that conquest is the elevation of Christian, Protestant, and Pietist particulars to the status of universals by which to judge the particulars of all religious others.

In this regard, Schleiermacher participates in a general European/neo-European trend, which Paul Barry Clarke labels "excessive and unwarranted universalization." Clarke finds such universalization in Kant, Hegel, and Marx, as well as more recently in Francis Fukayama's claim that liberalism is the "end of history."[67] The practice of elevating European/neo-European particulars to universal status, Clarke says, "writes out the variety of experiences that people have and interprets them under one rubric. In doing this it eliminates variety in history."[68] Clarke notes the consequence of this move: "When the particular becomes universalised it inverts itself and turns into ideology. As it inverts itself that which is merely contingent appears as necessary."[69] Consequently, the presentation of universals "is a mirage[,] for they are little more than particular expressions of vested interests."[70]

Schleiermacher's elevation of his own religious experience to universal status reveals a side of his theology that differs starkly from Reynolds's depiction of "robust and dynamic sharing of differences" between religions, without "religious narcissism and ethnocentrism."[71] Schleiermacher's apparently positive view of religious others masks an underlying colonizing dynamic, in which Schleiermacher replaces the witness of religious others with the agenda of the modern Christian self. There can be no "sharing of differences" when the voices of one's dialogue partners are suppressed. What we find instead is an a priori and one-sided *attribution* of difference, on the basis of unsubstantiated characterizations, and for the overall purpose of asserting the superiority of "the Christian."

In fact, religious narcissism and ethnocentrism turn out to be embedded in the very fabric of Schleiermacher's theological discourse. As Rieger notes, narcissism is a key element in the discourse of the self. We see it in Schleiermacher's use of religious others as little more than props for his arguments concerning the nature of Christianity. Narcissism is also manifest in Schleiermacher's choice of criteria for constructing "religion": he elevates characteristics important in European Christian Protestant Pietism into universals by which all other religious traditions are judged. This is narcissistic in that it presumes that the experience and categories of the theologian himself—without consulting the experience and categories of others—are of universal validity. Even Schleiermacher's apparently promising refusal to characterize other religions as sheer error in contrast to Christian truth turns out to manifest a narcissistic manipulation of religious others. Schleiermacher's stance is driven not by appreciation of truth in religious others, but by the inner logic of his supersessionist argument: religious others would be unable to convert to the Christian faith if they were wholly in error.[72]

Reynolds admits that Schleiermacher gives at least the appearance of ethnocentrism in "absolutizing history in the person of Christ."[73] Yet there is more than the mere appearance of religious ethnocentrism in Schleiermacher's theological discourse. For one thing, he assumes the superiority of Christianity a priori, and sees no need to provide evidence for this belief.[74] More serious, however, is his actual treatment of religious others: misrepresenting their beliefs, neglecting features that weaken his assertion of the uniqueness of Christianity, and excluding evidence that suggests the essence of religion may be something other than "feeling."

The Badiouan conceptual framework enables us to investigate how Schleiermacher constructs religious others as the void of his two situations, "religion" and "the Christian." Largely ignoring the witness of non-Christians, Schleiermacher selects criteria drawn from his own Pietist Protestant tradition to set the bounds for the religion situation, and then organizes that situation according to a hierarchy of development. At the top of that hierarchy Schleiermacher locates Christianity, which is itself structured according to a hierarchy of development, with Protestantism at the top. Throughout this process, the voices and experiences of religious others are excluded or marginalized. They become the void of Schleiermacher's two situations.

Theological Effects of Schleiermacher's Discursive Construction

As noted earlier, the discursive construction of "the Christian" is not an innocent activity. It has consequences. It entails the exercise of power—the power to draw boundaries, to establish what is "Christian" and what is not, to decide whose voices will be heard and whose voices will not. What, then, are the consequences of Schleiermacher's discursive construction of the religion and Christian situations?

Certainly the fact that he effectively marginalizes and excludes vast large segments of humanity does not foster good relations between Christians and their religious neighbors. It would be hard to blame religious others for taking exception to being depicted as lower species of religious development—let alone having their voices excluded from the discussion about what constitutes religion.

However, facilitating interreligious relations is not the task Schleiermacher sets for himself in the *Glaubenslehre*. It is, rather, to isolate Christianity's "peculiar essence" and on that basis to present the Christian faith systematically. How, then, does Schleiermacher's discursive construction of the religion and Christian situations affect these theological efforts?

Although Schleiermacher presents the religion situation as the context in which Christianity exists, it is clear that he operates from within the narrower Christian situation. As we've seen, his criteria for defining religion and for ranking religions in a hierarchy of development come from a narrowly Pietist Protestant Christianity. By universalizing the religious experience of his own subset of humanity, making it the norm by which to judge the religious practices of religious others and excluding the different experiences and perspectives of religious others themselves, Schleiermacher constructs "knowledge," in the Badiouan sense of that which is limited by what is included in the situation and how those elements are arranged by the governing order. Schleiermacher limits what can be "known," not only about religious others and how they in fact relate to Christianity, but also about Christianity itself. The result is a theology that is robbed of important insights and distorted by misrecognition.

Exclusion of Other Voices

Since Schleiermacher's religion situation largely blocks out the voices of religious others themselves, its "knowledge" excludes important features of human religious experience and practice. By insisting on the fundamentally interior character of religion, Schleiermacher excludes those religious traditions (or aspects thereof) that orient their adherents to the Ultimate primarily in terms of communal praxis. Judaism, for example, has traditionally stressed living a holy life as coextensive with the interior qualities of faith, feeling, and consciousness. Comparing Christian and Jewish views of religious others, Ruth Langer notes that whereas the main question Christians ask regarding another religion is whether the latter's "structures and beliefs create the conditions for the salvation of its adherents," traditional Judaism instead asks, "[Do] the religion's structures allow its members to fulfill God's commandments"?[75] In other words, Langer contends, where Christianity emphasizes interior *conditions*—faith, contrition, Schleiermacher's feeling of absolute dependence—Judaism emphasizes a holy *life*. While we may take issue with Langer's generalization about Christianity (as we will see in Chapter 6, Gustavo Gutiérrez strongly emphasizes that Christians must *practice* their faith), her depiction of Judaism captures its stress on "a process of learning to live like a Jew and committing oneself to an observant lifestyle."[76] This is not to say that Jews do not "live by faith," or that they do not experience something like Schleiermacher's feeling of absolute dependence. It is to say, however, that in Judaism the distinction between interior and exterior is not as sharp as Schleiermacher's system makes it.

Equally problematic is Schleiermacher's insistence on feeling as the fundamental characteristic of religion. Admittedly, it is possible to locate examples from other religious traditions that support this emphasis—although, again, Schleiermacher does not do so. For instance, Shinran's variant of Pure Land Buddhism stresses salvation by grace through faith in the Amida Buddha, and fosters a kind of "feeling of absolute dependence" upon the power of Amida's love and compassion.[77] Arguably, the Hindu bhakti (devotion) tradition, for which the *locus classicus* is the *Bhagavad Gita*, stresses the affective dimension of religion. For example, in the section of the *Gita* titled "The Way of Love," the divine avatar Krishna celebrates those who "set their hearts on me and worship me with unfailing devotion and faith."[78]

Nonetheless, the *Gita* also suggests the problem with too closely identifying religion with the affective. Although in some places the *Gita* seems to favor the yoga of bhakti, it also recognizes the value of other ways, including that of wisdom (*jñana yoga*), action (*karma yoga*), and meditation (*raja yoga*).[79]

Furthermore, it is difficult to see how the emphasis on feeling could apply to Buddhism (apart, perhaps, from Shinran). While one can find in Buddhism forms of devotionalism at least superficially similar to Christian Pietist forms, there is a strong cognitive element to much Buddhist teaching and practice. This can be seen in the comments of Buddhist scholar K. N. Jayatilleke. While acknowledging that Buddhism requires at least tentative faith, Jayatilleke contends that it also requires a critical outlook. He quotes the Buddha: "Just as the experts test gold by burning it, cutting it and applying it on a touchstone, my statements should be accepted only after critical examination and not out of respect for me." Commenting on this passage, Jayatilleke writes, "The Buddhist accepts the 'right philosophy' of life (*samma-ditthi*) as the basis of his living because he finds it reasonable and in fact more reasonable than any other way of life. Such faith which eventually culminates in knowledge is called a 'rational faith' (*akaravati saddha*) as opposed to a blind or 'baseless faith' (*amulika saddha*)."[80]

Misrecognition of Religious Others

Given the exclusion of the voices of religious others from Schleiermacher's discussion of religion, it is not surprising that his claims about them would be highly questionable. However, Schleiermacher's discourse does not simply misrepresent religious others; it misrecognizes them. By *misrecognition* I have in mind Rieger's Lacanian notion of that psychosocial process (discussed in Chapter 2) by which the self turns the other into an object "as a prop for the self."[81] That is, the other is regarded purely in terms of the subject's own self-image and desires.

Schleiermacher's depiction of religious others in the *Glaubenslehre*—particularly his reasons for placing them below Christianity in the hierarchy of "development"—function mainly to prop up his case for the superiority of Christianity. Case in point is his treatment of Islam and Judaism. Not only does Schleiermacher offer no relevant examples from these traditions to substantiate his claims about them, he also glosses over or omits characteristics in each tradition that call into question his understanding of religion and his supersessionist developmental hierarchy.

For instance, when Schleiermacher refers to "the influence of the sensible upon the character of religious emotions" in Islam, he does not specify what he means, how this influence is manifested, or even where he gets this idea.[82] Since he associates this "influence of the sensible" with polytheism, the clear implication is that Islam, though monotheistic, is tainted by polytheistic elements, and thus that it falls lower on the scale of "development" that leads to Christianity.

However, given the Prophet Muhammad's uncompromising assertion of the oneness of God and the Qur'an's vigorous rejection of Arab polytheistic practices, it is difficult to interpret Schleiermacher's characterization as anything other than misrecognition, however unintentional.[83] Furthermore, Islam would seem to express at least as forcefully as Christianity a feeling of absolute dependence on "God as the absolute undivided unity."[84]

Islam also stresses the problem of God-forgetfulness and the need for regeneration, which for Schleiermacher sets Christianity apart. Take, for instance, the *Fatihah*, the opening surah of the Qur'an and an obligatory feature of Muslim prayer: "All praise is due to Allah, the Lord of the Worlds. . . . Thee do we serve and Thee do we beseech for help. Keep us on the right path. The path of those upon whom Thou hast bestowed favors. Not (the path) of those upon whom Thy wrath is brought down, nor of those who go astray."[85] Interpreting this passage, David Waines writes: "Allah is the sole source and sustainer of life. . . . He is Lord of the cosmic drama from the beginning of time at the act of creation, to the end of time, on the Day of Judgment. From the beginning of the drama humankind requires his guidance, without which the individual or entire communities would go astray, as indeed has been the case in human experience."[86] In short, quite contrary to Schleiermacher, a focus on the human tendency to God-forgetfulness and the need for repentance and regeneration would seem to be at least as integral to Islam as they are to Christianity.[87]

In Schleiermacher's portrayal of Judaism, the degree of misrecognition is, if anything, even more pronounced.[88] Consider his claim that Judaism "betrays a lingering affinity" with idol worship in "its limitation of the love of Jehovah to the race of Abraham."[89] Judaism simply is not as uniformly particularistic as Schleiermacher contends. Had Schleiermacher delved more deeply into the literature of Judaism, he would have found that Jewish teaching displays a range of opinions on this issue (as on many others). Rabbi Nicholas de Lange contends that universalism is at least as deeply rooted as nationalism in Jewish sacred literature. As an example of the former he cites a teaching from the Mishnah: "The fact that [in the Bible] one man was created [rather than the separate founders of each nation] teaches us that none of us can say to another: My father was greater than your father."[90] Furthermore, Schleiermacher might have found in the German Jewish philosopher Moses Mendelssohn the idea that the general truths of Judaism are revealed to all rational beings, not solely to the Jewish people.[91]

There is an important lesson here. The exercise of theological power—the power to set the boundaries of "the Christian"—can distort the work of the one exercising that power. Schleiermacher recognizes that in the theological context of religious diversity, the "essence" of Christianity can only be established by comparison and contrast with other religions. Yet by excluding and misrecognizing religious others, Schleiermacher weakens his own case. The representation of religious others in his discourse is largely a narcissistic fiction. If the depiction of Christianity's "peculiar essence" is based on a distinction from a fiction, how reliable can his claims about that "essence" be? Furthermore, since Schleiermacher's arguments for the superiority of Christianity are built upon that "essence," how trustworthy can those arguments be?

Implications for the Understanding of God

If, as Rieger claims, there is no encounter with the divine Other apart from encounter with human others, so there can be no encounter with human others apart from encounter with *religious* others. As long as religious others continue to lie outside the field of consideration and authority, the Christian self-critique of unconscious structures of authority and power will remain incomplete. Equally important, our encounter with the divine Other will be blocked, and our understanding of that Other will be distorted.

The problem with Schleiermacher's theological discourse lies not only in the ways in which he marginalizes and excludes religious others, thereby participating in and perpetuating wider social-economic-political marginalization. The problem lies also in the consequences of those structures and processes for an understanding of God and of the relationship between God and humans.

Rieger expresses the problem in terms of Schleiermacher's tendency to confuse the nature and interests of God with the self-image and aspirations of his own European middle class, then on the rise socially, economically, and politically—especially in the global project of colonialism. Rieger writes, "In its eagerness to shape the world for the better, the middle class does not realize that it is perpetuating structures of exclusion which leave out huge parts of humanity. The middle class does not realize that its freedom depends on the unfreedom of others. . . . Ultimately this failure to truly connect with others who are members of a different class affects the relation of the self and divine Other as well."[92] Because of this basic blindness toward the social-political-economic others, and despite Schleiermacher's desire "to leave open the place of the infinite," Rieger writes, ultimately "God is . . . pulled into the force field of the self."[93]

As noted earlier, it is the *Christian* self that Schleiermacher takes as the reliable guide for theological reflection. Despite Schleiermacher's claims to universality, this self has its roots in Protestant and Pietist experience, with piety seen as fundamentally a matter of feeling. It is *this* self and *this* experience that are the essence of "the Christian" for Schleiermacher, and the ultimate source and norm for his theology. He dismisses deviations as the result of the influence of "alien" elements from religions at "lower" forms of development of the God-consciousness. The structure of Schleiermacher's theological discourse marginalizes some religious traditions and excludes others altogether. The voices of religious others are barely heard, even in the discussion of the supposedly universal category, "religion."

Consequently, the understanding of God and of the divine-human relationship is tightly restricted. There is no sense that other understandings—either from religious others or from within Christianity (e.g., from Catholicism)—might be valid or even worth considering. Indeed, there is no indication that Schleiermacher has even attempted to find out, given the paucity of citations to non-Christian sources in *On Religion* and the *Glaubenslehre*.

While Schleiermacher structures his theological discourse so as to prevent the distorting influence of "alien" elements, he seems not to have contemplated the possibility that the Christian witness could be distorted by the formation and structure of "the Christian" itself (i.e., as situation). And that, I argue, is precisely what happens in Schleiermacher's discourse.

Schleiermacher seems not to have considered the possibility that religious others might have a different experience of the Ultimate and of human relation to it, and that their experience might be equally valid. Since Schleiermacher's religion and Christian situations block out the witness of religious others, God is reduced to what *Christians* experience as "God," and God's redemptive action is reduced to the activity of the Church. Even access to the Holy Spirit is restricted to members of the Christian communion.[94] God is reduced to that which the Church mediates and what members of that Church experience.

This distorts the Christian understanding of God in four important ways. First, it suggests that God makes Godself known fundamentally through human *feeling*, through interiority, and not through "knowing" or "doing." This renders a priori invalid other paths to the Ultimate to which religious others witness: for instance, the Hindu belief that knowledge of the gods comes by listening (*shruti*) and remembering (*smriti*); the Muslim belief that God can be known directly by listening to the recitation of God's own speech in the Qur'an; the Jewish combination of faith in God's Torah and life lived according to *halakhah*; the Hindu yogas of selfless service, knowledge, and meditation; and Vodoun "service" to the spiritual intermediaries (*servi loa*). How can Schleiermacher be sure that these different forms of religious experience and practice are inferior to "feeling" as ways of coming to know God? Surely such certainty can only come *after* dialogue with religious others—dialogue that Schleiermacher's theological discourse excludes.

A second distortion follows from the first. A major thrust of Schleiermacher's theology is that reliable knowledge of God is restricted to those who are members of Christianity, which is the sole repository of the truth because it, alone among the religions, reflects the full development of the religious consciousness and is the sole mediator of the influence of Christ and the Holy Spirit. In effect, Schleiermacher is claiming that his own religion has sole possession of knowledge of the Divine. While religious others ("the unregenerate") also "experience gleams of blessedness through the God-consciousness latent in them . . . as preparatory workings of grace," Schleiermacher nonetheless holds that "the whole non-Christian world . . . hover[s] between idolatry and godlessness."[95] Furthermore, since God in Christ intended the foundation of the Church, and since God's own "laws" are in some sense responsible for the fact that not all humans are members of the Christian fellowship, the implication is that God in some sense intends this discrepancy of knowledge.[96]

There are at least two problems with Schleiermacher's case here. First, Schleiermacher assumes a priori what needs to be demonstrated: that religious others do not in fact know the God to whom Christians witness. Since the voices of religious others are largely excluded from Schleiermacher's Christian situation, he does not substantiate this claim. Second, the idea that it is in some sense divinely willed that some know God fully and others do not contradicts the Christian belief in a loving God. If regeneration and redemption are consequences of the flowering of the latent God-consciousness, surely a loving God desires that all humans reach that state. As James Fredericks notes, while the New Testament affirms that salvation comes through faith in Jesus Christ, it also affirms "that God's saving love touches every human being. . . . The God preached by Jesus of Nazareth and witnessed to in the New Testament is not indifferent or even hostile to the vast majority of the human race."[97]

However—and this is a third distortion—Schleiermacher's sense of divine love, so important in the Christian faith, is skewed by his focus on the religious experience of Christians. Since Christian doctrines are for Schleiermacher "accounts of the Christian religious affections set forth in speech," such doctrines can only reflect what Christians *experience* of God. Presumably, the doctrinal system can only affirm that God is love because there is an experience of that love, not, for example, because scripture proclaims it. Furthermore, Schleiermacher's system can only affirm that God is love because *Christians* experience that love, since he excludes all but Christian witness to that love. Consequently, he depicts divine love only as manifested in the activity of redemption, which occurs only through Christ.[98] Moreover, he claims that only those who *recognize* the divine love—those who are redeemed, that is, Christians—*receive* that love. Although "in virtue of their capacity for the God-consciousness all men certainly are also objects of the divine love," Schleiermacher claims, "the divine love does not realize itself in them simply as such"; they get only as far as "the negative consciousness that the Supreme Being is devoid of jealousy."[99] Consequently, "in so far as they do not love God, He cannot love them. . . . He loves them only as He sees them in Christ."[100] God apparently loves only those who recognize God's love—a legalistic, quid pro quo representation that conflicts with the scriptural sense of God's a priori and unconditional love, reflected in the Fredericks quote. Here Schleiermacher backs himself into a corner, because his comments elsewhere on the salvific status of non-Christians suggest that he resists the idea that some humans are forever shut out from salvation.[101] However, the systematic privileging of *Christian* experience leads him to contradict his own inclination toward universalism in favor of a legalistic depiction of God.

A fourth and final distortion is related to the preceding three. If God in some sense authorizes the variation in knowledge of God, then God must also authorize existing social, economic, and political structures of marginalization and exclusion. Although Schleiermacher is careful to separate the Kingdom of God from civil authorities and other worldly institutions, it is telling that Schleiermacher speaks approvingly (or at least uncritically) of "the great advantage in power and civilization which the Christian peoples possess over the non-Christian."[102] This demonstrates an important connection: a sense of superiority in religious matters often bleeds over into a sense of superiority in the social, cultural, political, and economic spheres.

Evental Sites and Blind Spots in Schleiermacher's Discourse

As we saw in Chapter 2, the void is not only excluded from a situation; it is also constitutive of its situation, haunting it as a kind of "absent presence" or "present absence." Where the situation meets its void is the evental site—the site where the truth that transcends a situation can break in, in the phenomenon of the event.

One potential evental site in Schleiermacher's situations is the recognition of a fundamental continuity between religious others and Christianity: as one religion among many, Christianity shares certain basic characteristics with religious others. Therefore, the relationship between Christianity and religious others cannot be reduced simply to one of truth versus error. Recognition of this continuity can offer a basis, or common ground, for encounter with, and meaningful dialogue between, Christians and religious others.

Had Schleiermacher attended to this fundamental continuity, he might have avoided at least some of the limitations and distortions that plague his religion and Christian situations. For instance, had he taken note of the importance of communal praxis in Judaism, he might have been led to inquire whether it might be as essential to Christianity as "feeling." This exploration might have led him to question the workability of his Pietist-influenced assumptions that a sharp distinction between interiority and exterior practice, between "feeling" and "doing," is in fact essential to Christianity. Strands of my own Anglican tradition do not make such a sharp distinction between the interior life and exterior practice. For example, the baptismal rite in the Episcopal Church emphasizes that the baptized are to "seek and serve Christ in all persons," and to "strive for justice and peace among all people."[103] In this respect, Anglicans have much in common with Judaism's stress on living a holy life.

Similarly, had Schleiermacher taken note of the importance of reason in Buddhism, he might have been led to investigate whether reason might play an equally crucial role in Christianity. If I may cite the Anglican tradition again, Richard Hooker holds that reason is God's instrument for guiding the world; God therefore leads people to truth both through revelation (i.e., scripture) and through reason.[104] Additionally, the Anglican scholar of mysticism Evelyn Underhill argues that thinking, feeling, and willing or acting are equally important in the spiritual life; indeed, when the "purely emotional" aspect dominates, "it often degenerates into an objectionable sentimentality, and may lead to forms of self-indulgence which are only superficially religious."[105]

In his a priori elevation to universal status of a Christian and largely Pietist understanding of religious experience, Schleiermacher evinces a blind spot toward religious others: a failure, rooted in the narcissism of the modern European/neo-European colonizing self, to engage those who differ and to come to grips with the implications of the fact that there are many different ways of being religious. Consequently, he reduces religious others to abstract categories rather flesh-and-blood human realities, just as the colonialist powers of Schleiermacher's day presumed to act in the "best interests" of their colonized subjects but did not bother to listen to what the colonized had to say in the matter.

Another potential evental site is Schleiermacher's elevation of the self to theological authority and the accompanying emphasis on personal religious experience. Christians and religious others appear to have fundamentally different experiences not only of that which is ultimately real but also of the human condition. Recognizing the value of personal religious experience—that of religious others as well as Christians—opens the possibility for Christians to listen to, grapple with, and learn from the experiences of religious others, thereby deepening and making more meaningful Christians' understanding of their own experience(s).[106] Additionally, Christians could learn a great deal from the ways religious others experience Christianity. For instance, in the lived experience of religious others, do Christians actually live up to their self-image as bringers of a liberating gospel of love? By grappling with religious experiences very different from their own, Schleiermacher might move beyond the mere "knowledge" of the Christian situation, to encounter the "truth" that transcends it.

Once again, however, blind spots in Schleiermacher's theological discourse prevent him from realizing the potential of this evental site. The suppression of the voices of religious others closes off his theology to the benefit of their perspectives. His a priori decision that the true character of religious experience is the feeling of absolute dependence effectively shuts the window to encounter with religious difference. There is no need for conversation with religious others if the character of their experience is already settled in advance. In other words, Schleiermacher is on the right track when he understands the importance of religious experience in theological reflection. Where he goes astray is in reducing such experience to that of his own subset of humanity and thereby blocking off the possibility of meaningful encounter with others.

A third evental site is Schleiermacher's recognition that any religious tradition, Christianity included, contains a mixture of truth and error. He strikes this cautionary note repeatedly in the *Glaubenslehre*, and in several different registers. As noted previously, he holds that the religious self-consciousness (the feeling of absolute dependence) is always accompanied by the sensible self-consciousness, and that this introduces distortions into religious expression, such as anthropomorphic characterizations of God. Even in the Christian consciousness, "the feeling of absolute dependence never purely by itself fills a moment of religious experience."[107] He approaches the problem of error in Christian teaching along similar lines. "In every act of the religious consciousness," he writes, "truth is more or less infected with error."[108] This applies to the Church as well: "The Church cannot form itself out of the midst of the world without the world exercising some influence on the Church"; "the Church is . . . ever anew admitting worldly elements."[109] A similar process of distortion occurs on the level of the individual Christian. As soon as the believer seeks to express the innermost Christian consciousness outwardly in "definite ideas," it is distorted by the person's former unregenerate nature.[110]

The recognition that Christian teaching remains to some extent provisional and always in need of reform injects a much-needed note of humility into Schleiermacher's theological discourse. It also has the potential to open his theology to encounter with religious others, leading him in a direction quite different from the supersessionist path he in fact takes. Acknowledging limitations in one's own viewpoint is a crucial first step toward transformative encounter with others. It places the theologian on equal footing with others; it removes at least some of the barriers to listening to the insights of others. Furthermore, Schleiermacher's recognition of distorting "worldly" influence on theological expression could warn him of the influence of Eurocentric and colonialist culture on his theology (e.g., in his notions of religious "progress").

Sadly, Schleiermacher does not take advantage of this evental site. Indeed, as we have seen, he blames *religious others* for errors that crop up within the Christian situation. He ascribes the lower stage of development of some Christian groups to the continued influence of non-Christian elements; the "errors" of Roman Catholicism, for example, derive from a persistence of elements from Judaism and "Heathenism."[111]

Schleiermacher seems not to have recognized the possibility that distortion and error can result from the construction of the Christian situation itself—from the boundaries he draws around "the Christian," from the processes of marginalization and exclusion of religious others, and from the assumptions that govern those processes.

In his way of handling religious others, Schleiermacher's theological discourse participates in, or at least does little to counter, the political and economic structures of exclusion, which were in his time already taking on their current shape. Religious others—non-Christians—made up then, as they do today, the largest segment of those who are on the receiving end of the colonialism and imperialism of Schleiermacher's time and the neocolonialism of global capitalism in our own. While it would be an overstatement to claim that the victims of colonialism and neocolonialism were victims because they were non-Christians, there is no doubt that the ideology motivating colonialism and neocolonialism arose in a Western European and largely Christian context; it was and is influenced by Christian ideas, such as a teleological view of history (seen in Schleiermacher's idea of religious "development"), supersessionism (seen in his assertion of the supremacy of "the Christian"), and the consequent devaluing of the beliefs and perspectives of those outside the community of the "chosen" (seen in his repression of voices of religious others).[112] Far from critiquing these structures and processes, Schleiermacher participates in them through the very structure of his theological discourse.

Conclusion

By constructing "religion" and "the Christian" on criteria drawn a priori from his own experience and that of his subset of humanity, and by repressing the voices of religious others, Schleiermacher creates a theological "knowledge" that is structurally closed to difference, to otherness. True, "the Christian," to be coherent and meaningful, depends on the drawing of boundaries that mark off differences with religious others. Nevertheless, establishing the criteria for those boundaries only from one side—that is, failing to listen to the different voices of religious others, to what they testify, rather than how they can be arbitrarily categorized and characterized in order to boost the Christian self-image—leads to a solipsistic vision of Christianity that confuses the interests of God with those of the self. In short, Schleiermacher's handling of the concept "religion" becomes a way to block, not to facilitate, encounter with those who are different.

Religious others point to the limitations of Schleiermacher's boundaries and to a truth greater than the knowledge available within his situations—truth not only about the situations themselves but also about God and human religious experience. This chapter has offered many examples of that truth: that Schleiermacher's religious "universals" are not so universal after all; that his depiction of religious others is highly inaccurate and distorted; that religion is a much more complex phenomenon than Schleiermacher's stress on *Gefühl* suggests; and that Schleiermacher's depiction of God is distorted by the very structure of his theological system.

These limitations and distortions, however, are not visible from within Schleiermacher's situations because the voices of religious others cannot be heard there. No matter how well-intentioned Schleiermacher may have been, the structure of his theological discourse—the criteria that form its boundaries, and its governing order—conceals otherness and difference. When Christian theology fails to hear the voices of religious others, it loses a critical perspective on itself and its witness. Theological discourse that does not open itself to encounter with religious others remains trapped in its own circular self-affirmation.

CHAPTER 4

Barth

Revelation in Service to "the Christian"

I f Schleiermacher is the father of modern liberal Protestant theology, Karl Barth is the father of the reaction against that theology.[1] Throughout his long career, he sought to counteract the theological dominance of the modern self by restoring to the place of authority God as divine Other. Whereas Schleiermacher grounds Christian theological reflection in immediate interior experience, Barth seeks to ground theology upon divine revelation, specifically that which Christianity recognizes in the biblical texts.

Although Barth does not develop a comprehensive theology of religions, his attempt to shift the authority structures of Christian theology has important consequences for his discourse about religion and religious others.[2] Like Schleiermacher, Barth recognizes that Christianity is one religion among many religions: it "is a species within a genus in which there may be other species."[3] And like Schleiermacher, Barth constructs a religion situation to organize this plural reality. His Christian religion is a subset of this wider religion situation.

Despite these structural similarities to Schleiermacher, Barth's understanding of religion differs dramatically from that of his predecessor. While Schleiermacher looks favorably upon the religious impulse and builds his theology upon it, Barth views religion from the standpoint of (what he takes to be) divine revelation, and finds it wanting—indeed, finds religion to be a mark of the utter fallenness of humanity. Barth therefore differs critically from Schleiermacher by placing alongside "religion" and "the Christian religion" a third category, "revelation"; by rethinking the first two categories in terms of his understanding of revelation, and by regarding revelation as opposed—dialectically opposed but opposed nonetheless—to all religion, including the Christian religion.

Barth's insistence upon the utter freedom of the divine Other and his warnings against absolutizing the Christian religion could open the way for encounter with religious others. Yet, as we shall see, the structure of Barth's theological discourse closes off that possibility, marginalizing religious others, blocking meaningful encounter with them, and, ironically, compromising the very freedom and otherness of the divine Other he so strongly stresses.

Given this ambivalence toward religious others in Barth's project, it is not surprising that scholars interpret his view of non-Christians and of interreligious dialogue in dramatically different ways. Many cite Barth as a prime example of the exclusivist approach to religious diversity. Paul Knitter, for example, stresses Barth's claim that there is an "exclusive contradiction" between Christianity and other religious traditions, and cites his warning to Christian missionaries to avoid looking for points of contact with other religions.[4]

Other scholars disagree vigorously with the characterization of Barth as an exclusivist. Joseph Di Noia contends that such a characterization reflects a basic misreading of Barth's theology. "Barth," he writes, "is . . . less concerned with what Christians should think about non-Christians than . . . with how modern concepts of religion, religious experience, and religious consciousness have influenced what Christians think about being Christian."[5] Di Noia also cites passages where Barth admits the possibility of divine revelation in other religions ("other lights").[6] Peter Harrison goes one step further: he contends that "Barth's evaluation of the religions was in reality quite positive."[7] Appealing to Barth's "incipient universalism" and (like Di Noia) to Barth's discussion of "other lights," Harrison concludes that Barth is best categorized as an inclusivist.[8]

Although Di Noia and Harrison raise important points, they seem to have overlooked the possibility that the *structure* of Barth's theology may contradict its *content*. As with Schleiermacher, the key is to examine not just what Barth *says* about religious others, but also what he *does* in and through his theological discourse. And, as with Schleiermacher, an understanding of Barth's theology is incomplete without an examination of what it excludes.

This chapter will focus on the two sections in Barth's *Church Dogmatics* (CD) that treat religion and other religions: section 17 of CD I/2 and section 69 of CD IV/3. Once again, our investigation will focus on three questions:

1. How does the discourse construct religious others?
2. How does the construction of religious others affect the resulting theological formulations and particularly those concerning the Divine?
3. What are possible eventual sites and blind spots in the discourse?

Barth's Construction of Religious Others

In many ways, Barth is the paradigmatic Badiouan theologian. He finds his identity in a truth event, in his disillusionment and very public break with his liberal Protestant teachers in 1914. His subsequent career is shaped by his effort to remain faithful to the insights he gained from this event.[9] In Badiouan terms, Barth depicts religion, including Christianity qua religion, as a situation. What religion excludes—its void—is divine truth, revelation. The truth of the void must break into religion from the outside; Barth even calls this in-breaking an "event" (*Ereignis*).[10] The Christian religion, which arises in faithfulness to this in-breaking event of divine revelation, constitutes the evental site within the religion situation, calling religion itself into question.

Accordingly, Barth purports to take the perspective of revelation, which stands outside, and in judgment upon, all religion including the Christian religion. What he actually does, however, is quite different. In fact he constructs revelation and religion from firmly *inside* the Christian situation. As a result, the structure of Barth's discourse works to undermine the very insight he seeks to communicate.

Barth's Truth Event

Early in his theological career, Barth shared the perspective of the dominant Christian situation of his time and context, the liberal Protestant theology that had developed after Schleiermacher, with its emphasis on inward personal experience. However, what Eberhard Busch calls a "portentous shift" from Barth's earlier liberal stance was motivated by a "new insight," which was in turn occasioned by two shocks. While serving as a small-town pastor beginning in 1911, Barth was shaken not only by his encounter with the social and economic misery of workers and peasants but also by the realization that the church had been co-opted by the bourgeoisie to protect the social-political-economic status quo and to keep the workers and peasants docile and submissive.[11] His dismay at this betrayal of the Gospel was compounded by the shock of seeing his liberal teachers endorse Germany's entry into World War I.[12] Barth realized that the Christian situation of German liberal Protestantism had been subsumed under the situation of bourgeois German nationalism. And what had been excluded from this Christian-bourgeois-nationalist situation was the very self-revelation of God that should have been the raison d'être of the Church. Busch describes Barth's "new insight" as follows: "'God' is in fact the designation of . . . the reality that is a '*new*' world in contrast with the present one. The new reality which the old world cannot itself posit can be posited only *from outside* of it, and it is posited by God. . . . God *posits himself* prior to all human reality. He does so by both setting himself against this reality ('judgment') and by setting himself in relation to it ('grace')."[13]

Barth's strong sense of the radical otherness of God and the externality of revelation decisively shaped his critical view of the Christian situation, religion, and revelation. The Christian situation of his time (and, as we shall see, religion generally) had been exposed as an all-too-human construct. While it presumed to witness to divine revelation, it in fact opposed and excluded it. What Christian theology thought was God may in fact not have been God at all.[14]

What was needed, Barth realized, was a complete overhaul of the Christian theological project. In fidelity to his truth event, Barth begins his own theological project not with religion, but with revelation (*Offenbarung*) as that which is excluded by religion and stands in judgment over it (and over all other human constructs).

Revelation, Religion, and Christianity

Revelation as Religion's Void

The proper object and standpoint of theology, Barth contends, should be revelation, not religion, nor the Christian religion qua religion.[15] What, then, is this revelation Barth believes is excluded by religion? To answer this question, it is helpful to differentiate the *content*, *source*, and *nature* of revelation as Barth construes it, keeping in mind that he treats all three as one.[16] For Barth, the *content* of revelation is Jesus Christ.[17] The *source* of revelation is the Bible, read through the eyes of faith.[18] As will be discussed later in this chapter, Barth closely associates the moment of revelation with encounter with the Bible.[19] It is important to note at this point that Barth directly associates divine revelation with what *Christians* recognize as revelation. We will explore the implications of this association later in this chapter.

For Barth, revelation is by *nature* something wholly other, external to humans and human constructs. In part this has to do with his sense of the radical otherness of God. Barth tends to speak of God as wholly "outside" humanity.[20] As "God's self-offering and self-manifestation," revelation "encounters man on the presupposition and in confirmation of the fact that man's attempts to know God from his own standpoint are wholly and entirely futile; not because of any necessity in principle, but because of a practical necessity of fact. In revelation God tells man that He is God, and that as such He is his Lord. In telling him this, revelation tells him something utterly new, something which apart from revelation he does not know and cannot tell either himself or others."[21]

Barth assumes that humans are radically fallen, and as such not only are incapable of knowing but are willfully opposed to God's Word.[22] There is no natural human point of contact for the divine message. Human reason is "intrinsically godless" and "inimical to belief"; thus there is no possibility of a natural theology, no possibility of reaching God by reason.[23] Barth writes that revelation is "the act by which in grace [God] reconciles man to Himself by grace. As a radical teaching about God, it is also the radical assistance of God which comes to us as those who are unrighteous and unholy, and as such damned and lost."[24] Accordingly, the appropriate human response to revelation is to listen and to obey.

Religion as Situation

Against revelation Barth posits the category "religion." If revelation is radically other than human, religion is human, all too human. Like Schleiermacher, Barth recognizes the roots of religion in a putative universal human experience of being "confronted by definite forces which stand over their own life and that of the world and influence it," a feeling of being in relation to "something ultimate and decisive, which is at least a powerful rival to their own will and power."[25] Natural though it may be, religion is nonetheless essentially idolatrous, the human attempt to do what only God can do.[26] It manifests the human desire for "truth above and certainty within, both of which he thinks he can know and even create for himself."[27] As such, religion "contradicts" and "opposes" revelation. "In religion," Barth writes, "man bolts and bars himself against revelation by providing a substitute, by taking away in advance the very thing which has to be given by God."[28]

In other words, religion is *Unglaube.*[29] As Di Noia notes, *Unglaube* is best translated "unfaith" or "faithlessness." Di Noia writes, "Human religiosity, according to Barth, is judged by revelation to be the absence or lack of faith: not simply an unwillingness to assent to certain truths, but an unwillingness to yield to the saving power of divine grace and revelation, and to surrender all those purely human attempts to know and satisfy God which together comprise human religion and religiosity."[30]

Consequently, religion cannot offer truth. "Religion is never true in itself and as such," Barth contends. "The revelation of God denies that any religion is true, i.e., that it is in truth the knowledge and worship of God and the reconciliation of man with God. . . . [For] revelation is the truth beside which there is no other truth, over which there is only lying and wrong."[31]

As Di Noia notes, it is important to keep in mind that for Barth "the judgment that all religion is unfaith is strictly a divine judgment rendered by revelation itself and knowable only by the grace of faith. This judgment is emphatically not one that is pronounced upon the world of non-Christian religions by Christianity nor by its representatives."[32] Although I will argue that this is a distinction without a difference, it is important to remember that Barth's explicit appeal is to divine revelation (as he understands it), not to the Church.

Since religion excludes divine revelation and instead attempts to know God from the human standpoint,[33] it generates (in Badiouan terms) knowledge, not truth. Thus Barth speaks of "the magic circle of religion":[34] it cannot see its own true character as idolatry, self-righteousness, and *Unglaube.* The truth of the void—revelation—must therefore break in "from outside the magic circle of religion and its origin, i.e., from outside man."[35] In terms similar to those of Badiou, Barth speaks of this in-breaking as an "event."[36]

Christianity as Evental Site

Where, then, does Christianity fit in? Barth clearly considers it to be a religion among other religions, since it bears strong phenomenological similarities to other religions (e.g., similar concepts of sacred scripture, similarities of outlook and piety).[37] Furthermore, Christianity qua religion is "idolatry and self-righteousness, unbelief [*Unglaube*], and therefore sin."[38]

Yet Barth does not let the matter rest there. He goes on to assert that Christianity is also the "true" religion. How can this be? The answer involves Barth's notion of revelation's *Aufhebung*, or sublation, of religion.[39] The dialectic of revelation not only negates but also rectifies and elevates religion.[40] Thus the realm of human religion is the *site* of divine revelation: "The revelation of God is actually the presence of God . . . in the world of human religion."[41]

However, Barth does not hold that God's presence makes all religion (or all religions) true. Only Christianity holds this honor: "God's gracious entry into the world of human religion renders the Christian religion the true religion of revelation."[42] Yet Christianity is not the true religion on its own merits. It is so only by divine election: as Barth puts it, we can only speak of Christianity as the "true" religion "in the sense in which we speak of a 'justified sinner.'"[43] As the sinner is justified by grace alone and remains a sinner, so the Christian religion, while qua religion remaining a species of *Unglaube*, "is snatched [by God] from the world of religions and the judgment and sentence pronounced upon it."[44] The Christian religion is the true religion only because "the righteousness and the judgement of God" characterize and differentiate it as true, rather than another religion.[45]

In Badiouan terms, Barth presents the Christian religion as the evental site within the religion situation. The Christian religion—insofar as it is true to its unique character and mission—is the site of the in-breaking event of divine revelation. It is "the religion of revelation."[46] It alone recognizes the true character of religion (including itself) as *Unglaube*, and it stands as witness to that truth and to the event that revealed it.

These comments might suggest that the "truth" of Christianity is bestowed purely from without, as righteousness is imputed to a person who remains utterly sinful. In some other passages, however, Barth suggests that there is something about the *nature* of Christianity that distinguishes it as true. More on this later.

In identifying the Christian religion as the "true" religion, Barth also implies a governing order for the religion situation, that which orders the relation of its elements to one another and to the situation as a whole. As we saw in the last chapter, for Schleiermacher the governing order of the religion situation is the concept of development from "lower" to "higher" forms of religiosity. Barth, on the other hand, suggests no such process of development: religions, being inherently opposed to revelation, do not progress toward it.[47] However, his characterization of the Christian religion does suggest a kind of ordering principle: truth as opposed to error. Christianity constitutes the only "true" religion, in contrast to "the religions of error," those that are "heathen, poor, and utterly lost."[48]

Barth's Christian Situation

It is fitting that we end the summary of Barth's purported theological project with that very negative depiction of religious others, for it indicates that Barth is actually doing something quite different from what he purports to do. The Christian religion as Barth constructs it is not merely a witness to the event of revelation. It is also a *situation*, with its own boundaries, governing order, and void. Although Barth claims to take the perspective of a revelation that is wholly other, he in fact builds revelation wholly from *within* the Christian situation. Although he claims to present religion from the perspective of revelation, he in fact constructs it on the basis of Christian "knowledge." To see how this unfolds, let us first look at Barth's Christian situation, then at the processes of exclusion by which he constructs its void.

As with Schleiermacher, the Christian situation in Barth's theology is bound up with the Church. According to James J. Buckley, Barth argues that "the election of Jesus Christ [i.e., as mediator between divine and human] is also the eternal and ongoing election of the community," that is, the Church; consequently, the Church must be "embodied as the special visibility of the body of Christ."[49] It is significant that Barth's *magnum opus* is titled *Church Dogmatics*. Barth sought to do theology explicitly from *within* the Christian community— to speak, as it were, *from* and *for* the church.[50]

How, then, does Barth draw the boundaries of that community—of the Christian situation? What sets it apart from other religions?

As we have seen, Barth tries to resist the tendency to turn the truth of the Christian religion into some essential or intrinsic property. Yet he does not succeed in resisting this tendency. Despite his claim that the Christian religion qua religion is not distinguishable from other religions, and is the "true" religion only by divine election and not by any features of its own, Barth also suggests that the Christian religion—and it alone—is *essentially* linked with divine revelation. He writes, "The true and essential distinction of the Christian religion from the non-Christian, and with it its character as the religion of truth over against the religions of error, can be demonstrated only in the fact, or event, that taught by Holy Scripture the Church listens to Jesus Christ and no one else as grace and truth."[51] Whereas Schleiermacher contends that in Christianity alone are God-forgetfulness and redemption fundamental, for Barth what sets

Christianity apart from other religions is its unique association with "the name of Jesus Christ," which for Barth "is the very essence and source of all reality"; the Christian religion is "the historical manifestation and means of . . . [the] revelation" of that "name."[52]

Furthermore, it is through that name that the Christian religion is *divinely created*. Unlike other religions, the Christian religion is created "by the name of Jesus Christ alone" and would not exist apart from Christ.[53] It is this aspect that gives it its status as the true religion.[54] Indeed, Barth holds that the "true Church" (discussed later) is not a human production, but is the subjective reality of God's revelation, the way that revelation comes to humans.[55] While God is not bound to the Church, the recipients of divine revelation *are* bound to the Church, because "the Church is the place in which God turns men into recipients of His revelation."[56] Barth even goes so far as to describe the Christian religion as an "annex" to the divine incarnation in Christ.[57] Elsewhere, he speaks of the Christian religion—and again, it alone—as created by the Holy Spirit: "The Christian religion is the sacramental area created by the Holy Spirit, in which the God whose Word became flesh continues to speak through the sign of His revelation."[58]

In light of Barth's assertions concerning Christianity's unique association with the name of Christ and its divine creation, it is hard to take seriously his claim that the Christian religion qua religion is not distinguishable from other religions. Instead, Christianity would seem to be qualitatively different from other religions.

The Christian Situation's Governing Order

As the governing order of Barth's religion situation is based on a dualism between true and false religions, so the governing order of his Christian situation is bound up with his sense of the true and the false Church. In CD I/2, he describes the true Church as "The place or area in history at which—and at which alone—reception of revelation is achieved, the visible and invisible coherence of those whom God in Christ calls His own and who confess Him in Christ as their God, in other words the Church."[59] This true Church always exists alongside the "false" church, the human production in which Christ is the predicate rather than the subject.[60] In CD IV/3, Barth indicates that the true Church consists in the "dangerous" confession that Jesus Christ is the one and only Word of God, to the exclusion of all other words, human and divine.[61] This confession, for Barth, functions as the governing order of the Christian situation. Those elements that, in Barth's judgment, stress this confession are favored; those that do not are marginalized.

Barth contends that Christians have been tempted to sidestep this confession; by doing so, they have been untrue to "what their name declares." Barth cites Roman Catholicism as an example of this deviation: Roman Catholicism, he contends, is "a system of evasion of confession."[62] While Barth considers it part of the Christian situation (part of "the Church"), its alleged failure to confess straightforwardly the uniqueness of Jesus Christ relegates it to the margins of the Christian situation.

The Void of Barth's Christian Situation

Although Barth focuses on Christianity rather than the religions, he recognizes that Christianity does not exist in isolation. Religious others form the context against which he draws the boundaries of the Christian situation and in contradistinction to which he asserts its truth. Thus, as with Schleiermacher, religious others are critical to Barth's theological discourse; they are the void that is both excluded by and constitutive of the Christian situation. I will discuss two forms of exclusion here: explicit and methodological.

Barth's theological discourse *explicitly* excludes the voices of religious others from the theological discussion by establishing criteria that they do not satisfy (at least according to Barth). As we saw earlier, Barth declares that the Christian religion is uniquely true not only because of divine election, but also because of Christianity's special relation with "the name of Jesus Christ." What is associated with, and witnesses to, that name is Christian; what does not confess that name is excluded from consideration, relegated to the void. Two instances of this form of exclusion stand out: Barth's discussion of Pure Land Buddhism in CD I/2, and his discussion of "other lights" in CD IV/3.

CD I/2 features a lengthy consideration of the "striking parallelism" of Pure Land Buddhism (which he calls "Yodoism") and "Christian Protestantism."[63] Ironically, this passage, one of the few occasions that non-Christian voices can be heard in Barth's work, also demonstrates how those voices are suppressed. Although Barth does not state explicitly what features of "Yodoism" he finds parallel to Christian Protestantism, we can infer that the main similarity is its founder Shinran's exclusive stress on a kind of salvation by grace through faith, salvation through "the primal promise of the compassionate redeemer Amida and on faith in him," that faith being "ultimately a gift of God" and available for everyone.[64] While Barth acknowledges fundamental differences between the two traditions, he does not consider these differences "decisive."[65] The similarities are more important, for they point to the decisive difference, to the fundamental distinction between true religion (Christianity) and false religion (everything else): "The Christian-Protestant religion of grace is not the true religion because it is a religion of grace"—nor because of any other features of Christian religion; instead, "the truth of the Christian religion is in fact enclosed in the one name of Jesus Christ, and nothing else."[66]

It is actually enclosed in all the formal simplicity of this name [Jesus Christ] as the very heart of the divine reality of revelation, which alone constitutes the truth of our religion. It is not enclosed, therefore, in its more or less explicit structure as the religion of grace, nor in the Reformation doctrines of original sin, representative satisfaction, justification by faith alone, the gift of the Holy Ghost and thankfulness. All this . . . the heathen, too, can in their own way teach and even live and represent as a church. Yet that does not mean that they are any the less heathen, poor, and utterly lost.[67]

In short, in order to exclude Pure Land Buddhism as irrelevant to Christian theology, Barth is forced to rely on a very minimal claim: no matter how similar to Protestantism in content and emphasis, a religion that does not confess "the name of Jesus Christ" remains "heathen" and "utterly lost."

In CD IV/3, Barth revisits the question of truth outside the boundaries of the Christian situation. Barth discusses the possibility of divine self-revelation through "other lights" and "other words" beyond the Church and the Bible. In fidelity to the radical freedom of the divine Other, Barth leaves open the possibility that God may choose to reveal Godself through "other words," even outside the Church and the Bible: "There are no good grounds not to accept the fact that such good words may also be spoken *extra muros ecclesiae* . . . through those who have not yet received any effective witness to Jesus Christ, and cannot therefore be reckoned with the believers who for their part attest Him."[68] Nothing can prevent God from "entering into . . . union with men outside the sphere of the Bible and the Church, and with the words of these men."[69] The implication is that divine truth cannot be restricted to the Christian situation alone. As Harrison notes, this "extramural knowledge of God" among non-Christians "is to be anticipated and welcomed by the Christian community, for . . . it may indeed play an important role in the formulation of Christian doctrine as the church strives ever to interpret the Word of God anew."[70] Indeed, Barth suggests that Christians should be prepared to listen to other words "not as alien sounds but as segments of that periphery concretely orientated from its centre and towards its totality, as signs and attestations of the lordship of the one prophecy of Jesus Christ, true words which we must receive as such even thought [sic] they come from this source."[71]

Yet any potential for openness toward religious others is effectively blocked by other parts of Barth's argument. He holds that Christians must confess that Jesus Christ is the *one and only* light of life and Word of God.[72] Although he recognizes the potential dangers of this exclusive confession, he insists that Christians have no alternative.[73] Jesus' truth and prophecy cannot be combined with any other. Consequently, Christians must not look for other divine words because "any such word can only be the word of another god which is *per se* false in relation to the one God."[74] Indeed, Barth argues that a pervasive weakness in the Church throughout its history has been its tendency to combine the one "Word of Jesus Christ with the authority and contents of other supposed revelations and truths of God."[75] Shades of Schleiermacher's practice of blaming error in Christianity on the influence of religious others.

Given his strong assertion of the uniqueness of the Word of Jesus Christ, how does Barth account for the possibility of other, true words outside the Christian situation? He does so by deploying an argument similar to that of inclusivists like Karl Rahner: other lights "shine" only because of the light of Christ; other words signify only because of the one Word, Jesus Christ. While other words are not per se "valueless, empty and corrupt," they are true only insofar as "they say the same thing as the one Word of God," as their intention is "to correspond to it and thus to confirm it," and as their speakers have been "commissioned, moved and empowered" by the one Word of God.[76] In short, while other words may be true and good, they cannot add anything new to the revelation of Jesus Christ. They are inevitably and necessarily incomplete: "None of them says what the life of Jesus Christ says."[77] Moreover, "this something different is inevitably a corruption."[78] Thus other words cannot be normative, and while Christians may listen to them, they remain "a mass of rudiments and fragments."[79]

In sum, while Barth recognizes the possibility of divine revelation outside the Christian situation, he denies that such revelation can add anything to the one and only Word of God. In other words, Barth insists on sameness at the expense of difference. While this stance toward other religions is somewhat more positive than the stance Barth takes in CD I/2, it effectively forecloses the possibility that what God may have revealed to religious others can both be true and differ substantially from what Christians deem God to have revealed to them.

In addition to his explicit exclusion of religious others, Barth also excludes religious others from consideration *methodologically*, through his choice of theological sources. Generally speaking, the only voices audible in Barth's discourses concerning revelation and religion are Christian voices. While Barth depicts revelation as something external to religion, including the Christian religion, the explicit sources for his claims about revelation are the texts recognized as authoritative within Christianity, particularly "Holy Scripture." True, Barth acknowledges that "the phenomena of revelations is only too plentiful" in the world of human religion; indeed, the divine incarnation is "not peculiar to the New Testament, but is also represented in the myths and speculation of every other possible religious area." Nonetheless, he does not pause to listen to those revelations. Barth closely identifies revelation with the Church's witness to the divine incarnation in the biblical texts. Furthermore, he insists that the incarnation "can be understood only from the standpoint of Holy Scripture, i.e., of the name Jesus Christ."[80] Despite his protestations about the utter otherness of revelation, the only revelation that matters to Barth is that recognized by Christians.

In CD I/1, Barth appears to distinguish the Word of God from scripture or from church proclamation by speaking of the "threefold form" of the Word: the Word revealed, the Word written, and the Word preached.[81] However, Barth refuses to distance scripture and church proclamation too far from the revealed Word: "The verbal form of this testimony is thought to be so indirectly identical with Jesus Christ that he continually discloses himself through it."[82] Barth characterizes his approach to revelation in CD I/2 as an attempt "to be faithful to Holy Scripture as the only valid testimony to revelation."[83] "The event of God's revelation has to be understood and expounded as it is attested to the Church of Jesus Christ by Holy Scripture."[84] In *Evangelical Theology: An Introduction*, Barth writes that "*the biblical witnesses of the Word*, the prophetic men of the Old Testament and the apostolic men of the New," enjoy "a *special* and singular, indeed a unique, position in their relation to the Word of God"; "they are its primary witnesses, because they are called directly by the Word to be its hearers, and they are appointed for its communication and verification to other men."[85] The only Word that counts is the Word recognized by Christians.

Barth's notion of "religion" comes as squarely from within the Christian situation as his notion of "revelation." While I would not go as far as Harrison to say that for Barth "religion" is purely formal and "devoid of any intrinsic significance,"[86] it can certainly be said that it is essentially an a priori category. Barth does not ground the concept upon evidence from empirical study of the religions. Barth seems to have admitted as much in his oft-cited exchange with D. T. Niles: "Karl Barth was asked how he knew that Hinduism was a form of unbelief, given the fact that he had never met a Hindu. . . . Hinduism can be known to be unbelief, according to Barth, a priori."[87]

As is the case with Barth's construal of revelation, it is Christian texts that serve as the explicit sources for his understanding of "religion" in CD I/2. In a long excursus, Barth traces the history of the term from Thomas Aquinas, through the Reformers, up to "the sad story of more recent Protestant theology."[88] In support of his axiom that religion is *Unglaube*, Barth cites Luther, Calvin, and the Bible, in particular passages in Jeremiah, Isaiah, Romans, and Acts.[89] There is no recognition that religious others might have something to contribute to the notion.

Theological Effects of Barth's Discursive Construction

Although Barth purports to take the standpoint of the revelation that stands in judgment of religion generally and the Christian religion particularly, it is clear that his understanding of revelation and religion derive from within the narrower Christian situation. In Badiouan terms, Barth constructs "knowledge" and thereby limits what can be "known," not only about religious others and how they in fact relate to Christianity but also about Christianity itself. Whereas Barth asserts the importance of distinguishing divine revelation from the Christian religion, in practice he tends to conflate the two. As a result, and contrary to Barth's insistence that the Christian confession should not be used to absolutize the form of Christianity or the Church,[90] he not only does precisely that but also blocks encounter with religious others.

Barth conflates revelation with the Christian situation in three ways. The first arises from his tendency to draw a sharp opposition between revelation and religion. Although the opposition is, as we have seen, a dialectical one, Barth nonetheless treats them as squarely opposed.[91] Since in CD I/2 Barth associates (explicitly or implicitly) the *religions* with *religion*—that is, with *Unglaube*—and since he holds that religion cannot and does not reveal God, the implication is that *the religions* cannot and do not reveal God. Thus he can call them "religions of error." This means that, in CD I/2, Barth has blocked off the *possibility* that God speaks in and through them.[92] While the discussion of "other lights" in CD IV/3 would seem at least to allow for that possibility, Barth renders this possibility theologically irrelevant by insisting that these "other lights" cannot offer anything not already contained in the revelation recognized within the Christian situation—that is, the Christian scriptures.

The second way in which Barth conflates revelation and the Christian religion involves his depiction of the nature of the latter. Despite his claim that the Christian religion qua religion is not distinguishable from other religions, and is the "true" religion only by divine election and not by any features of its own, Barth also suggests that the Christian religion—and it alone—is essentially linked with divine revelation. Barth speaks of the Christian religion not simply as elected by God, but also as divinely created, an "annex" to the incarnation of Christ and the sole means by which divine revelation comes to humans. Since he does not attribute these characteristics to other religions, it is difficult to credit his claim that the Christian religion is essentially indistinguishable from other religions.

Third, Barth tends to conflate revelation with the Bible—that is, with the texts recognized as authoritative within the Christian situation. As Rieger observes, while Barth wishes to return the divine Other to the position of authority in theology, he "ends up building theology around the textual reality of the Bible . . . as the factual authority."[93] For this reason, Rieger characterizes Barth's theology as the discourse of the Master, in which the texts of the Church take the place of prominence.[94]

When Barth discusses revelation, he restricts himself, for all practical purposes, to what *Christians* recognize as revelation. This is demonstrated by Barth's discussion of scripture in CD I/1. On the one hand, he seems to distinguish the

Word of God from the Bible; he also distinguishes God's utterance from that of the writers of scripture.[95] On the other hand, he also declares that "in the event of the Word of God" revelation and scripture become "one and the same thing"; he goes on to assert that "Revelation engenders the Scripture which attests it," and that "Jesus Christ has called the Old and New Testaments into existence."[96] In section 7.1 of CD I/1, Barth's identification of Bible and revelation is virtually complete. There, he speaks of the Bible "as the concrete form of the Word of God" and as "the Word of God by which all proclamation is to be measured."[97] Barth even goes so far as to declare that the Bible has not been chosen and adopted by the Church as criterion: instead, "it has been given to it."[98]

Certainly Barth has the right to hold that God has revealed Godself in and through what Christians recognize as holy scripture. However, he can do so only on the basis of the testimony of the Church—that is, on the basis of what is "known" (in Badiou's sense) within the Christian situation. By conflating revelation with the texts of the Church, Barth effectively restricts himself to the "knowledge" available within the Christian situation, not to the "truth" of the divine revelation, which (as even Barth admits) must transcend it and its texts. Concomitantly, he restricts divine revelation to what is recognized as such by the Church.

Barth's a priori definition of religion (to be discussed later) is a mark of his being bound by the "knowledge" of the Christian situation. As we saw earlier, Barth insists that it is only by the *Christian* revelation that we can recognize religion as *Unglaube*.[99] That means that Christians are epistemologically privileged: even if the source of this privilege is God and not Christians themselves, the clear implication is that only those who recognize the Christian revelation as authoritative are able to see the true state of things. True, Barth famously allows that the utterly free God can speak to us through Russian Communism or a dead dog[100]—and, by implication, through the *Bhagavad Gita* or the Qur'an. Nonetheless, Barth in CD I/2 does not seem to allow the possibility that God *has* revealed Godself outside the Christian scriptures. And although in CD IV/3 he speaks of "other words" as possible revelations of God, as we have seen he does not allow the possibility that they may be true and yet differ in any significant way from the revelation recognized by Christians.

In these ways, Barth's theology all too often becomes a theology of the governing order of the Christian situation, a theology that blocks encounter with religious others from the outset by restricting divine revelation to what Christians recognize as such. If divine revelation can be fully known within the Christian situation, why should Christians bother to explore the experiences and beliefs of religious others? Anything that Christians do learn from religious others will be wholly superfluous to what they already "know."

Implications of Barth's Discourse for the Christian Understanding of God

As with Schleiermacher, the problem with Barth's theological discourse lies not only in the structures and processes by which he marginalizes and excludes religious others, thereby participating in and perpetuating wider social-economic-political marginalization. The problem lies also in the consequences of those structures and processes for an understanding of God and of the relationship between God and humans. In this regard, Barth falters in his fidelity to the truth event that gave the impetus to his theological project.

Rieger's critique is helpful here. Drawing upon Lacanian discourse analysis, Rieger describes Barth's turn to the Other as an instance of the discourse of the Master: an attempt to replace the modern European self with the "master signifier." Mark Bracher describes master signifers as anything "that a subject has invested his or her identity in," anything that is "simply accepted as having a value or validity that goes without saying."[101] In Barth's discourse, the master signifier is God the Word, the divine Other. However, as Rieger notes, "We never have access to a pure master signifier." Thus the discourse of the Master may merely create the *illusion* of being founded upon the master signifier, when in fact its basis may be a mixture of other elements.[102] In Barth's case, the interests of the divine Other mingle with those of the modern self. Since his turn to the divine Other is not accompanied by a corresponding turn to human (and religious) others, his discourse merely represses the modern European middle-class self, enabling its return (so to speak) by the back door. Rieger writes, "The turn to the divine Other in and of itself does not seem to go far enough in countering the powers of exclusion, especially if it is not closely connected to an awareness of others, of those who are excluded."[103] Because of this basic blindness toward excluded human others, Rieger writes, Barth's theology is blind to the influence of the modern self on his theology.[104]

As with Schleiermacher, it is not only the modern European middle-class self but also the *Christian* self that Barth assumes to be the reliable guide for theological reflection. Despite his own well-founded warnings against absolutizing the Christian situation, Barth conflates divine revelation with what *Christians* recognize as divine revelation. As a result, the structure of Barth's theological discourse excludes the testimony of religious others. The voices of religious others are barely audible, even in Barth's discussion of "religion."

Consequently, the understanding of God and of the divine-human relationship is tightly restricted. There is no sense that other understandings might be valid or even worth considering. Indeed, apart from his discussion of Pure Land Buddhism and a few scattered comments in CD I/2, Barth gives us little indication that he has considered what religious others have to say about God or the Ultimately Real.

Furthermore, like Schleiermacher, Barth seems not to have contemplated the possibility that the Christian witness about the divine Other could be distorted by the construction of "the Christian" itself (i.e., as situation). And that, I argue, is precisely what happens in Barth's case. Barth's understanding of God and of the divine-human relationship are distorted by the structure of Barth's theological discourse in three respects. First, as Rieger argues, Barth fails to address the continuing influence of the modern self on his theology, and to recognize the crucial link between divine Other and human others. As a result, his theology fails to counteract power structures that conflate the interests of God with those of the (European middle-class) self—precisely the problem Barth criticizes in liberal Protestantism.[105]

Second, the elevation of the Christian scriptures to sole theological source and norm works against Barth's insistence upon the Otherness of God. The Christian scriptures constitute a particular community's experience of and witness to God and God's revelation; they are not that God or that revelation, as Barth himself seems to realize. The result of Barth's treatment of the Bible is to absolutize the Christian situation and to domesticate God accordingly. God, it seems, cannot speak in ways other than those in which God has spoken to Christians.

Because Barth's discourse blocks out the experiences of religious others, God is reduced to what *Christians* experience, and God's redemptive action is reduced to the activity of the Church. Access to the divine Other is limited because access to other human experiences of the Ultimate is also blocked. God is reduced to that which the Church mediates and what members of that Church recognize as authoritative.

Where Schleiermacher's theology sees the Church as sole repository of divine truth because it alone reflects the full development of the religious consciousness, Barth sees the Church as sole repository of divine truth because it alone witnesses to divine revelation. In effect, Barth is claiming that his own religion has sole possession of knowledge of the Divine. While religious others may also dimly know God via "other lights," they remain "heathen, poor, and utterly lost." Like Schleiermacher, Barth assumes a priori what needs to be demonstrated: that religious others do not in fact know the God to whom Christians witness. Since the voices of religious others are largely excluded from Barth's Christian situation, he is unable to substantiate this claim.

Third, when Barth insists that divine revelation justifies—indeed, necessitates—his claim that the Christian religion is the one and only true religion, he also implies that *God* authorizes the exclusion of the voices of religious others. This is an odd message for Barth to present, given his insistence elsewhere on God's preference for the marginalized.[106] Indeed, it raises the question of whether Barth really expects to learn anything of importance from the marginalized.

Evental Sites and Blind Spots in Barth's Discourse

As with Schleiermacher, Barth's theology manifests both evental sites and blind spots with regard to religious others. Perhaps the most important evental site is Barth's key recognition that divine revelation radically questions all human religious situations, including the Christian situation. This has the potential to foster, or at least not to block, encounter with religious others. First, it warns Christians and religious others alike that divine truth must not be confused with the human constructs that claim to witness to that truth. If Christianity, qua religion, actively opposes revelation, then Christians should beware of conflating divine revelation with their own texts and traditions; the same would apply, *mutatis mutandis*, to religious others. This insight should discourage Christians (and religious others) from absolutizing the boundaries of the Christian situation (and the Hindu situation, Buddhist situation, etc.).[107] Second, Barth's insight has the potential to level the field in preparation for interreligious dialogue. No religion may claim "our texts and traditions are better than yours," for, in the light of divine revelation, all religions are shown to be lacking. Third, by reminding Christians and religious others alike that they have not cornered the market on divine truth, Barth's insight predisposes them to humility, before human others as well as the divine Other, which is the prerequisite for mutually transformative interreligious dialogue.

Other aspects of Barth's theological discourse, however, hinder encounter with religious others. His theology all too often becomes—perhaps contrary to his own intentions—a theology of the governing order of the Christian situation, working to protect its boundaries against encroachment by the claims and witness of religious others. This plays out in three ways: his a priori approach to religion and the religions; his failure to follow out the implications of his insights about religious others; and his tendency to support Eurocentric power structures.

Apriorism

Barth gives no indication that he bases his understanding of "religion" on any in-depth study of, or dialogue with, religious others.[108] Rather, his a priori concept of religion serves only as a foil for his presentation of revelation, or, as Harrison puts it, "as the backdrop against which a positive understanding of revelation . . . may be projected."[109] In fact, Barth tries to have it both ways. He insists that his category "religion" is not derived from his beliefs about particular religions; yet he also insists on applying his understanding of "religion" as *Unglaube* to those religions, for example, classifying them as "religions of error."

It is difficult to avoid the admittedly uncharitable conclusion that Barth's claim that his category "religion" is not derived from his beliefs about particular religions is merely a move to forestall objections to his understanding based on contrary evidence from those more knowledgeable than Barth himself about other religions. Even if that conclusion is unwarranted, the question remains: can the category *religion* have any significance apart from what we know about *religions*? Surely the category only has meaning as a generalization drawn from particular instances. Indeed, Barth seems to have liberal Protestantism firmly in mind when he describes religion as *Unglaube*; and he clearly considers "Yodoism" to manifest *Unglaube*, despite strong similarities to Protestantism. If Barth really wished to dissociate "religion" from particular religions, he easily could have done so by using different terms; for instance, instead of "religion," he might have used the term *Unglaube* as the opposite of revelation. However, he does not. It is only natural that the reader associate Barth's category *religion* with particular religions, especially when Barth himself does so.

A more fundamental problem is the chilling effect that his a priori understanding of "religion" has on encounter with religious others. By asserting that religion is *Unglaube* without undertaking any dialogue with religious others, Barth effectively takes a first step toward blocking such dialogue. If Christians "know" in advance that the realm of religion offers only error and opposition to divine truth, why should they bother with the difficult work of interreligious dialogue? What could religious others have to offer but more *Unglaube*?

Barth's a priori treatment of "religion" also raises a nagging credibility problem. Apart from a deep familiarity with other religions, how can Barth be certain that they actually manifest the qualities he attributes to "religion"? How can he know that, say, Hinduism is (as he writes about "religion" generally) "a human attempt to anticipate what God in His revelation wills to do and does do," or that it attempts to replace "the divine work by a human manufacture"?[110] Surely this can only be known after an in-depth study of Hinduism, carefully comparing its beliefs and perspectives with those of Christians. Furthermore, such study will quite quickly reveal that Hindus do not understand their own revealed texts as human efforts. Indeed, Hindus distinguish what is divinely revealed or "heard" (*shruti*), such as the *Vedas*, from works that, while authoritative, are of human authorship (*smriti*), such as the *Mahabharata* and the *Ramayana*.[111] A similar distinction can be found in Islam, where the divinely revealed Qur'an is given greater authority than the humanly authored *hadiths*. If Barth is to be believed, Hindus and Muslims have simply "got it wrong" when they understand the *Vedas* or the Qur'an as anything more than "human manufacture." But, again, why should we accept Barth's judgment? How are Barth's readers to take his claims seriously when they are not supported by evidence that he actually understands the religions he criticizes?

A second way that Barth's apriorism blocks dialogue with religious others is his claim that Christianity is the one and only true religion. This claim is also made a priori, without evidence of any in-depth study of, or dialogue with, religious others. As Charles T. Waldrop notes, Barth bases his claim "only on faith in God's revelation. . . . It is a statement of faith, a confessional statement."[112] Thus it "is not . . . an inference based upon a comparison of Christianity with other religions. It is made as a response to the word which God speaks to us in the event of revelation."[113]

Barth contends that his claim that Christianity is the true religion, as well as his understanding of "religion," is demanded by faithfulness to divine revelation.[114] And, as we have seen, Barth closely associates that revelation with the scriptural texts recognized in the Christian situation. However, the Bible contains no explicit references to Islam, Hinduism, Buddhism, Confucianism, Daoism, the religions of sub-Saharan Africa, the religions of the Americas, or myriad other religious traditions past and present. One can, of course, take the Bible to refer *implicitly* to such religions; however, this is wholly a matter of interpretation, with all its attendant human limitations. Clearly, *Barth* has interpreted the revelation embodied in the Christian scriptures as classifying other religions as species of *Unglaube*, as "religions of error." But why should we accept his interpretation as authoritative? Barth gives us no reason other than his a priori "statement of faith."

Again, a credibility problem arises. Waldrop nicely describes the insupportability of Barth's claim: "It is difficult to see how a confessional approach can lead us to affirm either that other religions are false or that Christianity is the only true religion. On the contrary, since faith in God's revelation, according to Barth, leads us to affirm both God's freedom and God's love, it would seem that one who follows a confessional approach could be content with affirming simply that God speaks through Christianity and that, therefore, Christianity is true."[115] As Waldrop observes, confidence in the truth of Christianity does not require the additional claim that Christianity *alone* is true.[116]

Yet Barth does indeed make that additional claim, and in so doing blocks encounter with religious others—in fact, aborts such encounter before it can begin. If it can be known before the fact, on the basis of the revelation recognized by Christians, that Christianity is the one and only true religion, then there is no need to look any further afield. Other religions, already marked as species of *Unglaube*, cannot match what is offered in Christianity, the only religion elected by God. Any need for dialogue is effectively rejected.

Failure to Explore Implications

Barth's apriorism and his tendency to conflate revelation with the Christian situation also prevent him from exploring interesting and perhaps theologically revelatory implications raised in his remarks about religious others.

For example, while Barth recognizes the striking similarities between Pure Land Buddhism and Protestant belief, he fails to account theologically for them. Why would a religious tradition apparently untouched by the influence of Christian teaching develop an anthropology and a soteriology so similar to those of Luther, Calvin, or Barth himself? Might this constitute evidence of divine revelation outside the Christian situation? Furthermore, might that very similarity suggest that Protestant teaching is rooted less in faithfulness to divine revelation than in a human desire for "an easier and simpler road to salvation," which (Barth contends) is a prime motivation for Pure Land teaching?[117] In CD I/2, Barth does not explore these questions. He seems too concerned with protecting the boundaries of the Christian situation against encroachment by its void, religious others.

Similarly, Barth fails to investigate intriguing questions raised by his discussion in CD IV/3 about the possibility of extramural revelation through "other lights." How can Barth reconcile his overarching concern to affirm the utter freedom of the divine Other with his insistence that what God reveals outside the Church must correspond to the revelation recognized by Christians? Given the quite different historical and cultural contexts of those "other lights," is it not at least possible that an utterly free God might choose to reveal Godself in ways that would speak to their particular contexts and thus would differ markedly from the revelation recognized by the Church?

For example, the revelation in Jesus Christ, while universal in significance, is intimately linked with the particularities of Jewish life and belief in the first century CE. The very "name of Jesus Christ" of which Barth makes so much in CD I/2 takes its meaning from particularly Jewish hopes for a messiah (Greek *christos*) from the Davidic line. Those hopes are grounded in turn in an eschatological sense of salvation (Hebrew *Yeshua*, "one who saves") that looks back to the Exodus and that relies upon a belief that the fundamental problem of the human condition is sin, a falling away from God—as opposed to, say, delusion (as in forms of Hinduism), ignorance that leads to clinging (Buddhism), or an imbalance of yin and yang (Daoism). Given that "other lights" share neither the particularities of Jewish history nor the Jewish and Christian understanding(s) of the human condition, is it not reasonable—and consistent with Barth's stress on divine freedom—to expect that what God reveals through "other lights" will differ from the revelation in Jesus Christ? If so, is it not incumbent upon the Christian religion, which seeks to witness to God's self-revelation, to seek to listen to what those "other lights" have to say? Unfortunately, by insisting a priori that "other lights" can be true only if they "correspond to" and "confirm" the revelation in Jesus Christ, Barth gives Christians no good reason for taking the trouble to explore beyond the bounds of the Christian situation. Furthermore, by his stress on sameness, Barth effectively, and a priori, discredits the different historical and cultural contexts of religious others.

Eurocentrism

As we have seen, Barth excludes the voices of religious others as theological sources and norms, effectively reduces divine revelation to that which is recognized within the Christian situation, and holds that "other lights" are true only insofar as they correspond to what is recognized as revelation within the Christian situation. In these ways, Barth tends to equate difference with untruth, a tendency Emmanuel Levinas has characterized as Western imperialism's "horror of the other that remains other."[118] Barth in effect says that the sources and norms of European Protestant Christianity are sufficient for an authentically Christian theology, and that religious others have nothing new or different or even particularly interesting to contribute. Despite his insistence on God's preference for the marginalized, the structure of Barth's own theological discourse excludes those who are different, just as the power structures of colonialism and neocolonialism exclude non-Europeans. Since many (perhaps most) of those excluded are non-Europeans, Barth—like Schleiermacher before him—participates in the Eurocentric colonialist ideology in which, as Rieger puts it, "the modern European self affirms its own value and superiority on the back of the colonized other."[119] Barth's theological discourse echoes what plays out in the cultural, political, and economic realms: the assertion of European/neo-European experience, beliefs, texts, and institutions as normative for all humanity, and the concomitant exclusion of others.

Conclusion

In faithfulness to the event that opened to him the radical otherness of divine revelation, Barth seeks to counter the dominance of the modern European middle-class self by restoring the divine Other to the place of prominence in Christian theology. He advocates grounding theological reflection not in the experience of the self but in divine revelation, the self-disclosure of the divine Other.

However, he conflates that revelation with the texts recognized by Christians. While acknowledging at least the possibility that God reveals Godself through "other lights," Barth renders that possibility theologically irrelevant. In so doing, he absolutizes the Christian situation, blocks encounter with religious others, and domesticates the divine.

As was the case with Schleiermacher, Barth's example demonstrates that theological discourse that does not open itself to encounter with religious others remains trapped in its own circular self-affirmation, its own "knowledge." When Christian theology fails to hear the voices of religious others, it loses a critical perspective on itself and its witness. Barth's divine Other turns out to be not so "other" after all. This is ironic, for while Barth criticizes Schleiermacher for beginning and ending with the modern self, Barth's own theological discourse shows that a theology that begins with what Christians "know" can only end with what Christians "know."

CHAPTER 5

Lindbeck

Turning "the Christian" Inward

Neither Schleiermacher's turn to the self nor Barth's turn to the divine Other succeeds in transcending the confines of the Christian situation. In this chapter we examine how a third approach fares: George Lindbeck's postliberal turn to the texts and tradition of the Church.

In a sense, Lindbeck's theological project arose out of encounter with religious others, albeit within the Christian community. As a Lutheran engaged in ecumenical dialogue with Roman Catholics, he encountered an apparent anomaly: doctrinal "positions that were once really opposed are now really reconcilable, even though these positions remain in a significant sense identical to what they were before."[1] His landmark 1985 work, *The Nature of Doctrine: Religion and Theology in a Postliberal Age*, endeavors to account for this phenomenon. Yet *The Nature of Doctrine* is more than a mere explanation of a theological anomaly: it also offers a constructive proposal for doing theology.

This chapter will focus on *The Nature of Doctrine*, with glances at Lindbeck's other writings; I will also consult Bruce Marshall's important exegesis and defense of Lindbeck's project. Once again, the investigation will focus on the three issues examined in the chapters on Schleiermacher and Barth: how the discourse constructs religious others; how that construction affects the resulting theological formulations, particularly those concerning the Divine; and possible evental sites and blind spots in the discourse. Before moving to these questions, let us sketch the outlines of Lindbeck's postliberal project.

Lindbeck's Postliberal Project for Theology

As both David Tracy and Kenneth Surin note, *The Nature of Doctrine* undertakes two main tasks. The first is Lindbeck's avowedly nontheological task of formulating what Tracy calls a new paradigm, a "cultural-linguistic" model of religion and doctrine. The second task, as Surin writes, is "to develop . . . a 'way' of doing systematic or dogmatic theology, which he [Lindbeck] calls an 'intratextual' theology."[2]

A New Paradigm for Religion

Lindbeck proposes his cultural-linguistic model of religion as an alternative to what he contends have been the two predominant understandings of religion. In the first of these, which Lindbeck calls "cognitive-propositional," a doctrinal statement such as "Jesus is Lord" is a truth claim or proposition of the same order as "Water boils at 100 degrees C."[3] The second predominant understanding, the "experiential-expressive," regards religion as primarily interior religious experience; this presumably would include Schleiermacher's "feeling of absolute dependence." Such experience is expressed in the form of religious doctrines, which function as "noninformative and nondiscursive symbols of inner feelings, attitudes, or existential orientations."[4] Both models understand religion as being "about" some reality or experience external to it, and doctrines are true insofar as they accurately reflect that external reality or experience.

Although Lindbeck acknowledges the coherence of both models, he rejects their underlying assumption that religion and doctrine are intrinsically concerned with something external to them. Instead, Lindbeck turns this assumption on its head: his proposed cultural-linguistic model stresses "the degree to which human experience is shaped, molded, and in a sense constituted by cultural and linguistic forms," especially religion.[5]

Lindbeck follows the "linguistic turn" that became fashionable in philosophy and the social sciences in the 1960s and holds that culture and language shape, and perhaps determine, both our sense of reality and our experience. Along these lines, Lindbeck advances two claims, one stronger, one weaker. According to the stronger claim, Lindbeck holds that there is no experience without language. "It is necessary," he writes, "to have the means for expressing an experience in order to have it"; "There are numberless thoughts we cannot think, sentiments we cannot have, and realities we cannot perceive unless we learn to use the appropriate symbol systems."[6] Since he recognizes that this claim may be empirically falsifiable, he offers a (slightly) weaker version: "An experience (viz., something of which one is prereflectively or reflectively conscious) is impossible unless it is in some fashion symbolized, and . . . all symbol systems have their origin in interpersonal relations and social interactions."[7]

According to Lindbeck's model, religion functions like language. Rather than merely reflecting experience or reality, religion shapes (or, according to the stronger claim, determines) what its adherents experience or regard as real.[8] Religions, he contends, "are producers of experience"; they shape "the entirety of life and thought."[9] Religions are "not expressions of the transcendental heights and depths of human experience, but are rather patterns of ritual, myth, belief, and conduct which constitute, rather than being constituted by, that which modern people often think of as most profound in human beings, viz., their existential self-understanding."[10] Thus religions function as "the lenses through which human beings see and respond to their changing worlds, or the media in which they formulate their descriptions. The world and its descriptions may vary enormously even while the lenses or media remain the same."[11]

It is interesting, and more than a little ironic, that although Lindbeck speaks of religion as determining experience and thought, his own cultural-linguistic model seems to arise not from within a religious tradition, but from the literature of the social sciences and philosophy—specifically from the neo-Kantian epistemology popular in academic circles since the 1960s and reflected in the work of scholars such as Wayne Proudfoot.[12] That is not in itself a weakness in Lindbeck's approach; drawing as I do on Badiou, I would be the last person to criticize Lindbeck for appropriating a philosophical framework. But the very fact that Lindbeck finds it necessary to draw from outside religion suggests at least that there are limits to the extent to which religion shapes life, thought, and self-understanding.

Whatever the source of Lindbeck's cultural-linguistic paradigm, it has dramatic effects on the understanding of what it means to be religious. Whereas an experiential-expressivist like Schleiermacher would argue that religiosity is a matter of experiencing (to some degree) the feeling of absolute dependence, Lindbeck contends that it is instead a matter of interiorizing "a set of skills by practice and training. One learns how to feel, act, and think in conformity with a religious tradition"[13]—much as becoming a speaker of Japanese entails thinking and expressing oneself in that language.

Rule Theory of Doctrine
In the cognitive-propositional approach to religion, doctrines function as truth claims; in an experiential-expressive approach, as symbols of a more fundamental experience. In Lindbeck's cultural-linguistic approach, on the other hand, doctrines are to a religion what grammatical rules are to a language. They function "as communally authoritative rules of discourse, attitude, and action."[14]

According to Lindbeck's account, the evaluation of particular doctrinal formulations is comparable to testing the grammaticality of a sentence by appealing to competent speakers of a language. Those who are best able to judge doctrines "are those who have effectively interiorized a religion."[15]

Untranslatable, Incommensurable

Since, according to Lindbeck, each religion shapes (or determines) experience, there can be no experiential core common to some or all religions. In fact, Lindbeck suggests, adherents of different religions have radically different experiences: "Adherents of different religions do not diversely thematize the same experience; rather they have different experiences. Buddhist compassion, Christian love and . . . French Revolutionary *fraternité* are not diverse modifications of a single fundamental human awareness, emotion, attitude, or sentiment, but are radically (i.e., from the root) distinct ways of experiencing and being oriented toward self, neighbor, and cosmos."[16] Unfortunately, Lindbeck does not provide evidence to support this claim of radical difference.

Furthermore, since each religion is a comprehensive framework with its own set of rules (doctrines), its terms cannot be translated into those of another religion. Consequently, religions are fundamentally incommensurable: they cannot be compared to determine, for instance, whether one is truer than another.[17]

How far does Lindbeck think religions are untranslatable and incommensurable? The answer is complicated by the fact that once again, he advances both stronger and weaker claims. The stronger claim is suggested by Lindbeck's assertions not only that adherents of different religions have radically different experiences but that attempts to translate one religion's terms in terms of another religion inevitably distort those concepts.[18] (In a 1997 essay Lindbeck asserts that "untranslatability" is "common to all world religions."[19])

The weaker claim is hedged about by conditionals. Lindbeck writes that "the cultural-linguistic approach *is open to the possibility that* different religions . . . *may* have incommensurable notions of truth, of experience, and of categorial adequacy, and therefore also of what it would mean for something to be most important (i.e., 'God')."[20]

In his interpretation of Lindbeck's argument, Bruce Marshall stresses Lindbeck's weaker claim. Marshall holds that Christians can, with "some effort and sympathy," come to understand what the central concepts of religious others mean to them—for example, what "nirvana" means to Buddhists.[21] Yet even in this weaker sense, Marshall insists that this process of "redescription" is not a matter of translating the religious other's concept into Christian terms—for example, of finding equivalents to "nirvana" among the central concepts of Christianity. Rather, it is a matter of assimilation: because Christians employ a different set of concepts than do Buddhists, Christians will likely make different judgments about "nirvana" and its place in the overall scheme of things than do Buddhists.[22] Once assimilated into the Christian situation, "nirvana" will no longer mean what it meant for Buddhists.

An "Intratextual" Theology

Having laid out his postliberal, cultural-linguistic paradigm for understanding religion and doctrine, Lindbeck proceeds to sketch its implications for systematic theology. The postliberal view promotes what Lindbeck calls an "intratextual" theology. Whereas an "extratextual" theology (employed by cognitive-propositionalists and experiential-expressivists) "locates religious meaning outside the text or semiotic system either in the objective realities to which it refers or in the experiences it symbolizes," an intratextual theology regards religious meaning as wholly immanent to a given religion. For instance, according to an intratextual theology, "the proper way to determine what 'God' signifies . . . is by examining how the word operates within a religion and thereby shapes reality and experience rather than by first establishing its propositional or experiential meaning and reinterpreting or reformulating its uses accordingly."[23]

According to Marshall, the "plain sense" of scripture is for Lindbeck the primary criterion for evaluating the truth of Christian doctrinal statements: "The coherence of sentences (interpreted in their practical as well as linguistic context) with the plain sense is at least a necessary, and in some cases a sufficient, criterion of their truth . . . the more a given discourse addresses matters central to a Christian vision of the world (that is, one shaped by the plain sense of Scripture), the more coherence with the plain sense of the text will tend to be the decisive test of its truth."[24]

It is not surprising that Lindbeck, a Lutheran, elevates the "plain sense of Scripture" to supreme authority. However, he gives it a postliberal twist. He construes "plain sense" to be a function of the Christian community: "What a participant in the community automatically or naturally takes a text to be saying on its face insofar as he or she has been socialized in a community's conventions for reading the text as Scripture."[25] Note that "plain sense" has taken on both communal and intrasystematic significance.

All this means, according to Marshall, "that beliefs and practices 'internal' to Christianity are the primary criteria of truth," where "internal" means "when a Christian community, in a given historical context, regards that belief or practice as (maximally) necessary or (minimally) beneficial in order for it to be faithful to its own identity."[26] "All other belief and practice can be called 'external,' or 'alien' in William Christian's formal sense."[27] However, according to Marshall, the internal-external distinction may in practice be "merely provisional," since "the Christian community will naturally strive to 'internalize' initially alien discourse."[28]

In the intratextual theology that Lindbeck advocates, what is theologically normative is the religious text: "It is the text, so to speak, which absorbs the world, rather than the world the text."[29] This statement is pregnant with implications for a postliberal approach to religious others since the latter, presumably, constitute at least a part of the "world" to be absorbed.

To unpack Lindbeck's statement, we must first understand what Lindbeck means by "text," and then turn to his metaphor, "absorb the world." In both respects, Bruce Marshall's sympathetic reading of Lindbeck helps to fill gaps left by Lindbeck's rather sketchy account. I should also note that although both Lindbeck and Marshall discuss these concepts in terms of their application within Christianity, we can assume that they extend to other religions, *mutatis mutandis*, as well.

By "text," Lindbeck refers to Christian scripture. This he understands "as a canonically and narrationally unified and internally glossed (that is, self-referential and self-interpreting) whole centered on Jesus Christ, and telling the story of the dealings of the Triune God with his people and his world in ways which are typologically . . . applicable to the present."[30] In the notion of a "self-referential and self-interpreting" text, we again see Lindbeck's stress on the intrasystematic.

This brings us to Lindbeck's metaphor, "absorbing the world," a process by which the Christian scriptures serve "not simply as a source for precepts and truths, but [as] the interpretive framework for all reality."[31] Marshall interprets absorption as a process in which Christians attempt to "redescribe" alien elements—in other words, to interpret them according to "the community's own primary idiom, that is, by its ruled reading and use of the biblical text."[32] Yet this "redescription" must also be guided by what Marshall calls a "principle of charity," by which Christians, working from "the community's scripturally encoded criteria of truth," will attempt to hold "alien" elements to be true, and thus to make a claim on the Christian community's "scripturally normed project of interpretation and assessment."[33]

In fact, in Marshall's reading of Lindbeck, a religion's "assimilative power"— its ability to "absorb the world"—is not merely a matter of charity toward "alien" elements. It constitutes the primary warrant for upholding the truth of that religion's "web of belief and practice":

> The scripturally shaped web of Christian belief will be warranted as the primary criterion of truth by its capacity . . . to internalize or assimilate initially alien discourse, that is, to give persuasive interpretations in its own terms of such discourse which allow that discourse to be held true, or which give compelling reasons in light of its own criteria to account for rejecting that discourse as false. Conversely, repeated failure to assimilate alien discourse or to give compelling reasons for rejecting it will argue that we are not warranted in ascribing justificatory primacy to the plain sense of Scripture.[34]

Yet, as Marshall notes, assimilative power is not an external test, but is itself intrasystematic, the power "*of* a specific web of belief and practice and its associated criteria of truth."[35] It is a function of the *community's* beliefs and "the justificatory practices which it regards as primary."[36]

While this process of "redescription" sounds like a form of interreligious translation—which Lindbeck, as we have seen, contends is (or may be) impossible—Marshall contends that it is not. Because Christians work with a set of concepts different from that in which the alien element originated, once redescribed that alien element will likely take on a different meaning in the Christian context.[37] This has important implications for encounter with religious others, as will be discussed in the following sections.

Lindbeck's Construction of Religious Others

Religions as Situations

In line with the postmodern stress on diversity, Lindbeck presents us with *religions* instead of *religion*. He focuses on how religions—most prominently, the Christian religion—relate (or, perhaps, do not relate) to one another. I argue that Lindbeck presents religions, including Christianity, as tightly bounded situations, each with its own void and governing order.

Establishing the situational character of Lindbeck's depiction of religions is complicated by the fact that he resists defining "religion." C. John Sommerville writes that Lindbeck "turns verbal back-flips" to avoid such definition.[38] While Lindbeck may resist *defining* religion, he does *describe* it in a number of different ways, some substantive (i.e., in terms of what religion *is*), others functional (i.e., in terms of what religion *does*). In Badiouan terms, the substantive descriptions relate to religions as situations; the functional, to the "knowledge" available within a given situation.

To judge from his substantive descriptions, it appears that Lindbeck recognizes religions as ordered groupings of multiplicities: he refers to religions as "patterns of ritual, myth, belief, and conduct," and as "system[s] of discursive and nondiscursive symbols."[39] As we have seen, he also depicts religions as bounded and self-contained, each discrete from the others, each incommensurable with the others. He does not discuss what constitutes the structuring operation—the criteria for inclusion of some things in (and the exclusion of others from) one religion rather than another.[40] However, he clearly takes it as given that there are a number of entities that can be called "religions," one of which (his primary focus) is Christianity.

The situational character of religions comes across in two ways. The first involves his assertion of untranslatability. If the terms of a given religion cannot be translated in the terms of any other given religion, and more importantly, if adherents of different religions necessarily have different experiences because those religions determine what can be experienced, then there is no common ground, no conceptual or experiential "overlap" between religions. As Lindbeck puts it, there is "no common framework."[41] In terms of set theory, we could say that, according to the "cultural-linguistic" view, the intersection of any two religions is empty.

Second, the situational character of religions in the postliberal account is underscored by the strong inside-outside character of Lindbeck's discourse. Lindbeck's stress on intratextuality (as well as on intrasystematic coherence, discussed later) emphasizes relations and processes *internal to* a religion. The meaning of a particular term in a religion is wholly a function of how that term relates to other terms within the religious system, not to any referents beyond or outside it (only the religion as a whole refers to the Ultimately Real, as we will see shortly). As Marshall puts it, "beliefs and practices 'internal' to Christianity are the primary criteria of truth" for Christianity;[42] presumably, the same goes, *mutuatis mutandis*, for any given religion.

Given this strong inside-outside character, it is with good reason that Paul Knitter compares the postliberal understanding of religions with the fenced-in backyards of North American suburbia. For postliberals, Knitter writes, "Each religion has its own backyard. There is no 'commons' that all of them share. To be good neighbors, then, let each religion tend to its own backyard, keeping it clean and neat. In talking with one's religious neighbor . . . one is advised to do so over the back fence, without trying to step into the other's yard in order to find what they might have in common with oneself."[43]

"Knowledge" in Religions

While Lindbeck's substantive descriptions establish the situational character of religions, his functional descriptions suggest what Badiou calls "knowledge": that which can be known within a given situation. According to Lindbeck, religion "is first of all a comprehensive interpretive medium or categorial framework within which one has certain kinds of experiences and makes certain kinds of affirmations."[44] Religions are "the lenses through which human beings see and respond to their changing worlds, or the media in which they formulate their descriptions."[45] In other words, religions delimit what their adherents "know" about themselves and others.

True, Lindbeck does hold that any given religion refers, and seeks to correspond, to something outside itself, to that which it considers the Ultimately Real.[46] However, it does so only as a whole, not on the level of individual utterances (e.g., doctrines); Lindbeck says that "a religion may be pictured as a single gigantic proposition."[47]

Yet this "last-instance" appeal to a correspondence theory of truth should not distract us from the basically inward-turning, essentially coherentist nature of Lindbeck's approach—and thus, in Badiouan terms, Lindbeck's essential turn to "knowledge" rather than "truth."[48] This is particularly clear in Lindbeck's notions of categorial adequacy and intrasystematic coherence.[49]

Categorial adequacy follows from Lindbeck's neo-Kantian stance that experience is impossible without a symbol system to express it. By categorial adequacy Lindbeck refers to how well the categories of a system (situation) enable speakers of a religious "language" to make meaningful statements about whatever the religion holds to be most important or ultimately real. It "does not guarantee propositional truth, but only makes meaningful statements possible."[50] In his reading of Lindbeck, Bruce Marshall holds that categorial adequacy is a precondition for truth, in that we must have appropriate categories in order to make true statements about what the religion considers most important or ultimately real.[51] Categorial adequacy also offers a criterion for comparing religions: "The questions raised in comparing religions have to do first of all with the adequacy of their categories";[52] we will explore this claim later in this chapter.

How, then, is the adequacy of a religion's categories to be measured? Not by any external standard. Instead, Lindbeck's criterion involves what he calls "intrasystematic coherence." Marshall explains, "A given utterance [i.e., a category] will . . . be judged to be true by adherents of a religion to the degree that it coheres with the wider web of belief and practice which constitutes the religion, especially with the paradigmatic patterns of belief and practice 'encoded' in the religion's scriptures."[53] Lindbeck gives an example: "For a Christian, 'God is Three and One,' or 'Christ is Lord' are true only as parts of a total pattern of speaking, thinking, feeling, and acting. They are false when their use in any given instance is inconsistent with what the pattern as a whole affirms of God's being and will."[54] In short, Lindbeck holds that truth depends on intrasystematic coherence but not vice versa.[55]

Clearly, Lindbeck's notion of truth is quite different from Badiou's or my own. Rather than that which exceeds the situation, truth is for Lindbeck a function of the way parts of the situation hang together. In Badiouan terms, what Lindbeck calls truth is in fact knowledge.

Lindbeck's insistence on intratextuality also suggests the "knowledge" component of religions as situations. The meaning of a particular religious term (Lindbeck's example is "God") is "intrasemiotic": it is wholly a function of how that term relates to other terms *within* the religious system (or its texts). For instance, he understands the Bible as a "canonically and narrationally unified and internally glossed (that is, self-referential and self-interpreting) whole," which should "absorb the world."[56] While this might at first glance suggest a basic openness to the influence of the world beyond the biblical text, in practice it means that the world is *interpreted* in terms of the text. Encounter with "alien" elements (i.e., from the void) may lead insiders to revise their understanding of the authoritative text (at least on Marshall's reading of Lindbeck). Yet they do so not on the basis of the alien elements themselves, but on the "redescription" of those elements in terms of the "knowledge" of the insiders' religion. As Rieger puts it, in the cultural-linguistic approach the desired result is "conformity" with what is already known.[57]

The Void of Lindbeck's Religions

If religions truly are mutually untranslatable and incommensurable, then the terms and experiences of one religion are excluded from, and incomprehensible within, another religion. Thus from within a given religion, all other religions are truly void, in Badiou's sense.[58] Lindbeck recognizes that his approach "balkanizes" religions, since they are conceived as sharing neither common themes nor a common "universe of discourse."[59]

Furthermore, Lindbeck seems not to recognize that the "inside" of a religion depends in any way upon the "outside," as Badiou's situation depends on its void. For Lindbeck, religions are wholly self-contained, as is indicated by his insistence that religions are "comprehensive interpretive schemes" that shape "the entirety of life and thought."[60] This would seem to exclude the possibility that the "interpretive scheme" might actually depend on something outside itself. Instead, whatever is "outside" is interpreted (redescribed) according to what is "inside."

An odd consequence of this insistence on comprehensiveness is that it would seem to rule out dual or multiple religious identities: one, presumably, cannot be simultaneously Confucianist, Buddhist, and Daoist, as is the case with millions of Chinese, or simultaneously Catholic and Vodounist, as millions of Haitians claim to be.

Doctrines as the Governing Order of Religions

In Lindbeck's account, doctrines serve as the governing order of a given religion, arranging and relating its elements so as to preserve the situation's integrity and governing interests against the disruptive potential of the void.

According to Lindbeck's rule theory, doctrines function as the "grammar" of a religion. In Badiouan terms, they specify how elements within the situation may be grouped, ordered, and used. Doctrines serve to keep the void from "breaking into" the situation and disrupting or dissolving it. They do so by providing the interpretive framework for "understanding" (redescribing) alien elements. Doctrines also limit what is possible within a given situation, insofar as they "exclude certain ranges of . . . propositional utterances or symbolizing activities."[61] For instance, the doctrine of the Trinity limits the range of ways

Christians can talk about the divine reality. To speak of "three gods" or "one *ousia* in 5,000 *hypostases*" would be as ungrammatical in the Christian situation as "Irving have brung Shirley flowers" is in Standard English.

Lindbeck's Christian Situation

Lindbeck clearly considers Christianity an instance of his category "religion." As such, it is a situation, a bounded and structured multiplicity with its own "knowledge," governing order, and void. As is the case with Schleiermacher and Barth, Lindbeck's discussion of Christianity implies a structuring operation that presents certain things as distinctively "Christian" versus others that are "non-Christian." Although Lindbeck does not explicitly state his own criteria for inclusion within the Christian situation, he suggests them in several places.

In line with his general view about the nature of religions as language-like shapers of experience, Lindbeck understands Christians as those who (we might say) have learned to "speak the Christian language," those who experience themselves and the world generally in terms of the story told in the Christian scriptures. Christians "allow their cultural conditions and highly diverse affections to be molded by the set of biblical stories."[62] "To become a Christian," Lindbeck writes, "involves learning the story of Israel and of Jesus well enough to interpret and experience oneself and one's world in its terms."[63] We can safely assume that Lindbeck's construal of Christianity includes whatever "symbols" legitimate the "basic patterns of thought, feeling, and behavior" that uniquely characterize Christians, those whose experience is shaped by the biblical story.

It should also be noted that there is a circularity to Lindbeck's sense of the Christian situation: Christians are those who allow their experience to be shaped by the symbol system *recognized by Christians*.

The Void of Lindbeck's Christian Situation

Given Lindbeck's depiction of Christianity, it follows that the void consists of those persons (and their systems of "discursive and nondiscursive symbols") who do *not* interpret their experience and the world in terms of the story told in the Christian scriptures.[64]

Unlike Schleiermacher and Barth, Lindbeck does not assume that Christians and religious others share common ground. In Lindbeck's schema, religious others are not simply excluded from the Christian situation; they are, so to speak, walled off. Since religious others are assumed to be decisively shaped by their own comprehensive symbol systems, they have little or nothing in common with Christians. Since their core concepts either are "untranslatable" in Christian terms or can only be "redescribed" with consequent change of meaning, religious others in Lindbeck's depiction really do constitute a "void": they are effectively unknowable, in themselves, from a Christian perspective. This is underscored by Lindbeck's choice of language as metaphor: the relation of Christians to religious others is equivalent to that between speakers of, say, English and Turkish; it is a relation of mutual incomprehensibility. As Fredericks writes, Christianity as construed by Lindbeck "constitutes a world of its own, established by its sacred texts and structured by the grammar of its doctrine. . . . Lindbeck's intratextuality cannot relate Christianity dialogically with what lies outside the [purview] of its normative texts."[65]

In depicting "the Christian" as a self-enclosed world, Lindbeck seems unaware of the extent to which Christian identity and self-understanding depend on religious others—in Badiouan terms, the extent to which the Christian situation is constituted by its void. The reader of *The Nature of Doctrine* gets the impression that Christianity exists on its own, essentially untouched by what goes on outside its borders.[66]

The Governing Order of the Christian Situation
Doctrines, understood according to Lindbeck's rule theory, constitute the governing order of the Christian situation. Functioning as the grammar of the Christian religion, they order its various elements with respect to one another and to the situation as a whole. More importantly, insofar as doctrines "recommend and exclude certain ranges of . . . propositional utterances or symbolizing activities" within the Christian situation, they work to prevent potential disruption from its void. The concepts of assimilation and redescription demonstrate this prophylactic function. While Lindbeck's notion of "absorbing the world" (particularly in Marshall's reading) recognizes that Christians may encounter and grapple with elements from religious others, the overall web of Christian doctrines works to domesticate or neutralize any potential serious disruption by redescribing them in Christian terms.

Doctrines also limit what can be known within the Christian situation. For instance, the doctrine of the Trinity limits the ways Christians can think and talk about the divine reality; statements about "three gods" are ungrammatical in the Christian situation. While this regulative function helps Christians work out what statements are authentically Christian, it also a priori rules out "alien elements" that do not fit neatly within the overall framework of Christian doctrines. The Buddhist concept of nirvana is a good example. The web of Christian beliefs, doctrines, and practices seems to allow no room for nirvana, despite the fact that Buddhists attest to its reality and the possibility that people may attain it.

Theological Effects of Lindbeck's Discursive Construction

As noted earlier, what seems to have spurred Lindbeck to create the cultural-linguistic model was his own encounter as a Lutheran in dialogue with religious others (in this case, Roman Catholics). Ironically, his model winds up fostering distance and detachment toward religious others, not engagement and transformative dialogue.

To his credit, Lindbeck takes pains to reject a narrowly exclusivist view. He fully recognizes the fact that Christians now find themselves in a religiously plural context. Where once "non-Christians were distant or unknown," he writes, Christians now find that "unbelievers are neighbors, friends and relatives." Indeed, Lindbeck's own *experience* of "unbelievers" seems positive. Quoting Karl Rahner, Lindbeck notes that in this new pluralistic context, Christians find themselves relying on non-Christians' "humanity, reliability and decency just as much as on the corresponding qualities in [their] fellow believers (in which process one sometimes gets the staggering impression that one can rely much more on the former than the latter)."[67] Unfortunately, Lindbeck does not follow up on the intriguing and potentially revolutionary questions this insight raises. For example, what is it about Christians that compromises their "humanity, reliability, and decency," qualities that would seem to be the hallmarks of a life shaped by the Gospel? Is it a problem with individual Christians or a systemic problem—a problem with the Christian situation? And given that religious others are shaped by fundamentally different symbol systems, how is that they can embody qualities prized by Christians, in some cases more fully than Christians themselves?

Lindbeck acknowledges that this new, more intimate experience of religious others constitutes a radical challenge to traditional Christian exclusivist attitudes about the salvific status of religious others; in Badiouan terms, he seems conscious of the experience of religious others as an event. "It has become psychologically and sociologically impossible for most Christians and Christian communities to assign non-Christians *en masse* to damnation," he writes. "Only sectarian groups whose basic attitudes seem to most church people both inhuman and unchristian succeed in doing this."[68] Furthermore, Lindbeck contends that Christians can benefit from dialogue and cooperation with religious others.[69] While Christians may legitimately hold that their language "is the only one that has the words and concepts that can authentically speak of the ground of being, the goal of history, and true humanity (for Christians believe they cannot genuinely speak of these apart from telling and retelling the biblical story)," this belief does not rule out the possibility "that other religions have resources for speaking truths and referring to realities, even highly important truths and realities, of which Christianity as yet knows nothing and by which it could be greatly enriched."[70] And, Lindbeck suggests, the process can work in the opposite direction: "One of the ways in which Christians can serve their neighbors may be through helping adherents of other religions to purify and enrich their heritages, to make them better speakers of the languages they have."[71] Clearly, unlike many exclusivist Christians, Lindbeck does not believe that the only goal of interreligious dialogue is conversion.

Despite these intimations of openness, however, what we might call Lindbeck's "knowledge-focused" approach—his turn inward to the Christian situation and the coherence of elements therein—is reflected in his general distance toward religious others. I mentioned earlier that Knitter sums up the postliberal approach to religious others with the proverb "good fences make good neighbors." This aptly suggests Lindbeck's basic attitude toward religious others, which follows from his stress on religions as mutually untranslatable. Since Christians have "ways of experiencing and being oriented toward self, neighbor, and cosmos" that are "radically (i.e., from the root) distinct" from religious others[72]—in Badiouan terms, since Christians are shaped by the knowledge of the Christian situation—Christians and religious others can have little in common apart from their mutual isolation. By defining religions as frameworks that shape *all* life and thought, Lindbeck implies that any given religion crowds out all other religions, since, logically, one cannot have more than one framework that shapes *all* of one's "life and thought."

This knowledge-focused approach is also reflected in the fact that the voices of religious others are virtually inaudible in his discourse. For a proposal about religions in general, *The Nature of Doctrine* offers surprisingly little supporting material drawn from religions other than Christianity. Although Lindbeck often begins by referring to "religions," he often reasons from the Christian situation— what, he believes, obtains (or ought to obtain) with regard to Christianity—then generalizes to other religions, and usually ends up returning to Christianity. This may result from a lack of direct familiarity with religions other than Christianity and Judaism.[73] His footnotes in *The Nature of Doctrine* suggest a reliance on second-hand (and, in some cases, rather dated) literature (Otto, Evans-Pritchard) and on theoretical works (Geertz, Berger).[74] Whatever the cause, it is significant that, to judge from *The Nature of Doctrine*, Lindbeck *assumes* religious untranslatability from the start—a priori—and not after long and in-depth comparative study of religious others. It seems that Lindbeck's presumption of untranslatability stems from an underlying preconception about Christianity and religious others: that Christianity differs radically ("from the root") from other religions, and that Christian theology must not compromise this fundamental difference (as, Lindbeck argues, experiential-expressivists have done).

Lindbeck's distance and detachment toward religious others can also be seen in his discussion of their place in a Christian understanding of salvation. While, as we have seen, Lindbeck spurns a narrow exclusivism, he remains troubled by the fact that a more optimistic attitude toward the salvific status of non-Christians seems to run counter to the traditional witness of the Church regarding the *sola Christi*, salvation through Christ alone. He puts the problem this way in a 1973 essay: "Many church members are troubled by the easy assumption that non-Christians can be saved, and this is not always because they are narrow or self-righteous. . . . What concerns them, rather, is a logical problem, a problem of cognitive dissonance. Scripture affirms, liturgy celebrates and the churches have historically asserted the *sola Christi*, salvation through Christ alone. How then can men and women be saved outside the visible church, that is, apart from explicit faith in God's redemptive action in Jesus Christ?"[75] While Lindbeck speaks in terms of "church members," the subsequent discussion shows that he shares their concern, and it is easy to see why. Christians' *experience* of religious others seems to conflict with the Christian symbol system that, according to postliberalism, should *shape (or determine) that experience*. Cognitive dissonance indeed!

However, in that same early essay, Lindbeck proposes a way out of this (apparent) dilemma. His solution reflects and reinforces his basic detachment toward religious others. Lindbeck advances what he calls an "eschatological" view of salvation, which turns upon the Reformers' emphasis on *fides ex auditu*, "the faith which comes through hearing the gospel proclamation." On the one hand, Lindbeck wants to preserve the Protestant position that "it is only through explicit faith in Christ that men and women are redeemed." Does this, then, consign unbelievers to damnation? Not necessarily: if one does not come to explicit faith in Christ during one's life, "then the beginning of salvation must be thought of as occurring through an encounter with the risen Lord in or after death."[76]

Lindbeck contrasts this view with an "ontological" view of salvation, by which "salvation is primarily an inward grace which is articulated and strengthened by explicit faith." Lindbeck's eschatological view understands explicit faith in Christ, "not as expressing or articulating the existential depths, but rather as producing and forming them."[77] Thus, for believers and unbelievers alike, it is only in dying that "the final decision is made for or against Christ. . . . All previous decisions whether of faith or unfaith are preliminary. The final die is cast beyond our space and time, beyond empirical observation, beyond all idle speculation about 'good' or 'bad' deaths. . . . We must trust and hope, though not know, that in this dreadful yet wondrous end and climax of life no one will be lost. And here, even if not before, salvation is explicit. Thus it is possible to be hopeful and trusting about the ultimate salvation of non-Christians no less than Christians."[78]

This proposal manages to kill two birds with a single stone. By postponing to the afterlife the "final decision" for or against Christ (that is, the decision that ultimately *counts*), Lindbeck is able to defer troubling questions about the salvific status of religious others. At the same stroke, by maintaining that it is still faith *in Christ* that saves, and by grounding that salvation in the *fides ex auditu*, Lindbeck preserves the integrity of the Christian symbol system, which for postliberalism shapes (or determines) experience.

Again, one gets the distinct impression that it is the symbol system—the knowledge of the Christian situation—that must be preserved. The central problem for Lindbeck seems to be not how to regard religious others as included in salvation, but rather how to protect the symbol system against challenges arising from the witness of religious others and from Christians' (increasingly positive) experience of them.

Toward one group of religious others, Jews, Lindbeck's detached attitude seems to lessen a bit. He regrets that Christians traditionally have taken a supersessionist and triumphalist view toward Judaism, a view he firmly opposes.[79] Lindbeck contends that Christian supersessionism and triumphalism in the early church "resulted from self-serving gentile Christian misappropriation of intra-Jewish polemics over Jesus' messiahship, and . . . these errors are blatantly opposed to much of the New Testament witness, especially Paul's."[80] Indeed, Lindbeck calls for a Christian ecclesiology that is an "Israel-ology," that is, "an Israel-like understanding of the church"; "the Hebrew bible," he writes, "is the basic ecclesiological book."[81]

While these comments indicate Lindbeck's sincere openness to Jewish others, it is important to note that his stance results not from an encounter with the Christian void (with what Jews themselves have to say), but from his focus on the overarching narrative of the (Christian) biblical texts. Of course, this is exactly what we should expect, given Lindbeck's intrasystematic approach: he practices what he preaches. Lindbeck finds no *biblical* evidence that any nation besides Israel "is especially beloved by God as a means of blessing to all peoples"; consequently, Christian supersessionists and triumphalists miss the irrevocable nature of God's election of Israel.[82] As these comments indicate, Lindbeck's openness to Judaism stems from his understanding of the message of the biblical texts; they do not result (at least in any evident way) from encounter with Jewish persons as outside the Christian situation.

Furthermore, in that same 1973 article, Lindbeck does not display even this degree of openness with regard to any other religious outsiders. He writes, "Scripture read classically by Christians agrees with rabbinic Judaism in not ascribing the possibility of a universal redemptive role to any communal traditions except those of biblical faith."[83]

Implications of Lindbeck's Discourse for the Christian Understanding of God

As with Schleiermacher and Barth, the problem with Lindbeck's theological discourse lies not only in the structures and processes by which he marginalizes and excludes religious others but also in the consequences of those structures and processes for an understanding of God and of the relationship between God and humans.

Lindbeck's discourse can be seen as a reaction against that of Schleiermacher and of Barth (despite Lindbeck's own Barthian roots). As we have seen, Schleiermacher's discourse, seeking to ground the modern theological project in experience, runs the risk of replacing the divine Other with the modern European middle-class self. While Barth attempts to rectify this problem by turning to the divine Other, he fails to see that, as Rieger puts it, "we never have access to a pure master signifier,"[84] and that the turn to the divine Other is incomplete without a corresponding turn to human others. Consequently, Barth's theological discourse only represses the self, enabling it to exert its influence from the theological unconscious.

To his credit, Lindbeck takes to heart the insight that there is no unmediated access to the divine; indeed, his theological project is founded on that insight. Yet he moves too far in the opposite direction. His focus shifts almost completely to what mediates, that is, to language and the tradition of the Church (including the biblical texts).

True, Lindbeck does hold that a religion, as a "single gigantic proposition," seeks to correspond to that which it considers "the Most Important, the Ultimately Real."[85] Yet it is hard to see how this is meaningful in Lindbeck's theological framework. For one thing, it is difficult to see how that Ultimate Reality can transcend the "knowledge" of a religion's situation. The reader will recall Lindbeck's comment that "the proper way to determine what 'God' signifies . . . is by examining how the word operates within a religion and thereby shapes reality and experience rather than by first establishing its propositional or experiential meaning and reinterpreting or reformulating its uses accordingly."[86] If a religion and its texts shape or determine what its adherents experience or regard as real, then that religion and its texts constitute the only source for knowledge (in *both* the usual sense and Badiou's sense) about the Ultimately Real. That is, the Ultimately Real turns out to be a function of the religion's web of beliefs, practices, and rules—the knowledge of a religion's situation, not what exceeds it. It is also difficult to see how a religion's correspondence (as "single gigantic proposition") to Ultimate Reality could ever be tested. How would one go about determining whether so diverse and complex a phenomenon as Christianity (or even a comparatively small subset such as my own tradition, Anglicanism) constitutes a form of life that does indeed correspond to what Christians (or Anglicans) consider Ultimately Real? Individual elements, perhaps, but not the religion as a whole.

Apart from these few references to what religions consider Most Important or Ultimately Real, concerns about the divine Other are conspicuously absent in Lindbeck's discourse in *The Nature of Doctrine*. In a sense, this is inevitable, given the avowedly "nontheological" character of Lindbeck's project in the first five chapters, and his cultural-linguistic shift away both from propositions about God (in a cognitive-propositional approach) and from experiences of the divine (an experiential-expressive approach). Yet Lindbeck's discourse gives the impression that God is somehow intrinsically bound up with, and does not exceed, the language and tradition of the Church. As Ronald Thiemann comments with respect to *The Nature of Doctrine*, Lindbeck risks replacing "God" with the "text."[87] Put differently, Lindbeck's turn to the text loses sight of the otherness of the divine Other.

The exclusion of religious others in and from Lindbeck's discourse also has important consequences for the understanding of God. As I argued in Chapter 1, the turn to the divine Other is incomplete without a corresponding turn to human others, including religious others. At worst, Lindbeck's discourse blocks the turn to religious others by turning Christian theology inward, toward the intratextual; at minimum, it neutralizes the transformative power of encounter with religious others by "absorbing" what they have to say and redescribing their witness in Christian terms.

In Lindbeck's discourse, the conflation of God with the texts of the Church, which was implicit in Barth's discourse, is fully manifest.[88] Whatever Lindbeck's intentions, his discourse directs Christians away from a concern for the otherness of the divine Other—that which exceeds any human situation, including the Christian—and toward the "knowledge" of the Christian situation, as that knowledge is constrained by the doctrinal rules that constitute that situation's governing order. What exceeds the Christian situation is regarded either as inaccessible or as comprehensible only in terms of Christian "knowledge."

But God is not the knowledge of the Christian situation; God is not the language and tradition of the Church. While God no doubt can and does reveal Godself through the knowledge of the Christian situation, that knowledge can only prepare Christians for encounter with that which exceeds it, the otherness of the divine Other. And a vital part of that encounter is encounter with religious others. The comments of the Benedictine monk Abhishiktānanda are pertinent here: "Man [*sic*] only begins to know God truly when he realizes that he knows nothing about him. . . . As long as man attempts to seize and hold God in his words and concepts, he is embracing a mere idol."[89]

What place is there, in Lindbeck's system, for surprise? What place is there for the Spirit, which blows where it will, to startle us with the not-thought, the unrealized, an otherness that disturbs the good order of our symbol-systems? As far as I can see, in Lindbeck's approach such a "holy surprise"—a truth event—even if it could be recognized, would quickly lose its ability to surprise: it would be assimilated, and thus neutralized, by the process of redescription in terms of the existing web of Christian belief and practice. As a result, Lindbeck's theology effectively domesticates the divine, neutralizing the radical otherness of the divine Other by confining that Other to the "knowledge" available within the Christian situation.

Evental Sites and Blind Spots in Lindbeck's Discourse

Several aspects of Lindbeck's situations (those for religions generally and for Christianity) serve as potential evental sites. First, unlike Schleiermacher and (to an extent) Barth, Lindbeck neither assumes the superiority of the Christian religion over other religions, nor arranges religions in a hierarchy of development according to some external standard. Instead, his cultural-linguistic model sees Christianity as *functionally* similar to other religions. Unlike Schleiermacher, Lindbeck does not base this commonality on some core experience generalized from Christianity to other religions; nor, in contrast to Barth, does he regard this commonality as fundamentally negative. Rather, Christianity shares with other religions the fact that it functions as a comprehensive framework in terms of which adherents experience and talk about the world. Furthermore, Lindbeck makes no judgments as to whether some religions are truer than, or functionally superior to, others; all, apparently, are presumed equal in this respect (pending an evaluation of their ability to "absorb the world").

To say that all religions have the same function, however, is not to say that all religions are the same, or that they are all "about" the same thing (such as Schleiermacher's feeling of absolute dependence or Barth's religion-as-*Unglaube*). Lindbeck clearly respects the fact that religions may be radically different from one another. The assertion of radical difference is an evental site in that it could open Christians to transformative encounter with religious others. It reminds Christians not to judge religious others by Christian categories. More importantly, it suggests that religious others may have something genuinely new and different to say, something Christians have never considered.[90]

Perhaps most significantly, some aspects of Lindbeck's discourse work to counter notions of Christian superiority, such as we saw in Schleiermacher and Barth. Viewed as language-like entities, religions cannot be evaluated against one another any more than languages can: it makes as little sense to claim that Christianity is "truer" or "better" or "more highly developed" than, say, Hinduism, as it does to claim that English is superior to Japanese. The only standard Lindbeck offers for evaluating a given religion, or for comparing it with other religions, is its assimilative power, its capacity to "absorb the world," which is in turn a matter of its categorial adequacy. Furthermore, while Lindbeck frames categorial adequacy in terms of the comparison of religions, it seems to be more a question internal to a given religion, concerning how well the religion's overall web of belief and practice assimilates new conditions. Lindbeck's refusal to assert Christian superiority removes a major traditional barrier to mutually transformative encounter with religious others, and thus serves as an important evental site in his Christian situation.

Despite these real and significant merits, other aspects of Lindbeck's theological discourse tend to block encounter with religious others and to close off the possibility that Christians can really hear and be transformed by such encounters. Here again, Rieger's analysis is helpful. According to his Lacanian framework, Lindbeck's is the "discourse of the tradition."[91] As Rieger notes, the discourse of the tradition opposes the liberal theological paradigm, the discourse of the self, in that postliberalism aims at a "self shaped by tradition"; its goal "is to integrate the uninitiated . . . into the system, enabling them to repeat and reproduce the language and tradition of the church."[92]

While Rieger notes that the discourse of the tradition is able in some respects "to resist the powers of exclusion produced by the modern self," he also identifies a critical blind spot: a tendency to promote conformity and to block the possibility of resistance. As Rieger writes, "when everything is subordinated to language and tradition, virtually no place is left from which a given language or tradition might be questioned or transformed. . . . The possibility of resistance against the governing discourse . . . is lost."[93] In Badiouan terms, the cultural-linguistic approach becomes—no doubt contrary to Lindbeck's own good intentions—a theology of the governing order of the Christian situation, working to protect its boundaries against encroachment by the claims and witness of its void, religious others.

This is borne out by Lindbeck's discourse regarding Christianity and religious others. Rather than opening Christian theology out toward encounter with its void, Lindbeck's approach turns Christian theology inward. The stress is on the *intra*textual, the web of beliefs *internal* to the Christian situation.[94]

Ironically, this insularity is particularly evident in Lindbeck's treatment of his notion of the religious text "absorbing the world." At first glance, the "absorption" process would seem to open a given religion to external influences. Yet given Lindbeck's stress on religions as comprehensive webs of belief, in which concepts only have meaning in relation to all other concepts, it is difficult to see how Christians can even begin to understand what they are attempting to "absorb," without themselves becoming initiated into the religious other's whole web of religious discourse. That is, it is difficult to see how such assimilation can occur without Christians becoming "speakers" of the other religion's language, taking on the "basic patterns of thought, feeling, and behavior uniquely characteristic of a given community"[95]—in short, without converting to the other religion. For instance, it would seem that to understand what Buddhism means by nirvana would entail "effectively interiorizing" the web of Buddhist categories that give nirvana its meaning.[96] One wonders whether, given Lindbeck's framework, Christians could ever meet these criteria, and if so, whether they would still be Christians, since they would have then taken on another comprehensive framework (Buddhism), one that shapes "the entirety of life and thought."

Even if we set aside this question, it is difficult to see how the absorption process could in fact transform the Christian situation. Marshall acknowledges that as a result of redescription, assimilated elements will likely take on "a different sense than they originally had [i.e., in the religious other's context]."[97] Since Christians employ a different set of concepts than do Buddhists, Christians will likely make different judgments about nirvana and its place in the overall scheme of things than do Buddhists.[98] Assimilated into the Christian situation, nirvana will no longer mean what it means for Buddhists. It seems to me that, in such an approach, interreligious dialogue becomes a matter of mutual *mis*understanding rather than mutual transformation.

Whatever else redescription and assimilation may do to "alien" elements, they work to minimize, or even to prevent, the transformative potential of encounter with religious others as truth event. However charitable the intent, the practical effect of redescription is to domesticate and neutralize alien elements, to assimilate them to the "knowledge" of the Christian situation. Rather than reshaping the Christian situation in light of the "alien," the latter is interpreted in such a way as to minimize disruption of the Christian situation's signifying chain, its status quo. Redescription and assimilation rob alien elements of their transformative and revelatory power. It is difficult to see how Christians could actually hear anything truly new and prophetic.

In these respects, the cultural-linguistic approach works to discourage Christians from encounter with religious others, to turn inward and to be concerned primarily with what is "known" within the Christian situation. The cultural-linguistic approach renders interreligious conversation difficult if not impossible. As James Fredericks notes, "Lindbeck's intratextuality cannot relate Christianity dialogically with what lies outside the [purview] of its normative texts."[99] As Paul Knitter puts it, postliberalism turns religion from a prism (for viewing the world) into a prison: "It's one thing to see religion as the perspective from which we always view everything else; it's quite another to announce that we are stuck in that perspective or that the perspective can never change profoundly."[100]

It would also seem to blind Lindbeck to the reality of interreligious encounter experienced by (among others) Asian Christians, summed up by Michael Amaladoss: "For us Asian Christians, Hindus, Buddhists, Muslims, and others are part of our life. We share a common culture and way of life. We belong to a common economic and political system. We have a common history. Our religious differences have cultural, political, and even economic implications. In this ongoing dialogue of life we have begun to appreciate the believers of other religions. We respect and read with profit their scriptures and other sacred writings. We learn from their sadhana, methods of prayer, and religious experience. We regard positively their moral conduct."[101] Though not explicitly directed at Lindbeck, Amaladoss's word of caution is apt: "It is not helpful to isolate and reify the religions as systems in themselves, set apart from this experiential complex."[102] Lindbeck's approach does indeed isolate religions as systems in themselves, and pays a high price in doing so.

Conclusion

To his great credit, Lindbeck has enriched the theological discussion considerably. His postliberal project underscores several key facts that any authentically Christian theology must confront: that language mediates the experience of the divine; that the biblical text shapes Christian perspectives and experience; that doctrines function more like grammatical rules than propositions. Furthermore, Lindbeck recognizes the very real possibility that religions may be fundamentally different, and he sounds an appropriate warning against attempting to reduce the witness of religious others to Christian categories.

However, as I have attempted to show, these considerable contributions come at a high cost: the loss of encounter with religious others. Although he resists exclusivism and allows for the assimilation of "alien" elements into the Christian situation, Lindbeck renders encounter with religious others theologically irrelevant: he turns Christian theology inward, toward intrasystematic relations in which religious others, being extratextual, can play no part. His discourse, like that of Barth, ends up absolutizing the Christian situation, blocking encounters with religious others, and domesticating the divine. Here again, theological discourse that does not open itself to encounter with religious others remains trapped in its own circular self-affirmation, its own "knowledge."

CHAPTER 6

Gutiérrez

A Turn to *Christian* Others

Each of the theologians we've looked at so far ends up hardening the boundaries of the Christian situation, and consequently misses out on the possibility of transformative encounter with religious others and thus, potentially, with the divine Other. In this chapter we examine how a fourth theologian fares: Gustavo Gutiérrez. Gutiérrez is the only one of our four theologians to make an explicit turn to the marginalized and to focus on their struggles for liberation from the structures that marginalize them. Indeed, he envisions "Liberation from every form of exploitation, the possibility of a more human and dignified life, the creation of a new humankind."[1] Thus it is reasonable to expect that his theological discourse will be more open to encounter with religious others than that of the other three. The picture, however, is more mixed than we might expect.

I will focus on Gutiérrez's *A Theology of Liberation* and *Las Casas: In Search of the Poor of Jesus Christ*, with occasional reference to his other writings.[2] Once again, our investigation will focus on the three issues examined in the previous chapters: how the discourse constructs religious others; how that construction affects the resulting theological formulations, focusing on those concerning the Divine; and possible evental sites and blind spots in the discourse. We will begin by looking at Gutiérrez's truth event and the theological method that he developed in fidelity to it.

Gutiérrez's Truth Event and Turn to the Marginalized

As with Barth, Gutiérrez's theological project is rooted in a truth event that led him to question the nature and method of Christian theology as he knew it. This event involved his own personal experience of marginalization in Peru and his participation in the liberatory struggles of the poor and oppressed in Latin America.

As a mestizo in Peru, where economic status has traditionally been correlated with the whiteness of one's skin, Gutiérrez experienced both discrimination and poverty from an early age.[3] Later, during medical studies in Lima, he encountered the writings of Karl Marx and "joined student Christian movements that were protesting social and economic inequalities in Peruvian society." After graduate studies in Europe, he returned to Peru in the 1960s to take up parish ministry, and became involved in the base ecclesial communities movement in the slums of Lima. His encounter with the poor in his parish "challenged the traditional theological education he had received."[4] Gutiérrez wrote *A Theology of Liberation* in fidelity to this truth event, his first-hand experiences of poverty, oppression, and marginalization.

Gutiérrez's theological project responded to the revolutionary struggles of Latin America in the late 1960s. At that time, Latin America was the site of political, cultural, and intellectual ferment. Since the days of European colonial rule, Latin America had been characterized by stark inequality. Conservative elites, supported by national military forces as well as U.S. business and government interests, held power over a much larger majority of poor and dispossessed persons, in most cases Indian or mestizo. The Catholic Church was complicit in this arrangement; aligned with the conservative elites, leaders of the Catholic Church in Latin America had traditionally "set themselves firmly against popular activism and protest."[5] However, the success of the socialist revolution in Cuba in 1958 inspired the poor and oppressed in Latin America to seek liberation from centuries-old social-political-economic oppression and injustice. Leftist (usually Marxist) guerrilla movements and student protests erupted throughout Latin America.[6] The conservative elites generally responded to popular unrest by backing brutal authoritarian regimes (often supported by the United States[7]), which sought to quash dissent by means of disappearances, torture, and state-sanctioned murder.

For Gutiérrez the profound injustice, in which the church was often complicit, was not only a political problem; it was also an *evangelical* problem, an obstacle to the Church's proclamation of "the Kingdom of Life."[8] Yet in spite of the Catholic Church's long-standing and deep-seated complicity in unjust social-political-economic power structures, Gutiérrez did not reject the Church in favor of, say, Marxism. Instead he chose to rethink the Christian situation, by rereading the Bible and the Catholic tradition in light of the revolutionary context. What he found was the Gospel's call for liberative praxis, as Curt Cadorette observes: "Christians must scrutinize the societies they live in, grapple with their problems, and, informed and motivated by the gospel, take concrete action to overcome those sinful forces that cause pain and destroy life. . . . The liberative praxis of the Christian is his or her way of collaborating with that ultimate utopic and eschatological symbol we call the reign of God."[9]

Rethinking Theological Method

As with Barth, Gutiérrez's fidelity to his truth event leads him to radically rethink the way Christians should do theology. He seeks to do theology from an explicitly Latin American perspective.[10] While he notes that the process of liberation pervades all human life, he contends that Latin America is "the only continent among the exploited and oppressed peoples where Christians are in the majority"; this makes the Latin American situation "especially interesting" for reconsidering "the 'practice' of the church in today's world."[11] While he takes account of processes in the wider world and the history of the Church, his focus is on his own Latin American context and his own time.

For Gutiérrez, liberation theology offers "not so much a new theme for reflection as a *new way* to do theology."[12] It is a theology rooted in the perspective of the poor and oppressed; it is "an expression of the right of the poor to think out their own faith."[13] In liberation theology, their voices not only can be heard but also (at least theoretically) form the hermeneutical key for theological reflection.

Liberation theology is grounded in the realization that unless Christians listen to the voices of those who are different, particularly those who are socially and economically marginalized, they cannot speak in truth about the Christian God. Gutiérrez puts it this way: "We find the Lord in our encounters with others, especially the poor, marginated, and exploited ones."[14] This echoes Rieger's principle: no divine Other without human others.

Encounter necessarily leads to action. Rather than abstract speculation on other-worldly concerns, theology becomes "part of the process through which the world is transformed."[15] It contributes to this process primarily through prophetic critique of social structures that marginalize and oppress, including those of the Church itself. Accordingly, Gutiérrez understands theology to be "a criticism of society and the Church insofar as they are called and addressed by the Word of God";[16] it is "a critical reflection—in the light of the Word accepted in faith—on historical praxis and therefore on the presence of Christians in the world."[17] Furthermore, the authenticity of theology is verified by historical praxis, "by active, effective participation in the struggle which the exploited social classes have undertaken against their oppressors."[18] And since theology is an inherently critical endeavor, it cannot serve merely as an apologetic for Christianity. Rather—and this is crucial—it must assess both positive *and negative* aspects of Christian presence in the world.[19]

As Gutiérrez's references to the Word of God indicate, the Bible is fundamental to his theological method. Yet not the Bible alone, but the Bible in
dialogue with the lived experience of Christians, particularly those who are poor
and oppressed. James Nickoloff describes the dialogic process in this way:

> Because "the Word [of God is] contained in Scripture and transmitted by the
> living tradition of the church," Gutiérrez takes his cue in interpreting that word
> from the actual experience of the ecclesial community itself. What he has noticed,
> and repeatedly pointed out in his writings, is that Christians not only find answers
> to their questions in the Bible but also frequently discover that the Word of God
> puts new questions to *them*. Thus, while *we* read the Bible, it is also true to say
> that *the Bible* "reads" us. Through Scripture God questions believers about the
> adequacy of their discipleship.[20]

More generally, Gutiérrez contends that "the life, preaching, and historical
commitment of the Church" constitute a "privileged *locus theologicus*." Yet he
also insists that theological reflection must go beyond the "visible boundaries"
of the Church. Liberation theology "implies openness to the world, gathering
the questions it poses, being attentive to its historical transformations."[21] Quoting Yves Congar, Gutiérrez contends that theology must not use scripture and
tradition as its sole starting points, but must also begin with "facts and questions derived from the world and from history."[22]

Gutiérrez rejects the church-world dualism that has dominated Christian theology since the Patristic period (Barth's theology being a major recent example),
and in which the Church is regarded as "the exclusive depository of salvation."[23]
Not only does this rob the world of autonomy and authentic existence, Gutiérrez argues, it conveniently overlooks the fact that the Church has always been
involved in the world, "when by its silence or friendly relationships it lends legiti-
macy to a dictatorial and oppressive government"; this has been particularly true
in Latin America, where the Church has traditionally had close ties to the exploit-
ing classes. Gutiérrez notes that a church-world dualism works to the interest of
dominant groups, "who have always used the Church to defend their interests and
maintain their privileged position"; when they see "subversive" trends in the contemporary Church—that is, trends that threaten their own power—they hypo-
critically call for a return to a purely spiritual role for the Church.[24]

Gutiérrez also has theological, or more precisely, soteriological and eschatological grounds for rejecting a dualism between church and world. Contrary
to the traditional doctrine *extra ecclesiam nulla salus* ("No salvation outside the
church"), Gutiérrez argues, the church is not the realm of salvation, against the
world. Quite the contrary: it is in the world that Christ and his Spirit are "present and active," and their work, the work of salvation, is "a reality which occurs
in history"—that is, in the *world's* history, rather than in some otherworldly,

nontemporal, "spiritual" realm.[25] Christ's eschatological promises are not solely "spiritual," devaluing temporal and worldly realities. Instead, Christ gives these promises "meaning and fulfillment today (cf. Luke 4:21), but at the same time he opens new perspectives by catapulting history forward, forward toward total reconciliation."[26] Salvation "gives to the historical becoming of humankind its profound unity and its deepest meaning."[27]

Sin, Salvation, and the Kingdom of God

Despite the efforts of some to portray Gutiérrez as a Marxist, his principal categories come not from Marx but from the Bible: sin, salvation, and the coming of the Kingdom of God.[28] Yet these categories take on new meaning—or, arguably, regain their original biblical meaning—in light of Gutiérrez's truth event, the struggle for liberation in Latin America. For Gutiérrez, sin is "a personal and social intrahistorical reality."[29] It does not exist in and of itself, but is only evident in "concrete instances," in "oppressive structures, in the exploitation of humans by humans, in the domination and slavery of peoples, races, and social classes. Sin appears, therefore, as . . . the root of a situation of injustice and exploitation."[30]

Salvation, too, is "an intrahistorical reality."[31] Understood as "the communion of human beings with God and among themselves," salvation "embraces all human reality, transforms it, and leads it to its fullness in Christ."[32] Thus salvation "is not something otherworldly, in regard to which the present life is merely a test."[33] "Nothing escapes [the salvific] process," Gutiérrez writes, "nothing is outside the pale of the action of Christ and the gift of the Spirit. This gives human history its profound unity."[34]

As an "intrahistorical reality," salvation is for Gutiérrez intimately linked with historical and political liberation.[35] He writes, "Salvation embraces all persons and the whole person"; "the struggle for a just society is in its own right very much a part of salvation history."[36] Accordingly, Gutiérrez criticizes those who limit the work of salvation "to the strictly 'religious' sphere," who "refuse to see that the salvation of Christ is a radical liberation from all misery, all despoliation, all alienation," and who "in order to protect salvation (or to protect their interests) lift salvation from the midst of history, where individuals and social classes struggle to liberate themselves from the slavery and oppression to which other individuals and social classes have subjected them." Such thinking presents a real danger: "Those who . . . [try] to 'save' the work of Christ will 'lose' it."[37]

Accordingly, Gutiérrez contends that all persons, Christian and non-Christian alike, "are saved if they open themselves to God and to others, even if they are not clearly aware that they are doing so."[38] We will take up this topic shortly.

In line with his treatment of sin and salvation as "intrahistorical" realities, Gutiérrez portrays the Kingdom of God as very much this-worldly and historical, though not yet fully realized. The Kingdom is "a promise which is received in history," and "necessarily implies the reestablishment of justice in this world."[39] It also implies the end of poverty, since "poverty is an evil and therefore incompatible with the Kingdom of God."[40]

Las Casas

Before we turn to a consideration of Gutiérrez's Christian situation, we should touch on one further aspect of his work, which will have important implications for his treatment of religious others. In the 1980s and 1990s, liberation theology encountered an increasing conservative retrenchment in the Roman Catholic Church. Some liberation theologians were silenced, and Gutiérrez narrowly avoided episcopal condemnation.[41]

Quite contrary to the charge that he had abandoned the Christian tradition, Gutiérrez responded to this crisis by turning to that very tradition: he embarked upon an extensive study of the work of Bartolomé de Las Casas. This sixteenth-century Dominican priest and scholar was one of the few European voices in the colonial period who spoke out in defense of the indigenous Indian peoples of the Americas and in opposition to their maltreatment at the hands of European Christians. Though separated by four centuries, Gutiérrez finds in Las Casas a kindred spirit. Moved by the suffering of an oppressed people and outraged by the fact that their oppressors are Christians (who often have the support of the Church), Las Casas, like Gutiérrez, finds it necessary to break with the theological status quo and to "walk—like Abraham—toward an unknown land, along a desert trail where the only solid footing is faith in God and hope in the Reign of life."[42] In Gutiérrez's case the problem involves sinful social-political-economic structures that exploit the poor for the benefit of a wealthy elite; in Las Casas' context the problem is the enslavement and vicious maltreatment of the indigenous Indian peoples by Spanish Christians in the wars of the *Conquista* and in the subsequent *encomienda* system.[43] Both Gutiérrez and Las Casas are moved to denounce prophetically the injustices of the social system, and both face persecution within the Church for deviating from the party line.

Given these resonances, one detects a subtext in Las Casas: just as the Dominican friar's position has been vindicated by history, so perhaps will Gutiérrez's own liberation theology be vindicated. It is with good reason that one writer regards the Las Casas study not as "a defensive retreat to the comfort of the past," but as "a strategically *offensive* move that challenges Rome—indeed, the entire Catholic Church—with the imperative to reconstruct the very essentials of Christian systematic theology."[44] Indeed, so closely does Gutiérrez identify with Las Casas' thoughts, it is permissible to read the work as Gutiérrez letting his predecessor speak for him.[45] Of particular importance to our examination of Gutiérrez's treatment of religious others, *Las Casas* reflects Gutiérrez's own sense of the universality of salvation (which is only sketched in *A Theology of Liberation*), and of the working of divine grace in the religious life of non-Christians. We will consider these aspects of Gutiérrez's borrowing from Las Casas later in this chapter.

Gutiérrez's Christian Situation and Religious Others

As the reader has surely guessed, Gutiérrez's turn to the excluded has substantial implications for his understanding of "the Christian." Before turning to these, I should note that like Lindbeck, and unlike Schleiermacher and Barth, Gutiérrez is not primarily concerned with constructing what I have called a religion situation; that is, he is not concerned with establishing a "religious" domain distinguishable from other domains (such as the political, the aesthetic, or the cultural). Indeed, in contrast to our other three theologians, Gutiérrez seems relatively unconcerned with the category "religion." Consequently, we can move directly to Gutiérrez's construction of the Christian situation, its void, and its governing order.

Gutiérrez's changes in theological method affect the boundaries of his Christian situation in two ways: by expanding the range of theological sources and norms included in the Christian situation and by broadening the understanding of the category "Christian" itself.

Within his Christian situation, Gutiérrez includes as theological sources not only the Bible and the texts of the Christian tradition (including magisterial texts such as *Lumen gentium*) but also the voices of the poor and oppressed in Latin America, the historical praxis of the church, and "facts and questions derived from the world and from history." Additionally, Gutiérrez expands the range of theological sources by drawing upon the social sciences, including Marxist thought.[46] These nontraditional elements can be included in the Christian situation because it is in the world at large—not solely in the church—that Christ and his Spirit are "present and active." Although the primary norms for theological reflection remain the Christian texts (the Bible and the Christian theological tradition), these texts must be interpreted through the lived experience of the poor and oppressed in Latin America. In other words, Gutiérrez's Christian situation is potentially much more expansive than that of any of our other three theologians. And since he rejects a dualism between church and world, he also moves away (at least theoretically) from the relatively rigid boundaries of the Christian situation that we saw in Schleiermacher, Barth, and Lindbeck.

This more open and expansive construal of the Christian situation also carries over into Gutiérrez's recasting of the category "Christian" itself. He in fact uses the term in two senses, one descriptive and the other normative, which are both overlapping and mutually contradictory.

The first, *descriptive* sense denotes those who profess faith in Christ; "Christian" in this sense is coterminous with the Church. This sense is in play, for instance, in his remark that Latin America is "the only continent among the exploited and oppressed peoples where Christians are in the majority";[47] this clearly refers to the self-identification as Christians by marginalized persons in Latin America. This descriptive sense is also in play when Gutiérrez, in *Las Casas*, refers to the conquistadors and *encomenderos* as "Christians," since they were members of the Church, though their mistreatment of the Indians signifies their unfaithfulness to Christ's teachings.[48]

However, profession of faith and membership in the Church are neither necessary nor sufficient for Gutiérrez's *normative* sense of "Christian." Here, "Christian" denotes those who do the work of liberation—whether or not they profess faith in Christ. For example, Gutiérrez argues that Las Casas' profound sense of God and the requirements of the Gospel allowed him to see clearly "that it is not possible to be *a Christian and an oppressor* simultaneously."[49] Since oppressors in Latin America—in Gutiérrez's time as in Las Casas'—have been (at least nominally) Christian, it is clear that Gutiérrez understands "Christian" in this normative sense to involve considerably more than mere profession of faith in Christ and membership in the church. Through Las Casas, Gutiérrez asserts that being a Christian is not just a matter of baptism or of explicit profession of faith in Christ; it also depends on one's praxis, how one lives out that faith, and whether one practices justice and neighbor love: "Baptism is no warranty of eternal life. Unless the profession of faith be accompanied by the practice of justice and a love for one's sisters and brothers, that profession will be in vain. In fact, the 'Christian' who fails in this practice will be professing precisely a denial of faith in the God of love."[50]

"Christian" in this normative sense is *not* coterminous with the Church, although clearly many Church members also participate in liberation. As we've seen, Gutiérrez rejects the view that the Church is "the sole repository of religious truth,"[51] because it presupposes a church-world dualism that Gutiérrez considers wrong headed. Accordingly, he calls for the "uncentering" of the Church: "The Church must cease considering itself as the exclusive place of salvation and orient itself towards a new and radical service of people."[52] For Gutiérrez, the boundaries between the Church and the world should be permeable, or, as he puts it, "fluid."[53] He sees Church and world as interpenetrating realities: while the Church has a role to play in the world (to be discussed shortly), it must also allow itself "to be inhabited and evangelized by the world."[54]

While those who profess faith in Christ yet fail to practice Christian justice and love are excluded from Gutiérrez's Christian situation, so those who practice justice and love are included within it—even if they do not explicitly profess faith in Christ. The Christian situation consists of those who signify

Christ's liberation of humankind not simply by having faith in Christ but by doing the *work* of liberation—for it is by one's participation in that work that one manifests faith in Christ, even if unknowingly.

Here Gutiérrez seems to have in mind something along the lines of Rahner's "anonymous Christian," in which (as James Fredericks puts it) "those who are 'graced' in and through their own religions are also oriented toward the Christian church" and thus "are, in a sense, already Christians and experience what Christians experience and are directed toward what Christians have in Jesus."[55] Gutiérrez writes of "the single vocation to salvation, beyond all distinctions," which "gives religious value in a completely new way to human action in history, Christian and non-Christian alike." "The building of a just society," he writes, "has worth in terms of the Kingdom, or in more current phraseology, to participate in the process of liberation is already, in a certain sense, a salvific work."[56] Salvation depends less upon explicit profession of faith in Christ than upon one's attitude and behavior: "Persons are saved if they open themselves to God and to others, even if they are not clearly aware that they are doing so. This is valid for Christians and non-Christians alike—for all people."[57] Citing the episode of the gentile Cornelius in Acts, Gutiérrez contends that "not only is the Christian a temple of God; every human being is."[58] He cites Yves Congar: "'Many constitute the temple, but invisibly,' says Congar referring to the well-known expression of Augustine of Hippo: 'Many seem to be within who are in reality without and others seem to be without who are in reality within.' In the last instance, only the Lord 'knows his own' (2 Tim 2:19)."[59] In Gutiérrez's discussion of Mt 23, he notes that the "least of these" in whom Christ is present includes all persons, "pagans, Jews, and Christians."[60]

Gutiérrez finds support for this essentially inclusivist stance in what he calls "a beautiful, profound passage" of Las Casas. The friar contends that God's saving grace, though concealed, has always been at work among the Indian peoples, even *before* the historical moment of conversion to Christianity. Yet Las Casas goes further: he also claims that this saving grace has actually conferred on them forgiveness, and presumably salvation, despite their having "had no direct, explicit knowledge of the truths of faith."[61] It is not surprising that Gutiérrez implicitly approves of Las Casas' message that non-Christians may outnumber Christians at God's right hand on the Day of Judgment.[62]

For Gutiérrez then, non-Christians who are open to their neighbor and who do the work of liberation are Christ's subjects not only *in potentia* but *in actu* as well. They are members of the Christian situation (in the normative sense) just as much as those who profess faith in Christ and live out that faith by doing the work of liberation. At the same time, those who profess faith in Christ may deny him with their works; those who seem to be Christian insiders may be in fact outsiders, and the outsiders, insiders.

In other words, Gutiérrez implicitly draws the boundaries of the Christian situation to *exclude* those who are Christians in name only—that is, those who, though professing faith in Christ, deny that faith by oppressing and marginalizing others—and to *include* those who are open to the neighbor and who do the work of liberation, including many who would not self-identify as Christians.

The Void of Gutiérrez's Christian Situation

Undoubtedly Gutiérrez's Christian situation is, potentially, far more inclusive than that of any of the theologians we have considered here. Yet while some features of Gutiérrez's discourse incorporate non-Christians into the Christian situation, other aspects effectively exclude them—relegate them to the void of his Christian situation. In fact, Gutiérrez practices the two types of exclusion we identified in Barth's theological discourse: explicit and methodological.

As we've seen, Gutiérrez's Christian situation *explicitly* excludes those persons who are Christians in name only, as well as those, Christian or non-Christian, who oppress and exploit the poor. *Methodological* exclusion, on the other hand, involves Gutiérrez's choice of theological sources—the elements that make up his Christian situation. It is significant that he considers "*Christian* praxis (commitment and prayer)" to be the starting point for theology.[63] This Christian orientation carries through in the range of sources that actually figure in Gutiérrez's theological discourse. While his explicitly inclusivist stance would lead one to expect him to include non-Christian texts and traditions as theological sources, virtually the only *religious* voices audible in Gutiérrez's discourse are Christian voices, particularly scripture, the magisterial texts, and the Christian theological tradition. And while Gutiérrez asserts that these texts must be read through the experience of the marginalized, he does not explicitly discuss the non-Christian marginalized; he does not consider how their concerns and perspectives might differ from those of poor and oppressed Christians, or how it might be presumptuous and misleading to express non-Christians' experience of marginalization in terms of Christian texts and categories (e.g., sin, salvation) rather than their own.

Indeed, despite his significant widening of theological sources generally, Gutiérrez demonstrates little more familiarity with religious traditions outside Christianity than our other three theologians. Particularly puzzling is the absence of voices of religious others among the indigenous peoples of Latin America, and especially Gutiérrez's native Peru. If "our encounter with the Lord occurs . . . especially in the encounter with those whose human features have been disfigured by oppression, despoliation, and alienation,"[64] then we should also expect to "encounter the Lord" among the indigenous peoples of Latin America, who have often been the chief victims of poverty and oppression. Of an estimated 35 to 40 million indigenous persons in Latin America and the Caribbean today, Peru is home to about 9 million, making it one of the region's most indigenous countries.[65] Yet the voices of the indigenous peoples of Latin America are curiously absent in Gutiérrez's discourse. Given that they are among the poorest and most marginalized, their absence is striking.[66]

In Gutiérrez's theological discourse, then, we have the paradoxical situation that non-Christians who participate in the work of liberation are included in the Christian situation, yet remain outsiders—religious others—because their distinctive texts, traditions, and practices are excluded. This has substantial implications for Gutiérrez's theological reflection, as we will see shortly.

The Governing Order of Gutiérrez's Christian Situation

As we've seen, Gutiérrez's theological discourse establishes a distinction between normative Christianity and purely nominal Christianity. For Gutiérrez the criterion for this distinction is one's openness to one's neighbor and engagement in liberative praxis. This criterion functions as one part of the governing order of Gutiérrez's Christian situation. Those elements that, according to Gutiérrez, satisfy this criterion are favored; those that do not are marginalized. And, as we have seen, the deployment of this criterion raises the intriguing possibility that non-Christians may be in fact members of the Christian situation.

Yet there is another, tacit part of the governing order, which results from the methodological exclusion of non-Christian religious sources. While the voices of non-Christian poor and oppressed may theoretically be heard in Gutiérrez's Christian situation, they can be heard only *in terms of* Christian norms such as the Bible, rather than their own texts and traditions. It would seem that non-Christians are not in fact equal and full-fledged members of the Christian situation.

Theological Effects on Gutiérrez's Discourse about God

Gutiérrez is to be commended for creating a theology built on "the right of the poor to think out their own faith,"[67] which prophetically critiques society and the Church and which works toward the transformation of the world away from sinful structures that impoverish and oppress, and toward liberation for all. He also deserves praise for seeking to open the Christian situation to include the witness of non-Christians, by recognizing that they may contribute to the struggle for liberation as much as Christians (and in some cases, more so).

Yet as we've seen with our other theologians, the construction of the Christian situation, though necessary to an authentically Christian theology, can also work against the express interests and goals of the theologian. The construction of a Christian situation also constructs "knowledge" in the Badiouan sense, which can distort the theology that results. Gutiérrez turns out to be no more immune from this distorting effect than Schleiermacher, Barth, or Lindbeck.

As we've seen, Gutiérrez's discourse makes room for theological sources recognized as authoritative by the *Christian* poor and oppressed, but not those sources so recognized by the *non-Christian* poor and oppressed. Whether or not Gutiérrez intends it (and I doubt that he does), the methodological exclusion of non-Christian voices from Gutiérrez's theological discourse implies a double standard regarding the witness of the marginalized: although God's gracious presence is at work in the lives of non-Christians, their witness to that divine presence does not carry the authority of Christian witness.

How does Gutiérrez's discursive construction of the Christian situation and religious others affect his portrayal of God and of the relationship between God and humans? As with our other three theologians, the picture is mixed.

Gutiérrez fully recognizes that, as Rieger stresses, we cannot know and be faithful to the divine Other apart from encounter with, and service to, human others. Of the four theologians considered here, only Gutiérrez succeeds in opening Christian theological discourse to the witness of socially, politically, and economically marginalized persons, including, at least potentially, religious others. Indeed, he seeks to make such persons' experience of God the hermeneutical key for theological reflection on Christian texts and on the contemporary world.

The result of Gutiérrez's turn to the marginalized is, at least in some respects, a more balanced and arguably more faithful picture of the Christian God than that presented by the other theologians considered here. By adopting the experience of the poor and oppressed as hermeneutical lens, Gutiérrez is largely able (though not entirely, as will be discussed later) to avoid Schleiermacher's tendency to conflate the character and interests of God with those of the modern European middle-class self. As we have seen, by grounding theology in a "feeling of absolute dependence" Schleiermacher reduces the relationship to God to an identity between God and the self, and thus excludes other people. There is no critical or prophetic perspective—no *other*—from which the self's complicity in structures of oppression and exclusion can be revealed and critiqued. In contrast, by turning to the poor and oppressed, Gutiérrez restores to Christian theology a critical-prophetic perspective that illuminates both the sinfulness of social structures constructed by the modern self and God's commitment to those who suffer under them. It is not through some "feeling of absolute dependence" (or at least not by such feeling alone) that we come to know God; it is in doing justice to the poor and oppressed. By taking this approach, Gutiérrez recovers important aspects of the biblical understanding of God, aspects that have been neglected too long in the Christian tradition. He offers a more rounded picture of God—not an abstract and ahistorical being, but a God who acts in history and is involved in the struggles of the marginalized.

Additionally, contrary to our other three theologians, Gutiérrez contends that God's presence and activity cannot be restricted to the Church. Gutiérrez's turn to the poor and oppressed uncovers the Church's complicity in structures and oppression, and thereby reveals the danger of absolutizing the Church. While the Church is called to reveal and signify the plan of salvation and its fulfillment in history, it is not an end in itself, nor is it the exclusive locus of salvation. Unlike Schleiermacher, Gutiérrez does not hold that only the baptized have access to the Holy Spirit; instead, all humans are touched by the work of the Spirit. Unlike Barth, Gutiérrez does not regard the church as sole repository of divine truth, nor—at least in principle—does he hold that Christianity has sole possession of knowledge of the Divine. Unlike Lindbeck, Gutiérrez (again, at least in principle) resists identifying God with the language and tradition of the Church. Instead, by recovering the prophetic dimension of the biblical texts, Gutiérrez reminds us that God transcends the institutions and forms of Christianity—indeed, that God is equally active among Christians and non-Christians, in the Church and the world, wherever humans struggle for liberation.

As a result of Gutiérrez's reading the Bible through the eyes of those on the underside of history in Latin America, his understanding of God's nature and work both departs from traditional understandings and returns to a vision of God suggested in the biblical texts. This is not the god of the philosophers— Prime Mover, Pure Being, Anselm's "that than which nothing greater can be thought." Instead, Gutiérrez's God is radically present and active in human life and history.

Above all, God is *el Dios de la vida*, the God of life, as Gutiérrez titles his 1991 work of biblical theology, which is also his most developed meditation to date on the nature and work of the Divine. "Life and not death," he writes, "is what God desires for all, even evildoers, provided they abandon their evil ways and do 'what is right and just.'"[68] Because God is the God of life, God liberates: "The God of life manifests love by forming a family of equals through an act of liberation in which God does, and demands, justice amid the people and enters into an irrevocable covenant with them in history."[69]

As the last quote suggests, the God of life is intimately involved in the events and struggles of human history. Indeed, God saves in and through history; the Incarnation, Gutiérrez holds, is the paradigmatic expression of God's radically historical presence.[70] "The God of Jesus Christ is the God of the kingdom, the God who has a message and a purpose for human history." Furthermore, Jesus is God come into history to establish the Reign of God.[71]

While some of Gutiérrez's critics have accused him of reducing God to history, he in fact seeks to affirm both the biblical witness to God's otherness (holiness, transcendence) and the equally biblical witness to God's radically historical presence in and with humans.[72] On the one hand, Gutiérrez recognizes the biblical witness to the holiness of God, which he identifies with Barth's "Wholly Other," "the one who is completely different."[73] On the other hand,

Gutiérrez holds that "the Biblical God is close to human beings, a God of communion with and commitment to human beings."[74] Furthermore, Gutiérrez holds that the Holy Spirit dwells in *every* human being, not just the baptized—a teaching with clear implications for theological reflection on religious others.[75] Consequently (and as mentioned earlier), the "least of these" in whom Christ is present (Mt 23:31–45) includes all persons, "pagans, Jews, and Christians."[76] Thus Gutiérrez seeks to hold together the otherness and the nearness (the historicity) of God:

> The Scriptures teach us that the God of the Bible irrupts into history, but at the same time they show us that God is not as it were watered down by the historical process. On the contrary, as Paul says at the Areopagus, in God "we live and move and have our being" (Acts 17:28). We may therefore say that the holy God is a God who makes a covenant with the people and that the God of the covenant is the "Wholly Other," the Holy One. These are two distinct aspects of God but each implies the other.[77]

Both aspects carry implications for human behavior. On the one hand, God's holiness is "the source and model of human holiness"; "to proclaim the gospel is to transmit the holiness of God."[78] At the same time, human holiness is not a flight from the world, but an engagement in history that mirrors God's own engagement. Gutiérrez writes that "our holiness is to find expression in deeds, and it is by these that we shall be judged."[79] Just as God's holiness is manifested in history, so the knowledge of, and the worship appropriate to, this God cannot be separated from historical praxis. To know God is to do justice, and "the worship God desires is inseparable from the practice of justice."[80]

Idolatry—the rejection of God—is likewise a matter of praxis, of behavior in history and in the world. "The key question," Gutiérrez writes, "is this: Whom in practice, do you serve? The God of life or an idol of death?"[81] In the Latin American context, Gutiérrez argues, the principal manifestation of idolatry can be seen in those who profess to be followers of Christ "while in practice serving mammon by mistreating and murdering God's favorites, the poor."[82] "When the poor are oppressed and their rights trampled underfoot, their blood is shed; this is against God's will. The idolatry of money, of this fetish produced by the work of human hands, is indissolubly and causally connected with the death of the poor. If we thus go to the root of the matter, idolatry reveals its full meaning: it works against the God of the Bible, who is a God of life. Idolatry is death; God is life."[83]

Yet while Gutiérrez recognizes that there can be no encounter with the divine Other apart from encounter with human others, he seems to have missed the equally important corollary: there can be no encounter with human others apart from encounter with *religious* others. Like our other three theologians, Gutiérrez seems not to have contemplated the possibility that distortion of the Christian witness about the divine Other could result from the formation and structure of "the Christian" itself (as situation). As long as religious others are less than full participants in the theological conversation, the analysis of unconscious structures of authority and power will remain incomplete. Equally important, Christian encounter with the divine Other will be blocked, and Christian understanding of that Other will be distorted.

As was the case with Schleiermacher and Barth, Gutiérrez fails to address the continuing influence of the modern self on his theology. He certainly seems to buy into one of the foremost "grand narratives" of European/neo-European modernity, that of human history as the march of progress on the social, political, intellectual, economic, and scientific fronts. He characterizes history as "a process of human liberation" and freedom as "a historical conquest," involving greater human control of nature and evolution toward socialism.[84] Assertions like "God's presence and our encounter with God lead humanity forward" imply that God is in some sense the motive factor in human progress; a similar assumption seems to lie behind Gutiérrez's depiction of the "growth of the Kingdom," which is linked with "liberating historical events" and "greater human fulfillment."[85] In other words, human progress is conflated with what the *modern European/neo-European self* considers to be progress (e.g., scientific, technological, and economic "development"); God, it seems, is seen as the agent behind these developments, giving them divine sanction.

This modernistic view of liberation constitutes an obstacle to interreligious encounter. As Edward L. Cleary notes, by functioning as "a modernizing and rationalizing element," liberation theology has been seen as condemning traditional indigenous religious beliefs and practices, including the folk and popular Christianity of the poor and oppressed indigenous peoples of Gutiérrez's own Latin American context.[86] This has the effect of blocking out witness of the Divine that differs from the "official" Christian norm. Insofar as this is the case, Gutiérrez fails to counteract power structures that conflate the interests of God with those of the modern (European/neo-European middle-class) self.

Furthermore, by restricting theological sources to Christian texts—the Bible, the magisterial texts, the Christian theological tradition—Gutiérrez distorts the picture of God. The Christian texts used by Gutiérrez constitute a particular community's experience of and witness to God and God's revelation; they are not that God or that revelation.

Much as Schleiermacher makes "the christianly pious person into the criterion and context of his theology,"[87] Gutiérrez makes the "christianly pious" poor and oppressed persons in Latin America the principal focus of his theology. While Gutiérrez does not commit Schleiermacher's associated error of making the human self the sole subject of theology (his prophetic, almost Barthian insistence on God's holiness and demand for justice precludes such a move), Gutiérrez's depiction of God is reduced to what Christians experience as "God." In other words, God is reduced to what the church mediates and what poor and oppressed members of that church experience and recognize as authoritative. As Schleiermacher tends to confuse the nature and interests of God with the self-image and aspirations of his own European middle class, so Gutiérrez conflates the nature and interests of God with what *Christians* understand them to be. God, it seems, does not speak in ways other than those recognized by Christians.

Gutiérrez does not explore the possibility that non-Christian poor and oppressed persons have different experiences of the Ultimate and of the human relation to it, and that their experience might be as theologically valid as that of the Christian poor and oppressed. This oversight is odd, since Gutiérrez recognizes that those who do justice, including non-Christians, know God.

By restricting himself to Christian understandings and experience of God, Gutiérrez's theological discourse absolutizes the Christian situation and domesticates God accordingly. Access to the otherness of the divine Other is blocked because access to other human experiences of the Ultimate is also blocked. Consequently, the depiction of God, and of human relation to God, is distorted. This distortion is evident in at least two respects: the emphasis on knowledge of God through liberative praxis and the understanding of God's relation to history.

First, as we have seen, Gutiérrez insists that God is present in, and thus is known through, liberative praxis. While, unlike Schleiermacher and Barth, Gutiérrez does not explicitly rule out other ways of knowing God or Ultimate Reality, his de facto exclusion of the voices of religious others gives the impression (perhaps despite Gutiérrez's own intentions) that only one way—the Christian way—really "counts." This approach marginalizes other paths to the Ultimate to which religious others witness.

Interestingly, we find a very different path to the Ultimate in the religions of the indigenous peoples of Gutiérrez's native Peru. In a study of the religious experience of the Aymara people, Xavier Albó enumerates "the special signs, places and times through which God shows himself [*sic*] to the Aymara people." While the list includes the struggle for rights and encounter with the poor and needy, the Aymara also recognize a number of other places and times in which the Divine is revealed, including the home, the family, agricultural work, the multiplication of life (including plant and animal life), health, the community, festivals, and moments of crisis (e.g., sickness, death, natural disaster).[88] The Aymara also consider the landscape itself sacred and revelatory. Albó writes that, over the centuries, the Aymara "have developed a sacred relationship" with the wild and remote Andean environment in which live. "They see it as full of life, inhabited by powerful and extraordinary beings, as real as themselves, with whom they must learn to relate and to dwell amicably and whose presence they must acknowledge in all their activities." The Christian faces of God introduced by Europeans complemented, but did not replace, the Aymara's traditional and time-tested sense of the sacred: "The bearded men who in latter times have come from over the sea did not bring any alternatives so convincing that they [the Aymara] abandoned completely their previous personal experiences" of the Divine.[89] Since the voices of the Aymara and other indigenous peoples are not present in Gutiérrez's theological discourse, he is unable to benefit from their insights and to reshape his understanding of God accordingly.

A second distortion stems from Gutiérrez's understanding of the relation between God and history. While Gutiérrez (*pace* some conservative critics) by no means reduces God to human history, he does assert that God's holiness and otherness is manifested in history and thus cannot be separated from historical praxis. While he insists that God is not "watered down by the historical process,"[90] he nonetheless tightly associates God with the trajectory of human history. For Gutiérrez, the Christian God is "a God who saves in history."[91] As mentioned earlier, Gutiérrez's sense of history, and of God's action in history, is highly teleological; it is bound up with both Christian and modernist notions of progress and is expressed in terms of a beginning (creation) and an end (the eschaton): "The complete encounter with the Lord will mark an end to history, but it will take place in history."[92] Thus God's activity—and consequently, God's nature—is closely associated with history so construed.

In insisting on the unity of history, Gutiérrez speaks of overcoming "all" dualism (natural/supernatural, temporal/spiritual, profane/sacred, world/church).[93] However, from the perspective of some religious others, Gutiérrez remains quite dualistic. A Buddhist perspective, for instance, might well question how far Gutiérrez's understanding of history and of God's relation to it escapes dualism. Indeed, from a Buddhist standpoint, Gutiérrez's sense of history is not only dualistic but also may reflect an unenlightened perspective. As Masao Abe notes, "For Buddhism, history has neither beginning nor end."[94] Nirvana involves truly realizing "the beginninglessness and endlessness of history," and thus finding "the whole process of history from beginningless beginning to endless end intensively concentrated within the here and now. . . . We realize our true life and true Self at this moment in which beginning and end, time and eternity, and one and all are not seen in duality but in dynamic oneness."[95] To the one who has attained nirvana, history ends; the awakened one experiences a Reality beyond the dualism of time and eternity. At the same time (no pun intended), for the awakened one history also begins, "because those who, despite *the fact of* universal salvation realized by an awakened one, *think themselves* to be 'unsaved', remain innumerably in the world and will appear endlessly in the future. Thus history has a new [meaning] for an awakened one—it is an endless process in which he [*sic*] must try to actualize universal salvation in regard to those 'unsaved.'"[96] Thus, for the awakened one, "the present life is not a means to a future end, but is the end itself, while in the light of compassion life is an endless activity of saving others, an instrument for universal salvation."[97]

While Abe's Buddhist understanding of the Ultimate explicitly excludes the notion of a personal God, I think that his perspective captures an aspect of the Christian understanding of the Ultimate that Gutiérrez, in his efforts to place God firmly in history, neglects or at least underplays. While it is true that God acts in history, it is also the case that God's presence in history is the presence of a transcendence, of a Reality that transcends the temporal—the presence of eternity in history—that which constitutes the limit of the temporal and historical. Perhaps God not only saves humans *in* history, as Gutiérrez contends; perhaps God also saves humans *from* history. Perhaps, by participating in the divine Other's work in history, we also share in the divine Other's transcendence of history itself.

At any rate, to fail to consider alternative views such as those Abe expresses is also to fail to challenge the dominance of a European/neo-European worldview over the perspective of others. If liberation theology is serious about liberating the poor and oppressed, it must be wary of absolutizing its own very Western and very Christian assumptions.

Evental Sites and Blind Spots in Gutiérrez's Discourse

As is the case with our other theologians, Gutiérrez's theological discourse manifests both evental sites and blind spots with regard to religious others. Once again, Rieger's Lacanian analysis helps in identifying both. Rieger characterizes the theologies of liberation as instances of the "discourse of the marginalized."[98] In this discourse, that which is repressed takes the role of agent, confronting the self with its own processes of repression and misrecognition. Through this confrontation, the self can come to a better understanding of its own nature and dynamics: it is able to see that it is not independent or autonomous (as is assumed by the discourse of the Self), but is shaped by its repression of the other. And this confrontation with the other also reveals "the master signifiers—the gods—which the modern self follows without knowing it."[99] Furthermore, moving the other to the position of agent allows for reshaping both the self and its master signifiers, "reformulating them in ways that bring out their freeing and liberating potential for all."[100]

Both the revelatory and the transformative effects mentioned by Rieger are evident in Gutiérrez's theological discourse. First, by moving the poor and oppressed of Latin America to the agent position, Gutiérrez reveals the "gods" worshipped by the powers that be, in society as well as the church: power, status, social control, financial wealth. For example, as we saw earlier, Gutiérrez recasts idolatry as serving mammon by oppressing the poor.[101]

Second, Gutiérrez's theology works to reinterpret the Christian tradition's master signifiers, such as scripture and the magisterial texts, so as to bring out their liberating potential. His critics have seen his incorporation of social sciences as theological sources as diminishing the authority of traditional Christian master signifiers and distorting them according to "alien" frameworks (such as Marxist thought).[102] However, Gutiérrez does no such thing. In Gutiérrez's theological discourse, the traditional Christian master signifiers, and particularly the Bible, retain pride of place—a fact underscored by the absence of non-Christian religious sources in his discourse. Gutiérrez reveals how the biblical texts, read through the lens of the poor and the oppressed, speak profoundly and insightfully to the contemporary social-political-economic context, critiquing the structures of oppression and calling not just for "spiritual" salvation but for the this-worldly liberation of oppressed and oppressor alike.

This new focus on the biblical critique of oppression and the biblical message of liberation constitutes an eventual site insofar as it allows for the "uncentering" of the church and the associated recognition that non-Christians may contribute to the work of liberation as fully as Christians. The perspective of the poor and oppressed reveals the hollowness of any profession of faith in Christ that is not lived out in openness to the neighbor and in liberative praxis. One cannot be both a Christian and an oppressor; loyalty to the divine Other cannot be separated from service to marginalized human others. The logical implication of this stance is to recognize that one's salvation does not rest solely on profession of faith in Christ or membership in the church. Furthermore, since openness to the neighbor and liberative praxis may be exhibited by those outside the church, they may also be subjects of Christ, even if unknowingly. Indeed, they may be *true* subjects of Christ, unlike "Christian" oppressors. Of the four theologians we have considered, only Gutiérrez opens Christian theology (at least in principle) to non-Christians.

Despite these real gains, however, other aspects of Gutiérrez's theological discourse tend to block encounter with religious others. Here again, Rieger's analysis is helpful. He notes that in the discourse of the marginalized the position of the other must be kept open and flexible, "as a place where listening and self-reflection become possible."[103] Otherwise, the position can become fixed, creating what he describes as "a new authoritarianism . . . where the theologian who identifies with the marginalized plays God, putting certain things such as '*the* poor' or '*the* woman' into an absolute place of authority." In this way, the theologian in fact arrogates to herself a position of absolute power, which is related to wider power relations in the social-political-economic context.[104]

Sadly, this tendency can be found in Gutiérrez's discourse as well. The problem can be expressed in terms of center and periphery. Although liberation theology is at the periphery in relation to the conservative center of the Vatican under Popes John Paul II and Benedict XVI, it remains a theology of the center with respect to religious others, who remain on the periphery. As we've seen, it is methodologically Christian centered, in the use of Christian texts as principal theological sources and the exclusion of the religious texts and traditions of non-Christians—despite Gutiérrez's recognition that non-Christians may be included in the domain of salvation. This exclusion is ironic, since, as we have seen, he also advocates the "uncentering" of the church in relation to the questions of the world and the transformations of history, and seeks a theology in which the poor and oppressed speak for themselves.

Moreover, this methodological exclusion reflects underlying power relations between Christians and religious others. Mirroring relations of authority and power between colonial center and colonized periphery, Gutiérrez leaves it up to Christians to decide what is authoritative, what is the nature of the Ultimate, what constitutes salvation and liberation, and, ultimately, who is "in" and who is "out." In other words, Gutiérrez fails to keep the position of the other open and flexible, as Rieger recommends; instead, he fixes it on the witness of *Christian* marginalized, effectively excluding the many non-Christians, in Latin America as elsewhere, who are marginalized in theological discourse.

A notable example is Gutiérrez's tendency to treat the Christianity of the Latin American marginalized as monolithic (and more or less identical with Gutiérrez's own Christianity). In *A Theology of Liberation* he gives no sense of the diverse blend of Catholic and indigenous religiosities (and, more recently, Protestant variants) that other scholars have identified as "folk" or "popular" Christianity.[105] For a variety of reasons, including the continuing powerful attraction of native religious beliefs and practices, the indigenous peoples of Latin America have long practiced a kind of folk or popular Catholicism, which Edward L. Cleary and Timothy J. Steigenga describe as "a synthesized form of Catholicism, combined with greater or lesser degrees of native religion." Cleary and Steigenga note that "approximately 10 percent of Latin America's people are orthodox Catholic in their beliefs and practices, while 10 percent are orthodox native practitioners. The rest fall somewhere in between."[106]

Gutiérrez does not reflect on how the perspectives and practices of folk Christianity differ from the "official" Christianity of the liberation theologians, or what the latter can learn from the former. More importantly, he does not reflect on how the preservation of elements of indigenous religions in folk Christianity manifests the liberatory struggles of the indigenous peoples, their ongoing protest against the forced imposition of foreign (Christian) beliefs by their European conquerors. Studies of popular religion in Latin America (which, in fairness to Gutiérrez, appeared since *A Theology of Liberation* was first published) indicate that it empowers its adherents to control their world, to adapt to changing conditions, and to negotiate social and political divisions. Equally important, folk

Christianity gives adherents direct access to the sacred, obviating the need for mediation by representatives of "official" Christianity (e.g., priests).

For instance, the Saints' cult in central Ecuador operates in large part independently of the "legitimate" beliefs and practices of the Roman Catholic Church. While God is seen as a distant being, saints such as Sucre's San Francisco (popular accounts of whom bear little or no relation to official church history) are seen as more approachable and can be petitioned for assistance. Statues of the saints are seen as beings in their own right, rather than mere representations of Jesus, Mary, or the saints. Although the local Catholic priests tolerate these beliefs, they complain that the people venerate the saints above God, and are therefore not "good Catholics." The people, however, persist in their beliefs, which give them a measure of power unavailable through the official church.[107] By stubbornly insisting on their own vision of Christianity and their own religious practices (some of which take place alongside those of the institutional church), indigenous peoples assert their own authority and power in opposition to that of the official church.

While liberation theology has contributed to the rise of indigenous theologies by conscientizing (raising the social and political consciousness of) the indigenous poor and by making room (at least in principle) for their voices in Christian theological discourse, it has been seen in indigenous circles as an essentially hegemonic discourse, an imposition of dominant Christian perspectives. In his study of the rise of the indigenous theology movement in Latin America, Stephen P. Judd notes that while Gutiérrez is sympathetic to the movement, he "went to great lengths to differentiate" his own theology of liberation from it and spoke cautionary words to indigenous theologians.[108] In an article on Mayan indigenous theology, Chiappari criticizes Gutiérrez's theology in particular as inherently exclusivist (my term, not Chiappari's). Despite Gutiérrez's "tremendous solidarity with and respect for indigenous peoples and their cultures," Chiappari writes, his stress on evangelization indicates that he "ultimately cannot abide by their practice of their own, non-Christian religions."[109] In a study of indigenous religion and politics in Bolivia and Peru, Cleary notes that liberation theology, which became the dominant paradigm for many Catholic missionaries in the 1960s and 1970s, worked against the traditional religious practices of indigenous peoples. Functioning "as a modernizing and rational element in religious thought," Cleary writes, liberation theology consequently was understood in indigenous circles "not just as condemning traditional practices as out of touch with a modern understanding of Scripture, but also as portraying traditional practices as the continuation of the dominance of mestizo political and economic control and the subordination of Indian peasants."[110]

Gutiérrez seems not to recognize that the preservation of non-Christian indigenous religiosity in the Latin American context (as elsewhere) can also be a liberative praxis. Indeed, it may be key to disrupting the European/neo-European repression of indigenous peoples, who are attempting to preserve and assert their own identity and experience in opposition to centuries of oppression by European Christians. Consequently, to exclude their voices from theological discourse is a sign of complicity in the structures of exclusion and oppression against which indigenous peoples struggle.

Chiappari lays bare the power relations inherent in liberation theology and the contradictions with its stated goals: "If [liberation theology] is concerned with the powerlessness of the 'little ones of history,' then why not give more power to them, and specifically in the arena in which they are most able to do so, i.e., religion? . . . If indigenous peoples have a right to religious freedom, then they should be allowed to practice their own religions, rather than be proselytized by other religions."[111] What is involved here, Chiappari argues, are attitudes about power and self-determination, attitudes that mirror those of Latin American power elites toward indigenous peoples: "The worldview of [liberation theology] . . . includes the belief that Christianity is a better religion than all others, however subtly or implicitly this view might be held. And, like the various indigenist policies of Latin American states, this view presupposes that those with more power know better than those with less. Thus, however well intentioned either church or state may be, their position with regard to indigenous people has been that they must be 'de-Indianized' to some degree, whether by integration, incorporation, or inculturation."[112]

Moving beyond Latin America, Gutiérrez's statement that it is "the only continent among the exploited and oppressed peoples where Christians are in the majority"[113] implies a recognition that many (perhaps most) exploited and oppressed peoples in the world are not Christians. However, he does not consider what shape their own theologies of liberation might take, and how non-Christian beliefs, texts, traditions, and practices might figure in such theologies. While such reflection is technically beyond Gutiérrez's stated scope of constructing a theology for the Latin American context, the shape of non-Christian theologies of liberation could have important implications for Gutiérrez's own Latin American, Christian theology of liberation.[114]

Finally, the absence of non-Christian voices from Gutiérrez's discourse deprives it of interreligious support for the concept of liberation.[115] For example, the religions of the Indian subcontinent (Hinduism, Buddhism, Jainism) share the concepts *moksha* (liberation) and *mukti* (release), which both parallel and differ from Gutiérrez's understanding of liberation. Norman E. Thomas contends that Hinduism has its own liberation theology and philosophy, which is built upon the concept of *jivanmukti* (liberation in life) and issues forth in work for social transformation. "As such," Thomas writes, "it provides a parallel to liberation theologies in contemporary Christian thought, and a useful meeting point for Hindu–Christian dialogue and for ecumenical social action broadly conceived."[116]

Conclusion

In faithfulness to the truth event that opened him to the relation between the divine Other and marginalized human others, Gutiérrez seeks to ground Christian theological reflection in the experience of the poor and oppressed of his Latin American context. While he does not reduce salvation to political liberation, he shows that the two are intrinsically related: since sin is manifest in unjust social structures, all work toward a more just social order is salvific. This means that non-Christians and Christians alike may participate in the work of salvation—in other words, that non-Christians may in fact be subjects of Christ, even if unknowingly. Conversely, it means that those who profess faith in Christ and yet participate in injustice and oppression are outside the Kingdom of God, that is, the Christian situation in its normative sense.

Yet despite the potential of this move to open Christian theology to encounter with religious others, Gutiérrez effectively contradicts it by relying solely on the texts and traditions recognized by Christians. While insisting that non-Christians who do the work of liberation know God, he renders that possibility theologically irrelevant by ignoring their voices, their own experiences and understandings of the Divine Ultimate. Consequently, like the other three theologians, he winds up absolutizing the Christian situation, blocks encounter with religious others, and domesticates the Divine.

The sobering lesson is that even a theologian who is sensitive and committed to the marginalized can participate in marginalization and othering. Once again, theological discourse that does not open itself to encounter with religious others remains trapped in its own circular self-affirmation, its own "knowledge." When Christian theology fails to hear the voices of religious others, it loses a critical perspective on itself and its witness. As with Barth, Gutiérrez's own theological discourse shows that a theology that begins with what Christians "know"—in this case, poor and oppressed Christians—can only end with what Christians "know."

CHAPTER 7

Conclusion
Turning to Religious Others: A Proposal

A Look Back

As I stated at the outset of this work, for much of its two thousand-year history, Christianity has operated as if it were the only game in town, or at least the only game that mattered. In this respect, the four theologians we have examined end up offering more of the same. Despite dramatic differences in method, in their construal of "the Christian," and in the authority structures upon which they ground their theological formulations, they continue to operate as if religious others have nothing important or relevant to contribute to the Christian theological conversation.

Given the contemporary challenge of religious diversity, more of the same is no longer sufficient. Christian theology cannot ignore the voices of religious others any more than we Christians can ignore the religious others who are our coworkers and next-door neighbors, whose children attend school with our children, and whose places of worship contribute to the life of our communities as much as do our churches. If Christian theology is to remain relevant, to speak to our time, it must learn to listen and respond to our religious neighbors.

Yet there are deeper reasons for Christian theology to make this turn to religious others. As I have argued throughout this work, the question of religious others lies at the very heart of Christian theology. Encounter with religious others reveals the limitations of knowledge available within the Christian situation and opens Christians to the in-breaking of transcendent truth. Building on the work of Joerg Rieger, and deploying a conceptual framework drawing on the situation-void-event philosophy of Alain Badiou, I have attempted to show how four major types of Christian theological discourse construct religious others and repress their witness, and how this repression limits and distorts the resulting theological formulations.

What can we learn from this exercise? For one thing, we have seen that the problem is not boundary drawing per se; it does not lie in the formation of a Christian situation and its void. As I argued in Chapter 1, boundary drawing is necessary: we draw boundaries around certain concepts in order to use them, and Christian theology is no exception. Any theological discourse, Christian or otherwise, must begin somewhere. Christians naturally and necessarily begin with the truth event that is most important to us, that which (as Badiou would say) constitutes us as subjects: the truth of God revealed in Jesus Christ. Each of our four theologians—Schleiermacher, Barth, Lindbeck, and Gutiérrez—attempts in his own way to do theology in fidelity to that truth event as he understands it. And any properly Christian theology must establish some criteria to separate what is Christian from what is not. Accordingly, each of our four theologians establishes, explicitly or implicitly, criteria for what is Christian and what is not. That is, each sets the boundaries of the Christian situation.

Yet in so doing, each theologian discursively constructs religious others, the void of the Christian situation. Religious others do not exist as such prior to or apart from a given theological discourse. We cannot take for granted the "obvious" boundaries between religions, or between Christian and non-Christian, as all four of our theologians appear to do. We should not mistake the purely conventional for "the way things are," and certainly not as absolute, fixed, or (God forbid) eternally established. There are no "essential" religious others. Religious others are constructed as a result of the application of criteria for belonging or inclusion. Othering is a discursive process.

What is othered, however, is not merely excluded; religious others haunt Christian theological discourse as a kind of "present absence" or "absent presence." More formally, they are constitutive of the situation that excludes them, which does not exist qua situation apart from its void.

While the discursive construction of the Christian situation and its void is a necessary step for a properly Christian theology, it has a downside that none of our four theologians seems to have recognized. The construction of "the Christian" is also the exercise of power, with all the dangers power brings. It entails marginalizing or excluding voices that offer a critical perspective on what can be "known" within the Christian situation.

At the same time, as the void that is constitutive of the Christian situation, religious others point to the insufficiency and limitations of that situation, and reveal a truth greater than the knowledge available within it—truth not only about the Christian situation itself but also about the Divine or Ultimate and humanity. If no attempt is made to listen to the voices of those outside the Christian situation (as constructed by particular instances of theological discourse), Christian theology loses access to that truth and remains trapped in its own circular self-affirmation.

By failing to grapple with the relevance of the otherness of religious others, theology also tends to lose sight of the otherness of the divine Other. Without encounter with the witness of religious others, Christian theology risks reducing the divine nature to what is "known" within the Christian situation; insofar as it does, Christian theology robs itself of a critical perspective that can call into question its limitations and the repressions of its governing order.

It is at this point that power relations in the Christian situation can link up with power relations in the wider social-political-economic context. God may come to be confused with the modern European middle-class self (Schleiermacher and Barth) or with the language and texts of the Church (Lindbeck and Gutiérrez). I'm sure that none of those theologians intends such a conflation; each would probably have denied it if asked. Yet such a conflation does result from each theologian's tendency to absolutize the boundaries of the Christian situation and to exclude other, different visions of the Divine or the Ultimate.

Even though a theologian constructs her Christian situation in faithfulness to the truth event of God's self-revelation in Jesus Christ, if she hardens its boundaries she conceals otherness and difference. By blocking out the voices of religious others, Christian theological discourse fails to be fully faithful to the teachings and example of the very Christ in response to whom theologians construct the Christian situation in the first place. As I have attempted to show, faithfulness to Christ entails remaining open to the God who cannot be controlled, the God who may speak and act through those who are othered by the dominant systems and structures, including the Christian situation (however construed). Faithfulness to Christ does *not* entail ignoring the witness of non-Christians. Quite the contrary: it demands that Christians be ready to listen to what religious others are saying about the Ultimate that Christians call God and, more importantly, to attend to what the God Christians proclaim is saying in and through the experience and witness of religious others. Faithfulness to Christ *entails* and *demands* meaningful encounter with those who are different, especially those (like Jesus' compassionate Samaritan) who differ *religiously*.

Looking Forward

It is one thing to critique the work of others. It is far more difficult to imagine a theology that moves beyond them and that offers a better alternative to more of the same. Yet that is the final task of this work: to offer a constructive proposal for a Christian theology that will avoid the blind spots of the four theological discourses, a theology that will be faithful not only to the truth of God revealed in Jesus Christ but also to encounter with religious others as potential truth event witnessing to that God.

Since actual implementation of such a theology is beyond the scope of the present work, I will restrict myself to an all-too-brief sketch of its outlines and parameters. I hope to put muscle and flesh on this bare skeleton in my future work, and I invite others to join me in this work.

The proposed approach is organized around four principles, discussed in the following sections.

Emphasize the Critical and Self-Critical Task of Christian Theology

The revelation (in this work as well as that of Rieger) of blind spots and distortions in major instances of Christian theological discourse highlights the ever-present need for Christian theology to critique its own assumptions and formulations. Of course, I am not alone in construing theology as an inherently critical project. As we saw in Chapter 6, Gutiérrez recognizes theology's role as critical reflection on praxis and "on the presence of Christians in the world."[1] Similarly, Charles M. Wood defines theology as "critical inquiry into the validity of Christian witness," where "validity" has the three dimensions of authenticity, truth, and appropriateness to context.[2] "The engagement of Christians in theological reflection," Wood writes, "might best be seen as an exercise in self-criticism, aimed at enabling those so engaged to bear more adequate witness. It involves the raising of some hard questions concerning one's own or one's church's present activities, understandings, and commitments."[3] As Wood observes, "critical" means applying criteria. My proposal breaks new ground in the *choice of criteria*. While intra-Christian criteria (such as scripture or tradition) remain vital to an authentically Christian theology, they do not in and of themselves prevent or reveal the blind spots and distortions arising within Christian theological discourse. They must be complemented by encounter with religious others. I will discuss this further in the following sections.

Recognize That Christian Boundaries Are Both Necessary and Merely Provisional

A crucial part of the critical–self-critical task is to critique the discursive construction of the Christian situation. As I have noted, theological discourse must begin somewhere, and Christian theological discourse naturally begins in and with what is recognizably Christian. Yet while boundary drawing is a "necessary evil," we must not forget that it is (so to speak) an "evil" nonetheless; that is, it is a requirement, but it has costs and sometimes quite steep ones. For one thing, boundaries limit or block access to truths, most prominently the truth of the void of the Christian situation and the otherness of the divine Other, encountered in and through human others, including religious others.

For another thing, the setting of boundaries is a highly subjective and contentious process, varying significantly from one theologian to another. As we have seen, each of our four theologians constructs the Christian situation according to quite different criteria. For Schleiermacher, Christianity is the only religion in which God-forgetfulness and redemption are the focus of all religious emotions; for Barth, it is the only religion that, in response to divine revelation, understands all religion (including Christianity itself qua religion) as *Unglaube*. For Lindbeck, membership in the Christian situation involves speaking the Christian language and interpreting the world through its system of discursive and nondiscursive symbols; for Gutiérrez, it is a function of openness to the neighbor and participation in liberative praxis. This diversity of understandings about what constitutes "the Christian" suggests that it is not a straightforward, one-size-fits-all category. It means different things for different followers of Christ. While the construction of an authentically Christian theology requires the theologian to establish what is Christian and what is not, that ruling is at best an approximation.

For these reasons, Christian theology must recognize that its boundaries are provisional, not fixed, and are by no means absolute or impermeable. They serve only to mark out a starting point, a field in which to begin Christian theology. As that theology proceeds, it must recognize its limits, and be ready at all times to hear and respond to the truth that lies beyond. Gutiérrez's notion of keeping the boundaries between the church and the world "fluid" is relevant here.[4] Just as he sees church and world as interpenetrating realities, in which the church allows itself "to be inhabited and evangelized by the world" and vice versa,[5] so Christian theology needs to have a more fluid sense of inside and outside, in order, as Fredericks puts it, to keep the tension between Christian and non-Christian "creative."[6]

To do so, Christian theology must be ever mindful of three key questions: What is God saying and doing in and through religious others? What do religious others tell Christians about ourselves, our witness, the God to whom we witness, and our relationship with that God, with human others, and with other beings? What do religious others reveal about the power dynamics in our own theological discourse? Christians cannot answer these questions if we do not first listen to religious others—and not just in Christian terms, but also in terms of how religious others think and experience the Divine Ultimate.

Develop a More Comprehensive Comparative Theology

Given my overall argument in this book—and despite my mildly critical comments in Chapter 2—it should come as no surprise that I consider comparative theology to be one of the most promising forms of Christian theology to come along in some time.[7] Among the major proponents and practitioners of this approach are James L. Fredericks, Francis X. Clooney, and John P. Keenan.[8] Reflecting the postmodern distrust of a priori universals and grand narratives, comparative theology (as Fredericks writes) "does not start with a grand theory of religion in general that claims to account for all religions," nor does it "look for some abstract lowest common denominator or essence that all religions, including Christianity, share."[9] Comparative theologians contend that a complete and satisfactory theology of religions is not possible prior to in-depth dialogue with other religions. Instead, comparative theology is a matter of "doing before knowing," "a theology that arises *through* dialogue," "a Christian theology done by means of dialogue with those who follow other religious paths."[10] Fredericks and Keenan bring Christian theology into direct conversation with Buddhist texts and teachings; Clooney does the same for Hinduism.

This is a Christian theology explicitly open to the void of the Christian situation, a theology in which the voices of religious others are not only audible but share equal space with Christian voices. It embodies the second principle I laid out: by beginning the theological project in and with mutually transformative conversation with Hindus (Clooney) or Buddhists (Fredericks and Keenan), comparative theology recognizes the relevance of the witness of religious others to Christian theology.

In its present form, however, comparative theology does not go far enough. The principal problem lies in its assumption that theological reflection can be deferred until after dialogue with religious others. As I argued in Chapter 2, it is neither possible nor desirable to postpone theological reflection until after dialogue. The readiness for dialogue, based as it is on the assumption that religious others may have something true to say to Christians, itself implies a theological stance. It assumes that dialogue with religious others is not, as some exclusivists hold, simply an encounter with apostasy and unbelief, but is at least potentially a truth event. That assumption must be made explicit and defended theologically. In a sense, the present work contributes to that effort: it serves as at least a partial systematic theological basis for a comparative theology.

One side effect of the moratorium on (explicit) a priori theologizing is also a major deficiency in comparative theology to date: its lack of attention to the dynamics of power and repression in the religious discourses being compared. In the comparativists' defense, this omission probably stems from a reluctance to impose theological presuppositions or biases onto their dialogue partners or the dialogue itself. All the same, the effort to be fair results in neglect of the power dynamics within and around the discourses being compared. To date, the work of Clooney, Fredericks, and Keenan tends to focus on texts and teachings themselves, in isolation from the wider social, political, economic, and religious contexts in which those texts and teachings arise and function.[11] There is little or no attention to the question of who stands to gain from the discourses being compared and whose voices are repressed or ignored. In other words, the comparativists so far seem not to have attended to the question of the broader context within which the discourses operate, and the question of who is "inside" and who is "outside" and why.

I would also like to see the comparative theologians address the ways in which they themselves, the texts they compare, and the comparative project itself are embedded in wider structures of social, political, economic, and religious power and repression. Take, for example, Fredericks's comparison of the Buddhist scholar Nāgārjuna and Thomas Aquinas in *Buddhists and Christians*. What sort of power relations are at work in Fredericks's own selection of these particular representatives of their respective communities, rather than the countless other voices that might have been chosen? Is this a completely "neutral" selection, or does it reflect deeper assumptions about the authority and privilege of the comparative theologians to determine what sort of voices are comparable? Also, how does Fredericks's position as a neo-European Christian affect his discourse about Buddhism? Or, to approach the matter from a different angle: how does Fredericks's project fit within the power relations of his own Roman Catholic community? Does it represent a resistance to the antidialogical tendencies within the magisterium; if so, how does that manifest in the nature of the issues Fredericks selects to address and the conclusions he reaches?

Let me be clear: I am not criticizing Fredericks for making the choices he makes; indeed, I admire his work and hope to build upon it in future. Rather, what is lacking is the explicit recognition of the embeddedness of those choices in wider social, political, economic, and religious webs of power and repression, and the consequences that has for the content of his work. Yet here again, these issues only arise given some a priori theological framework that recognizes the dynamics of power and repression in theological discourse.[12] At the risk of repeating myself, some "knowing" is necessary before the "doing" of comparative theology.

A more comprehensive comparative theology requires dialogue partners to *look up* from their texts (scriptures, traditions, doctrinal debates, ritual practices, etc.) and to *look around* at the social, political, and economic contexts in which their dialogue takes place. I will flesh out this notion shortly.

Incorporate the Witness of Religious Others as Sources and Norms

This is clearly the most radical and potentially controversial element of my proposal, reaching as it does to the very roots of Christian theological reflection. Yet as I argued earlier in this work, it follows from liberation theology's fundamental insight, that we are unable "to see, recognize, or worship the God who walks with the poor" unless "we look at reality through their eyes."[13] If

Christian theology seeks to see reality through the eyes of the marginalized, it will necessarily be looking through Christian *and* non-Christian eyes.

What does it mean to "look through non-Christian eyes"? I do not see how it can mean anything other than drawing upon the experience and perspective of religious others, as both source and norm for theological reflection. To reprise my discussion of these categories from the introduction, a theological *source* is any element that one uses in doing theology, "any element that enters into the formulation of one's theology, anything that informs one's theology"; theological *norms* are criteria the theologian uses to evaluate the sources she uses and to structure the theological claims she makes.[14] By calling for the incorporation of the witness of religious others as sources and norms for Christian theology, I am calling for Christian theology not only to be informed by that witness but also to measure the adequacy of its theological formulations by that witness.

In a sense, comparative theology entails incorporating the witness of religious others as *sources* for Christian theology. When Christian theology truly listens and responds to the truth that lies beyond the Christian situation, it is necessarily informed by extra-Christian elements; those elements enter directly into the formulation of a Christian theology. This move works to correct the problem of exclusion, both explicit and methodological, which I noted in the chapters on Schleiermacher, Barth, Lindbeck, and Gutiérrez.

Simply including the witness of religious others as theological sources, however, does not go far enough. As we saw with Schleiermacher's treatment of Judaism and Islam, and with Barth's treatment of Pure Land Buddhism, theological discourse can draw upon the witness of religious others without being materially changed by it; theological discourse may misrecognize that witness (as with Schleiermacher) or cite it only to dismiss it out of hand (Barth). In Badiouan terms, while the witness of religious others may not be altogether excluded from the Christian situation, it can be marginalized by the governing order of that situation. Consequently, while incorporating the witness of religious others is a necessary step, it alone does not alter the power structures of the relationship between Christians and religious others.

In order to change those power structures, Christian theology must go a step further. It must also incorporate the witness of religious others as *norms* for Christian theology, alongside other norms more widely accepted within the Christian community, such as scripture, tradition, and human reason. In other words, the witness of religious others should serve, alongside other Christian norms, both to structure theological reflection and to contribute criteria for judging the adequacy or inadequacy of any given theological sources or formulations.

What I have in mind here is not some liberal welcoming of all voices to the table, all the while maintaining the power and authority of the dominant group (in this case Christians). If we welcome religious others to the table only to subordinate their witness to our own, we might as well not invite them in the first place. Rather, I envision something analogous to David Tracy's correlation of human experience and Christian witness, where both are brought into fully reciprocal, mutually critical conversation.[15] In like fashion, the witness of religious others can be brought into fully reciprocal, mutually critical dialogue with Christian witness; in this way, *both* Christian witness *and* that of religious others function as sources and norms for Christian theological reflection.

In other words, what I envision is a relationship between Christian and non-Christian witness that (a) is fully dialogical and (b) fully recognizes and seeks to overcome existing power differentials. Let me discuss these two characteristics in turn.

A fully dialogical relationship would proceed more or less as follows. The Christian theologian necessarily begins with the foundational truth event of God's self-revelation in Christ, as witnessed by the community of those who are constituted as subjects by fidelity to that truth event. That Christian truth event establishes certain givens—for example, that the universe is the good creation of God; that the basic human condition is sinfulness, construed as broken relationship with God; that God acts graciously to restore that relationship.

Yet the Christian truth event, and the witness thereto, also raises numerous problems and questions. For example: If there is only one God, why are there so many religions? How can God become human and remain divine? What does it mean for humans to be made "in the image of God"? Why has the Christian tradition legitimated the oppression of women, the poor, and non-European peoples? Why does Jesus describe the qualities of neighbor love by pointing to the hated outsider, the Samaritan?

The disruptive force of these and other questions is not to be quelled by turning inward and attempting some kind of intrasystematic coherence à la Lindbeck. Such questions are crucial to Christian theology because they suggest the limits to what is "known" within the Christian situation, and call for encounter with what lies beyond it—that is, encounter with those marginalized or excluded by Christian discourse, including religious others. The Christian theologian brings both the givens and the questions to the encounter with religious others; in like fashion, religious others bring their own givens and questions to the conversation. The resulting dialogue may suggest answers to some of Christianity's questions; it may also challenge some points that previously were assumed to be settled within the Christian situation. A similar process will occur on the conversation partner's side: the Christian witness may clarify some questions and may challenge what the conversation partner had assumed to be firmly established within her own religious tradition.

So far this proposal resembles the method of comparative theology. Where it differs is in taking stock of power differentials in the relationship and in taking practical steps toward surmounting them. Without such measures, interreligious dialogue remains (as someone once described the inclusivist approach) a conversation between the elephant and the mouse. No matter how much the elephant proclaims his willingness for dialogue, the mouse will be reluctant to speak freely.

As I stated earlier, an important first step in recognizing and overcoming power differentials is for dialogue partners to *look up* from their texts (scriptures, traditions, doctrinal debates, ritual practices, etc.) and to *look around* at the social, political, and economic contexts in which their dialogue takes place. In what ways is each partner's religious tradition implicated in wider structures of authority, power, and repression? Just as important, how does the dialogue itself contribute to or work against those structures? Who stands to gain from the dialogue, and in what ways? Second, each dialogue partner should examine structures of authority, power, and repression within her own religious situation. How do boundary drawing and other discursive processes facilitate or hinder encounter with others? How far has each religious tradition absolutized or hardened its borders, and what are the consequences? Above all, the dialogue partners should act in fidelity to the truth event of encounter with the void, and let that fidelity guide their praxis from that point forward.

There may be occasions, perhaps many occasions, where a strictly intra-Christian (or intra-Buddhist or intra-Hindu . . .) approach is appropriate. However, it must be recognized that such an approach contributes little if anything to altering the power relations between Christians and religious others, power relations that run counter to the teaching and example of Christ. It must also be recognized that those power relations may distort the theology that results, as we have seen in our test cases.

Finally, it should go without saying that in incorporating non-Christian texts as sources and norms, Christian theologians should not limit themselves to those texts that are similar to or support Christian witness. That would only perpetuate asymmetrical power relations between Christians and religious others. Again, in line with Rieger's principle that there is no encounter with the divine Other without encounter with human others who are different, Christian theologians must grapple with *real* differences—especially witness that seems to contradict what Christians take to be settled—*and* allow the possibility that these very differences may also be revelatory of the God to whom Christians seek to witness.

Possible Objections

As I have argued, the turn to religious others is consistent with the teachings and example of Jesus and with the broader historical movement of Christian theologies of liberation. Nonetheless, I recognize that it represents a marked departure from the theological status quo, "the way we've always done things." As such, it is certain to raise a number of objections. Indeed, a number of years ago, before my own personal encounter with the witness of religious others, I would have raised several of these objections myself. I attempt to address some of them here.

1. *It isn't Christian.* This objection might take two forms, depending on how "Christian" is construed. The first equates "Christian" with recognition of the *sole* authority of Christian sources and norms (e.g., the Bible, the Catholic magisterium). What lies beyond is either untrue (Barth's *Unglaube*) or irrelevant to Christian faith and reflection. Though I take this objection seriously, it need not detain us long here since it runs counter to the premise of this work as a whole: that the witness of religious others is both relevant and essential to authentically Christian theology. The best response I can offer is to ask those who have this objection to refer to my scriptural argument in Chapter 1 and ask themselves whether faithfulness to Christ either dictates exclusion of non-Christian witness or, as I believe, demands transformative encounter with that witness.

In a second variant of this objection, "Christian" entails recognizing the *primary* (not the sole) authority of Christian sources and norms. Those in this camp may be willing to accept the use of non-Christian witness as theological sources but not as norms. According to this viewpoint, the turn to religious others, by ascribing to that witness the same level of authority as Christian sources and norms (e.g., the Bible), produces a theology that, whatever else it may be, is no longer distinctively Christian.

To this objection I reply that Christian identity per se has no *intrinsic* value. It is of value only insofar as it transforms one's life and praxis. In other words, it is what one *does* with that identity that matters. Gutiérrez is correct: those who profess faith in Christ, yet do not live out that faith in loving service to the marginalized, are not Christians after all; it is necessary not just to profess faith in Jesus, but to follow his example. As I have argued, the example of Jesus necessitates a turn to religious others, a willingness to look at reality through their eyes. Thus, contrary to this objection, an authentically Christian theology *must* make the turn to religious others.

2. *It will render Christian theology internally incoherent.* This objection is founded on the notion, which I share, that the witness of religious others is (or may be) fundamentally different from that of the Christian tradition and community. Given this fact, the incorporation of the witness of religious others as sources and especially as norms will introduce fundamental and irremediable contradictions into Christian theology. To give two obvious examples, the witness of some Buddhists is that the Ultimate is not a personal and transcendent God as Christians understand God to be; the witness of Vaishnavites is that there have been many incarnations (*avataras*) of the supreme God (Vishnu),

whereas most Christians recognize only one divine incarnation. Surely—so goes this argument—only one of these visions can be right. Will not the raising to normative status of beliefs that so directly contradict Christian belief render Christian theology utterly incoherent?

My response to this objection is twofold. First, although I take this objection seriously, I find it a bit surprising because it seems to be based on the quite insupportable assumption that Christianity is itself free of internal contradictions. Christian theologians have long recognized the contradictions within the Christian witness itself and have long experience in coping with them. Some contradictions may be relatively minor: for instance, whether humanity was created after the animals (Gen 1) or before them (Gen 2). Other contradictions have had more serious implications for Christian theology. For example, the Pauline admonition that women remain quiet in church (1 Cor 14:33b–35) has been used to prevent women from entering the ministry, while the equally Pauline claim that in Christ there is no male or female (Gal 3:28) seems to deny discrimination on grounds of gender. Another important contradiction concerns the resurrection accounts. Paul suggests that the risen Christ appeared first to Peter (1 Cor 15:5–7), while two gospel accounts suggest that Mary Magdalene was the first witness.[16] Once again, this anomaly has important implications for the status of women in the church. Similarly, Luther's *sola fide* has been construed by some followers as sanctioning the belief that works are immaterial to salvation, contradicting numerous biblical passages that suggest otherwise (e.g., James 2:14–24, Mt 25:31–46).

Second, Christian experience in dealing with these and other contradictions in the Christian witness gives us guidance (positive as well as negative) for dealing with contradictions that may be introduced by the turn to religious others. Many Christian theologians have come to recognize that flattening out the Christian witness to remove the contradictions also robs it of its depth and richness of possibility. For example, an overemphasis on the oneness of God misses the divinity of Jesus and the Holy Spirit and fails to recognize the plurality and relationality that is inherent to the divine nature, which has important implications for human community.[17] Similarly, while the Chalcedonian assertion that Christ is both fully divine and fully human raises all manner of logical difficulties, its balancing of transcendent and immanent, eternal and temporal, allows for such creative expressions as Barth's "the humanity of God."[18]

Contradictions between the Christian witness and that of religious others can be handled in like manner, seeking depth and richness of possibility by preserving the creative tension between them. In this way, contradictions can serve as evental sites in the situations of both dialogue partners, pointing to the truth that transcends their boundaries.

For instance, in my own work in theological anthropology, I find especially intriguing the sharp difference between the Mahāyāna Buddhist doctrine of *anattā*, or no-self, and Christian understandings of human personhood as involving an individual soul that persists after physical death. As a Christian, I accept the truth of the latter view; yet I am unable to dismiss the doctrine of *anattā* since it is rooted in the experience and nondualistic perspective of Buddhists.[19] My sense is that both anthropologies are in some sense true, that each points to a limitation in the other, and that together they point to a mystery that neither captures fully. (I intend to pursue this question in future work.)

3. *This proposal is impractical, even utopian.* This objection takes two forms. The first rests on the postliberal article of faith that Christianity is incommensurable with other religious traditions. Accordingly, Christians either cannot really understand what religious others have to say (because they lack the vocabulary) or can only understand that witness in inescapably Christian terms. If this were the case, there would be no possibility of incorporating the witness of religious others as sources and norms.

However, I have serious doubts about the incommensurability thesis. As discussed in Chapter 5, it cannot be substantiated except through the very comparison it holds is impossible. Furthermore, it is empirically undermined by the fact that comparative theologians like Clooney and Fredericks are carrying out the very comparisons the thesis denies are possible.

A milder form of this objection, and one more worthy of serious consideration, stresses the difficulty (rather than the impossibility) of the turn to religious others. There seem to be at least three kinds of difficulty: pedagogical, methodological, and psychological. I will address each in turn.

The *pedagogical* difficulty concerns the training involved in making the turn to religious others. Given the long history and diversity of the Christian tradition, not to mention the sheer volume of the literature involved, it is difficult enough to train theologians to do theology in solely Christian terms, without introducing elements from other religions, any one of which may be of equal or greater complexity.

While no single theologian can be expected to be familiar with all religious traditions that lie beyond the boundaries of Christianity, I believe that it is feasible for theological training to include an in-depth study of pertinent elements of (at least) one other religious tradition; this could be implemented as a minor field or secondary concentration.[20] For example, a Christian systematic theologian specializing in soteriology might be required to minor in related notions from one other tradition (for instance, Hindu understandings of *moksha*, or Vodoun beliefs about the destiny of the various human spirits after death). Such training would sensitize the theologian to limits in Christian understanding and prepare her for ongoing encounter with religious others.

The *methodological* difficulty involves the natural and perhaps universal human tendency to interpret the unfamiliar in terms of the familiar. In Christian theology this tendency can be manifested in misrecognizing the witness of religious others according to Christian terms and categories, such as redemption or justification, which are meaningful in the Christian context but may have little or no relevance to what religious others in fact are saying. How, then, can Christian theology incorporate the witness of religious others without skewing that witness toward Christian terms and categories—that is, without losing sight of the otherness of the religious other? This is a thorny problem, made thornier by the unfortunate proclivity for Christians to proclaim rather than to listen. Although I have struggled with this problem throughout the present work, I doubt that, despite my best efforts, I have mastered it either.

The best I can offer here are some broad guidelines. First, it is crucial to be ever mindful of the otherness of the divine Other. This, after all, is the theological basis for the turn to religious others. Ultimately, neither the self, the ecclesial texts, nor excluded human others can occupy the position of ultimate theological authority: that position must be reserved for the divine Other. God is, as Rieger notes, different from what we expect; that is to say, God cannot be reduced to or identified with human ideologies. When the contours of the Divine start to become too sharply drawn and too familiar, it is time for a hermeneutics of suspicion.

Second, we need a consistent, yet revisable hermeneutic for Christian and non-Christian sources. It is not enough just to compare the *texts* of religious traditions in isolation from other factors. Non-Christian texts are just as susceptible as Christian sources to being co-opted by the powers of ideology.[21] Consequently, it is necessary to read non-Christian and Christian sources alike through the eyes of the marginalized.

How do we do this? Clearly, what would be most preferable would be face-to-face encounters with the marginalized themselves. The next best alternative is to keep up with scholarship on marginalization in the communities of religious others.[22] The receding of geographical constraints has also made possible truly global communication and information flow. The Internet already promotes the exchange of information, experience, and perspectives from marginalized religious others and those scholars who work directly with them.[23]

At the same time—and this is the third guideline—it is crucial that Christian theologians resist turning this hermeneutic of the marginalized into another absolute. As many others before me have asserted, we must see theological reflection as a process, a pilgrimage in faith in the divine Other revealed in the life and teachings of Jesus of Nazareth. As with any journey, the landmarks may look quite different as one nears them, and now and then, as we come to learn more about where we have been and where we are headed, it may be necessary to change course. James Fredericks puts it well: "One sign of the spiritual maturity of a religious believer is the ability to change one's mind well—that is, to change religiously in a way that opens the believer up to a greater appreciation of truth and a greater understanding of his or her tradition and those of others."[24]

My own starting point is the preferential option for the marginalized. This is a Christian norm, derived from a particular understanding of Christian teaching. However, what I have come to believe about the Christian God, and that God's preferential option for the marginalized, motivates my readiness to embrace the texts and experiences of religious others. Perhaps, in the course of dialogue with religious others, I will come to understand that the fundamental category *liberation*, or even the turn to the marginalized itself, is limited in some way. It will then be necessary to revise my position from that point on.

Having considered pedagogical and methodological difficulties with the turn to religious others, we move finally to what might be called, for lack of a better term, a *psychological* difficulty. Encounter with religious others can be profoundly unsettling. The witness of those who are different can shake our certainty and undermine whatever sense of stability we have managed to attain. It can call into question cherished beliefs and long-held assumptions. It can leave us in a strange territory of unknown and shifting landmarks, where the best maps are only approximations.

However, we should see this condition not as an obstacle to our journey but as a sign of being on the right path. For this unfamiliar land is where Christians are called to be—despite what some Christian voices may tell us, with their siren song of absolutes and certitude. I will have more to say about this later.

While I believe that the pedagogical, methodological, and psychological difficulties attendant to my proposal can be surmounted, I will admit that there is a "utopian" dimension to this proposal. However, it is utopian not in the sense of impractical dreaming or an evasion of reality, but as a form of thinking that, as Gutiérrez puts it, leads "to a praxis which transforms what exists." All of us, Christians and religious others alike, need such utopianism, because without it, we fall "into new structures which oppress humanity."[25]

Some Theological Examples

The reader need not take my word that the way forward I propose is eminently practicable. A number of contemporary theologians are already moving in that direction. Not surprisingly, they all have roots in Asia, where (as I mentioned in Chapter 1) Christians are particularly conscious not only that they are one religious group among many but also that they have been shaped in subtle ways by the religions that have traditionally dominated their cultures.

For example, in *Christophany: The Fullness of Man*, the Catholic theologian Raimon Panikkar sets out a christological investigation in which the boundaries of "the Christian" are quite permeable and in which elements of non-Christian witness function as both source and norm for a theological reflection that remains firmly Christian.[26] Noting that christology has been "a reflection pursued by Christians who, except in its first period of formation, have virtually ignored the world's other traditions," Panikkar recommends instead *christophany* (incorporating the Greek *phaneros*, "manifestation"), which he contends "is open to . . . a dialogue with other religions" (as well as with contemporary science).[27] He argues that christophany "should not be an exercise in Christian solipsism" (in my terminology, a theology of Christian "knowledge"); it instead "interrogates other cultures . . . as they in turn interrogate it."[28] The method he proposes "considers the other religions of the world not as Christians have often interpreted them but as they understand themselves . . . [as] *loci theologi*, proper and legitimate places for theological activity."[29] In discussing the ineluctable mystery of christophanic experience, he reaches out not only to conventionally Christian sources such as scripture and Teresa of Avila but also to Hindu *advaitin* thought.[30] Here is a theology that manages both to be authentically Christian and to blur the boundaries of "the Christian"—precisely in order to express the truth of the divine Other.

Much as I admire Panikkar's openness to religious others (who, in the course of his work, lose much of their "otherness"), I miss a fuller exploration of the question of power relations in christophany. True, Panikkar does set his work in the social-political context of "a human and ecological crisis of planetary proportions."[31] And near the end of his book, he notes perceptively that "a realistic christophany cannot avoid political problems," since Christ "is not a politically neutral figure"; Panikkar goes on to commend as "most convincing" the liberation picture of "the Jesus of the oppressed making us aware of the institutionalized violence of this our new world."[32] Unfortunately, he does not explore the implications of these important perceptions in the main body of his consideration of the christophanic experience. We are left with some important questions: What sort of power relations are at work in the communities and texts included in Panikkar's theological discourse? How might power relations distort the christophanic experience?

Of the Asian theologians I've encountered to date, only the Korean feminist[33] Chung Hyun Kyung brings together the interrogation of power relations with a more permeable Christian situation. The author of *Struggle to Be the Sun Again: Introducing Asian Women's Theology*, she has been at the forefront of emerging efforts to inculturate Christian thought in an Asian—specifically, Korean women's—frame of reference.[34] Chung's Christian theological work draws freely (though not uncritically) from non-Christian sources, including Korean shamanism.

Korean Christian women, she argues, define their Christian identity in terms of their "lived inherited experience" reaching back prior to the arrival of Christianity in Korea, not to mention the birth of Christianity itself; this religious inheritance includes the experience of shamanism, Buddhism, and Confucianism. Turning to the specific problem of the liberation of Korean women from oppression and suffering, she interprets the liberative power of the Christian gospel in terms of two key concepts drawn from Korean shamanism: *han*, which refers to the root experience of oppression, injustice, and suffering; and *han-pu-ri*, which can be translated as "liberation," but also carries the sense of collective healing.[35] By treating non-Christian resources as both source and norm for Christian theology, Chung implies that Christian encounter with religious others serves to enrich Christian theological reflection. Indeed, she holds as her main criteria not a clinging to some special Christian identity but the very Christoform values of "justice and peace, the integrity of creation, and building of a sustainable, life-giving earth community." She advocates a "fusion of [religious] horizons," in which "differences vivify, transform, and enhance each other."[36]

While Chung deserves praise for opening Christian theology out in response to oppression, some have charged her with syncretism. She responds perceptively in a 2003 interview: "If they ask me, 'Are you a syncretist?' I say, 'You are right, I am a syncretist, but so are you.' My response is that I know I am a syncretist, but you don't know you are a syncretist because you have hegemonic power . . . non-Christian cultures, when they try to interpret the gospel out of their life experience, they are syncretists! But they are just being true to their identity, history and culture."[37]

To Chung's response I would add my own, grounded in the conceptual framework I have outlined in this book. To view syncretism as a problem is to mistake the "knowledge" of the traditional Christian situation for the truth of the divine Other that transcends all knowledge, including the Christian sort. Chung recognizes that faithfulness to the truth of the divine Other *demands* opening the Christian situation to encounter with the religious others it has traditionally excluded. If this be syncretism, it is what the Gospel demands.

For Chung herself, encounter with religious others is not merely a theological exercise; she embodies it in her own religious life. She has discussed how her own Christian faith has been enlivened by Zen practice and work in the Korean shamanic tradition.[38] She writes, "When people ask what I am religiously, I say, 'My bowel is Shamanist. My heart is Buddhist. My right brain, which defines my mood, is Confucian and Taoist. My left brain, which defines my public language, is Protestant Christian, and, overall, my aura is eco-feminist.'"[39]

This brings up another potentially important resource for rethinking the boundaries of the Christian situation: multiple religious belonging (MRB). Those who practice MRB live out the "fusion of horizons" that Chung describes by identifying themselves as, say, Buddhist *and* Christian, or Jewish *and* Daoist. While MRB is quite common in Asia (many Chinese, for example, are simultaneously Confucian, Buddhist, and Daoist), it is a relatively new phenomenon in the West. Among a growing number of MRB practitioners is Ruben L. F. Habito, who identifies as both a Catholic and a practitioner of Zen Buddhism.[40]

Certainly MRB is not appropriate for every Christian, perhaps even for most Christians. I don't identify myself as an MRB practitioner, despite my ongoing dialogue with Buddhism. Yet those who do practice MRB make interesting dialogue partners for Christian theologians. By locating (to use set-theory terminology) intersections and possibilities for union between Christianity and other religions, they suggest the various ways in which the boundaries of the Christian situation—and other religious situations—may be drawn.

A Final Word

Throughout this work I have insisted on the limitations of the Christian situation. Yet if postmodernism has taught us anything, it is that each of us is radically situated: there is no Olympian vantage point from which to regard our world objectively. That said, I have also argued that, so long as we do not absolutize our situations, we have access to truth that transcends them, through encounter with those who are marginalized or excluded.

My own situation is a subset of the Christian community, the Episcopal Church. As I write this passage, on the fifth Sunday after Pentecost, I find that the lectionary readings for this day are particularly apt: they underscore the limitations of our situations and, in doing so, serve as an evental site for encounter with a wider and deeper truth.

In the readings from the Hebrew Bible (Ez 2:1–7) and the Gospel (Mk 6:1–6), Ezekiel and Jesus find that they are prophets without honor in their own land. They face the stubbornness and unbelief of their respective religious communities, which have their minds made up about the way things are. In the pericope from Mark, the people of Jesus' own hometown refuse to believe in him, because they know all about him—they have him "figured out." Yet theirs is clearly knowledge in Badiou's sense: a very circumscribed and restricted kind of knowledge, untroubled by all that has been excluded and generating nothing but more of the same.

Like the people of Nazareth, Christians have for too long assumed that, graced by the word of God in scripture and tradition, we know all that we need to know about those outside the boundaries of our community. Accordingly, we have proceeded as if it is unnecessary to take into account what religious others have to say. Caught up in our own circular self-affirmations, we have lost sight of the otherness of the divine Other. And our confidence in our "knowledge" has legitimized our exclusion and mistreatment of those who are different.

It has seldom occurred to us that faithfulness to Christ and to the God whom Christ reveals might involve turning precisely to those who differ from us—and not simply as targets for evangelism. It has seldom occurred to us that certainty—at least as traditionally construed—has little to do with the Gospel message.

The Gospel is not about certitude. It is about faith and trust. That, it seems to me, is the message of this day's epistle reading, from Paul's second letter to the Corinthians (12:2–10). Here, Paul makes the surprising admission that his having received special revelation from God gives him no special status. Nor does it make his life any simpler or easier. Quite the contrary: he faces continued "hardships" and "calamities." He has come to understand that God's power is made perfect not in the strength humans desire but in weakness. Christians, too, seek strength in many forms, most of all in the certitude of our own rightness.[41] Insofar as we do so, we miss the lesson Paul has struggled to learn and to pass along to us.

This serves as both a final caution and a note of promise. Like Paul, the Christian community has been graced with access to divine revelation. Yet this does not authorize Christians to claim superiority over those who are different. Nor does it simplify our lives by offering us an unshakable certainty in our own rightness. Instead, the revelation of the divine Other in Christ persistently reminds us of the limitations of the situations we create, the Christian situation included. These limitations serve, like Paul's thorn in the flesh, to remind us of our frailty. It is in this frailty that we need the witness of those who differ from us, and it is in their frailty that they need ours. It is for this reason that we embrace the stranger, the one who, in the words of poet Charles Olson quoted at the outset of this work, "makes the very thing you were doing no longer the same."

APPENDIX

A Crash Course in Alain Badiou's Philosophy

One of the most innovative and important voices in recent Continental philosophy, Alain Badiou has only recently begun to draw the attention his work deserves in the English-speaking world. Most of his work remained unavailable in English translation until the last few years. Yet even in translation, many of his texts remain largely inaccessible for nonspecialist readers. His philosophical writings are frequently complex and abstruse, with their own specialized and arcane vocabulary, much of which is drawn from mathematics.

In this appendix, I hope to make Badiou a bit more accessible (and perhaps spur others to read him) by providing a brief introduction to his career and to those concepts from his philosophy that I deploy in this book.[1]

Badiou's Philosophical Trajectory

Born in 1937, Badiou is a younger contemporary of such leading lights of postmodernism and poststructuralism as Michel Foucault, Gilles Deleuze, and Jacques Derrida.[2] Among Badiou's early influences were the psychoanalyst Jacques Lacan (whom Badiou has called "our Hegel"), and the structuralist Marxist Louis Althusser, with whom Badiou studied and worked in the late 1960s, but with whom he very publicly broke in the 1970s.[3] In the turbulent late 1960s and 1970s, like many French intellectuals of his generation, Badiou was attracted to Maoist thought. He worked out his own philosophical take on Maoism in *Théorie de la contradiction* (*Theory of Contradiction*, 1975), *De l'idéologie* (*On Ideology*, 1976), and *Théorie du sujet* (*Theory of the Subject*, 1982), only the last of which has so far appeared in English translation.[4]

By the late 1970s and early 1980s, he had begun to move away from the categories and terminology of Maoism and to develop his own distinctive philosophical voice.[5] Nineteen eighty-eight saw the publication of what remains Badiou's groundbreaking philosophical work, *L'Etre et l'événement*, which did not appear in English, as *Being and Event*, until 2005.[6] In this work Badiou responds to the postmodern and poststructuralist currents that were then at the height of fashion.[7] While he embraces their stress on plurality and multiplicity, he strongly opposes their rejection of the very possibility of universal truth, their equation of truth with coherence within a given symbol system, their consequent reduction of philosophy to a hermeneutics of the play of signifiers, and their tendency toward moral and political relativism.

As Jason Barker writes, for Badiou philosophy remains "*the means of seizing truths.*"[8] Drawing his ontology from the set theory of Georg Cantor and later mathematicians, Badiou militantly asserts the existence of truths—indeed, and quite unfashionably, *universal* truths. Yet this is no modernist universalism, which amounts to the absolutizing of the experience and thought of a subset of humanity (usually European/neo-European and male). Instead, truth for Badiou is at once universal and contingent: it has to do with specific constructs (situations) and is understood as that which "exposes the gaps in our understanding."[9] We will explore his notion of truth shortly. Suffice it to say at this point that *Being and Event* constitutes an ingenious and powerful antidote to the moral and epistemological relativism of much postmodern and poststructuralist thought.

At nearly five hundred closely argued pages, it is no work for the fainthearted. Badiou's arcane terminology, much of it drawn from mathematics, can be off-putting to nonspecialist readers. His more recent *Ethics* (2002) and *Saint Paul* (2003) offer somewhat more accessible treatments of the conceptual framework of *Being and Event*.[10] Readers with a theological background may particularly appreciate his *Saint Paul*, which presents the apostle as a revolutionary bearer of a new universal truth—themes crucial to Badiou's philosophy and Christian theology alike. (I should note that in recent work, most prominently *Logics of Worlds* [2009], Badiou has continued to develop his conceptual framework.[11])

In the following sections I will focus on some of the key concepts from Badiou's *Being and Event* period.

Situation and Void

Badiou is a philosophical pluralist: he holds that reality is fundamentally multiple, infinite, and inconsistent—the last term signifying that there is no inherent unity or organizing principle in reality.[12] He writes in his *Ethics*: "The multiple 'without-one'—every multiple being in its turn nothing other than a multiple of multiples—is the law of being. . . . Infinite alterity is quite simply *what there is*."[13] We do not, however, experience or interact with reality in terms of infinite, inconsistent multiples of multiples. Rather, we experience sets or groupings of entities and qualities and happenings: books, housing developments, jazz recordings, cats, religious systems, yucca plants, and so on. Badiou terms these sets *situations*.

A situation is "a state of things, any presented multiple whatsoever."[14] Roughly equivalent to the mathematical concept of a set, a situation can be made up of "circumstances, language, and objects."[15] It is a collection of multiples selected out of the wider plural reality and, in Badiou's terminology, "counted for one." Indeed, the situation *is* this counting-for-one.[16] Oliver Feltham and Justin Clemens provide a helpful explanation in their introduction to Badiou's philosophy:

> The term "situation" [for Badiou] is prior to any distinction between substances and/or relations and so covers both. Situations include all those flows, properties, aspects, concatenations of events, disparate collective phenomena, bodies, monstrous and virtual, that one might want to examine within an ontology. The concept of "situation" is also designed to accommodate anything which *is*, regardless of its modality; that is, regardless of whether it is necessary, contingent, possible, actual, potential, or virtual—a whim, a supermarket, a work of art, a dream, a playground fight, a fleet of trucks, a mine, a stock prediction, a game of chess, or a set of waves.[17]

One other aspect of the situation is very important: it stands on the distinction between inside and outside—those elements that are counted as "belonging," in contradistinction to those that are not. Any situation excludes some multiples.[18] Badiou calls that which is deemed not to "belong" the *void* of the situation. The void is the "unnamed" and the "not-thought" in the situation. It is not, however, a species of nonbeing, although it may *appear* to be "nothing" from within the situation. Rather, it is being that literally "does not count" according to the criteria that define the situation. Feltham and Clemens explain, "Badiou argues that, in every situation, there is a being of the 'nothing.' He starts by stating that whatever is recognized as 'something,' or as existing, in a situation is counted-for-one in that situation and vice versa. By implication, what is *nothing* in a situation must go uncounted. However, it is not as though there is simply nothing in a situation which is uncounted—both the *operation* of the count-for-one and the *inconsistent multiple* which exists before the count are, by definition, uncountable."[19]

Peter Hallward puts it this way: "Every situation . . . has its ways of authorizing and qualifying its members as legitimate members of the situation: the void of such a situation includes whatever can only be presented, in the situation, as utterly unqualified or unauthorized. It is precisely these unqualified or indiscernible capacities that make up the very being of the situation."[20]

Hallward's comments point to another key feature of the Badiouan void. More than merely what is excluded, the void is also the situation's ground of being. The void, that which is not "counted-for-one" in the situation, also *constitutes* the situation by the very fact of its exclusion. The situation cannot exist *qua* situation *without* that which is not counted as belonging to it.

Badiou's sense of the void as a situation's ground of being draws upon the mathematical concept of the null (empty) set. In set theory it is axiomatic that each and every set contains the null set (symbolized as $\emptyset$). The null set is defined as that which has no elements in common with a given set.[21] However, $\emptyset$—that which is not part of the set—is also *constitutive of* that set. The relationship between situation and void is equivalent to that between any set and the null set. Badiou writes, "At the heart of every situation, as the foundation of its being, there is a 'situated' void, around which is organized the plenitude . . . of the situation in question."[22] Badiou also characterizes the void as "the almost-being which haunts the situation in which being consists."[23] As Feltham and Clemens put it, "for Badiou, every situation is ultimately founded on a void. . . . The void of a situation is simply what is not there, but what is necessary for anything to be there."[24]

The State (Governing Order) of the Situation. In order to be of any use, a situation must be more than merely a jumble of elements; those elements must be ordered or organized. The operation of the count-for-one, which calls the situation into being, merely sorts out what belongs (the situation) from what does not (the void); it does not order the elements within the situation. Ordering is accomplished by what Badiou calls the *state* of a situation, which I term the *governing order* in this book. As Hallward explains, "A situation counts elements; the state of a situation counts its *parts*, the ways of combining the elements."[25] In Badiou's terms, the situation "presents" its elements, whereas the state of the situation "represents" (re-presents) them. The state serves as the metastructure of the situation, ordering the relation between the whole and the elements, "between the count and what is counted."[26] The state "ensures that the potentially anarchic organisation of social combinations remains structured in such a way as to preserve the governing interests of the situation. The state keeps things in their place."[27] It "arranges a situation in such a way as to ensure the power of its dominant group (or ruling class)."[28] By keeping elements in their place, the state works to prevent the revelation of the void fundamental to the situation. In other words, the state works to keep the void from "breaking into" the situation and disrupting or dissolving it.

The state also inscribes "what there is." It is what those within the situation "know." Badiou speaks of the state as the "language" of a situation: "The function of the language of the situation consists in gathering together the elements of the situation according to one or other predicative traits. . . . A subset—such as those of cats or dogs in a perceptual situation, or of hysterical or obsessive traits and symptoms in an analytical situation—is captured through concepts of the language on the basis of indices of recognition attributable to all the terms or elements that fall under the concept."[29]

For a contemporary example of these concepts, we can consider the plight of the *sans-papiers* of French society, the undocumented workers who have been a focus of Badiou's own political activism.[30] The *sans-papiers* live and work in France. Yet according to the dominant political discourse in France—the contemporary French situation and its state—they don't count as "French." They make up an important part of the French collectivity yet are not considered "French." As such, they live in a kind of shadow world. They constitute the void of the French situation. And yet they also constitute what it means to be "French," in the sense that the everyday lives of those who do "count" as "French" depend on the *sans papiers* doing the hard and dirty jobs essential to the smooth running of "French" society.

Truth versus Knowledge. Much more than a mere translation of set-theoretical concepts to philosophy, the situation-void framework allows Badiou to address a question that has become quite unfashionable in recent philosophy: the question of truth. Badiou swims against the tide of the linguistic turn in recent philosophy, in which "the question of meaning replaces the classical question of truth," and philosophy degenerates into little more than "an infinite description of the multiplicity of language games."[31] For Badiou, ignoring the question of truth and focusing instead on "the polyvalence of meaning" cripples philosophy, renders it unable to offer ways of resisting an inhuman world dominated by a scientism that excludes most of humanity, a world subordinated to "the merchandising of money and information," a world obsessed with security.[32]

For philosophy to oppose this situation, he argues, it must propose "a principle of interruption" that breaks with the status quo. This requires "the reconstruction or re-emergence of the category of truth." Badiou does not have in mind a retreat to classical metaphysical conceptions of truth as totality, but rather a move to truth "as we are able to reconstitute it, taking into consideration the world as it is."[33]

Badiou rejects coherence and constructivist models of truth favored by Gadamer and Foucault (and, in the theological realm, Lindbeck), which "privileg[e] language over being" and by which truth and meaning are reduced to "conformity to widely recognized norms."[34] At the same time, unlike advocates of a correspondence-realist theory of truth (in which truth is the correspondence between an assertion and the extralinguistic reality to which it refers), Badiou holds that truth is not independent of us: "It is we who make truth, but precisely as something that exceeds our knowing."[35] Furthermore, truth is itself multiple. There is no Truth in general, "there are only particular truths in particular situations."[36]

What, then, is truth for Badiou? In a word, it is *excess*. It is that which exceeds the bounds of a situation and its state; as such it is associated with (though not identical with) the void. Insofar as a situation is structured on the exclusion of some multiplicities, its presentation of reality must be accordingly limited. By definition, it cannot name those multiplicities that are neither presented by the situation nor represented by its state (such as the *sans-papiers* in the French situation). Badiou contrasts truth (*vérité*) with knowledge (*savoir*). The latter is whatever can be "known" within the structure of a situation.[37] From the perspective of what the situation "knows," the void is unnamable. Situated knowledge is a closed system: "What there already is—the situation of knowledge as such—generates nothing other than repetition."[38]

By contrast with the limited and relative knowledge of situations, truth (or more precisely, *a* truth, since Badiou holds that truth, like reality, is multiple) is universal: it is not limited by (or to) any given situation. And it is directly associated with a situation's void. Hallward explains that for Badiou truth "is nothing other than the process that exposes or represents the void of a situation—or, for it amounts to the same thing, that suspends the state of a situation."[39] A truth is always something new, something extra.[40] This does not mean that Badiou understands truth to be transcendent in a metaphysical sense.[41] However, truth is "heterogeneous to all the subsets registered by forms of knowledge" in a situation, because, unlike those subsets, a truth cannot be captured by means of any predicate of the language (the state) of the situation.[42] Thus, as stated previously, truth is a matter of excess: it "always says more than can be defined or proved"—that is, from within the situation and its state.[43]

The Event and the Badiouan Subject

As excess, a truth cannot be known from within a situation—that is, according to the situation's governing criteria (its originating count-for-one and its state). Rather, truth must "break into" a situation; it is revealed through encounter with the void of the situation. Picturesquely, Badiou says that a truth "punches a 'hole'" in knowledge.[44]

This appearance or irruption of the truth of the void Badiou calls an *event*. The event is what the state of the situation tries to conceal.[45] The event "brings to pass 'something other' than the situation, opinions, instituted knowledges; the event is a hazardous [*hasardeux*], unpredictable supplement, which vanishes as soon as it appears."[46] This "something other" is the revelation of the situation's void. Badiou writes that "the fundamental ontological characteristic of an event is to inscribe, to name, the situated void of that for which it is an event."[47] The point at which this happens is what Badiou calls the *evental site* (*site événementiel*) of a situation.[48] This site is associated with the void; in fact, its locus is the "edge" of the void, which is also the boundary of the situation: "This exposure begins with an event, the occurring of which is located at the edge of whatever passes as uncountable in the situation."[49] Encounter with truth calls into question what is "known" within a situation. It calls for a revolutionary rethinking of things and compels "a new way of being."[50]

Indeed, for Badiou, it is this encounter with a truth that calls the *subject* into being. Badiou writes, "Whatever convokes someone to the composition of a subject is something extra, something that happens in situations as something that they and the usual way of behaving in them cannot account for. Let us say that a *subject* . . . needs something to have happened, something that cannot be reduced to its ordinary inscription in 'what there is.'"[51]

Badiou's subject comes into being in fidelity to the truth revealed in an event. Badiou speaks of truth "inducing" the subject, who becomes the "bearer" (*le support*) of a process of truth.[52] The event prompts the subject to radically question the knowledge instituted by a situation and its state. Yet she need not reject everything within the situation. Acting in fidelity to the event, the subject collects "all those elements in the situation that respond or 'connect' positively to this revelation of its void."[53] The result is a new situation constructed in fidelity to the truth encountered in the event.

Summary. Badiou's philosophy offers a powerful and robust framework for talking about discursive processes of inclusion and exclusion generally, and for illuminating the dynamics of those processes. Equally important from a theological standpoint is the fact that Badiou's framework, unlike the various postmodern discourses, allows us to speak of universal truth, though that truth is intrinsically multiple and (in Badiou's terminology) inconsistent. Furthermore, the Badiouan approach affirms the possibility of transformative encounter with universal truth, through evental sites at which the truth of the void can break into a situation.

In other words, Badiou's philosophy is both realistic and optimistic. It recognizes the constructed and contingent nature of the historical situations in which we find ourselves. Yet it also refuses to descend into relativism, and it remains committed to the possibility not only that there exists truth "for all" but that such truth can be accessed—"the possibility of overstepping finitude," as Badiou puts it[54]—through the inbreaking of an event. Hallward sums up Badiou's contribution quite eloquently: "Badiou's most fundamental principle is . . . simply the belief that radical change is indeed possible, that it is possible for people and the situations they inhabit to be dramatically transformed by what happens to them. . . . Triggered by an exceptional *event* whose occurrence cannot be proven with the resources currently available in the situation, true change proceeds insofar as it solicits the militant conviction of certain individuals who develop the implications of this event and hold firm to its consequences: by doing so they constitute themselves as the *subjects* of its innovation."[55]

Notes

Introduction

1. A notable exception is the fifteenth-century bishop and scholar Nicolas of Cusa. Nicolas's *De Pace Fidei* (*The Peace of Faith*) presents a vision of a heavenly conference concerning the possibility of harmony between the different religions. In the course of this conference, the personified Word of God converses with representatives of the various "religions," including Eastern Orthodoxy, Roman Catholicism, Islam, and Hinduism.

2. I borrow the term "European/neo-European" from Alfred W. Crosby, *Ecological Imperialism: The Biological Expansion of Europe, 900–1900*. Crosby uses "Neo-European" to signify those cultures transplanted by Europeans outside of Europe proper—e.g., the United States, Canada, Latin America, Australia—as distinguished from the indigenous cultures of those areas (2–3). I use the term as a more precise equivalent of "Western."

3. See Eck, *A New Religious America*.

4. Throughout this book, the term "religious others" is roughly synonymous with "non-Christians." I prefer the former term for two main reasons. First, the negative term "non-Christian" can imply that "Christian" is somehow the norm. Second, the term "religious others" reflects the fact that Christian discourse constructs this category through a process of othering associated with the setting of boundaries.

5. Brockman, "Thinking Theologically about Religious Others."

6. This threefold characterization was first put forward by Alan Race in *Christians and Religious Pluralism: Patterns in the Christian Theology of Religions*. Though still widely used, Race's schema does not accommodate recent developments such as postliberalism and comparative theology, which do not fit neatly into any of the three slots; also, since it is bound up with attitudes about salvation, which is a major concern for Christians but arguably less so for some other religions (e.g., primal religions, Daoism), it cannot be applied easily outside the Christian context. Given these weaknesses, an alternative, fourfold taxonomy recently suggested by Paul Knitter is gaining increasing acceptance. See Knitter, *Introducing Theologies of Religions*.

7. Pamela Dickey Young defines a theological *source* as "any element that enters into the formulation of one's theology, anything that informs one's theology." She defines *norm* as "a specific criterion or set of criteria by which any given theological sources or formulations are judged to be adequate or inadequate for theology in general or for

the type of theology being done, and which is used as the structuring principle for a theologian's own theology" (*Feminist Theology/Christian Theology*, 19–20).

8. David Lochhead notes the pervasive presence of a "theology of isolation" among Christians (*The Dialogical Imperative*, 8–11). Recent works in comparative theology are a notable exception to this insularity in Christian thought. Examples include John P. Keenan, *The Meaning of Christ: A Mahāyāna Christology*; Francis X. Clooney, *Hindu God, Christian God: How Reason Helps Break Down the Boundaries between Religions*; and James L. Fredericks, *Buddhists and Christians: From Comparative Theology to Solidarity*. It is noteworthy that a number of non-Western Christian theologians evince a greater readiness to mutually transformative dialogue with non-Christians. Examples include Wesley Ariarajah, Stanley Samartha, Lynn De Silva, and Choan-Seng Song.

9. Lochhead, 81.

10. Cracknell, 112–16.

11. Paul Knitter, *One Earth Many Religions: Multifaith Dialogue and Global Responsibility* (Maryknoll, NY: Orbis Books, 1995), 57.

12. Ibid., 58.

13. Ibid., 71.

14. Ibid., 36.

15. As Michel Foucault puts it in *The Archaeology of Knowledge and the Discourse on Language* (49) discourses are not "groups of signs (signifying elements referring to contents or representations)," but rather are "practices that systematically form the objects of which they speak." In the sense that I use the term, discourse does not merely represent what it speaks about (although the words and symbols that make up discourse may themselves represent or refer to other things, such as the Divine) but instead actively creates its objects.

16. Habito, "Maria Kannon Zen," 152.

17. I discuss these issues at greater length in Brockman, "Encountering 'The Event' as Event: Transforming Christian Theological Reflection about Religious Others."

18. The reference to "the pillar and ground of truth" is from "An Outline of the Faith," *The Book of Common Prayer*, 854.

Chapter 1

1. This phrase is from John Dominic Crossan, *Jesus: A Revolutionary Biography*, 54, 66–70.

2. Fred B. Craddock characterizes the Samaritan in the parable as follows: "Ceremonially unclean, socially outcast, and religiously a heretic, the Samaritan is the very opposite of the lawyer as well as the priest and the Levite. The story must have been a shocking one to its first audience, shattering their categories of who are and who are not the people of God" (*Luke*, 150–51). John Bowman comments: "That the parable says this about a Samaritan allows [Jesus'] point to be made so much clearer. Indeed the Samaritan is no neighbor of the Jews from a Jewish-legalistic standpoint but an [alien] and outsider" (*The Samaritan Problem*, 69).

3. Other examples include Jesus' praise for the faith of the centurion, Mt 8:10; Jesus' unfavorable comparison of two Galilean towns with the "pagan" Tyre and Sidon, Mt 11:20–24; the story of the cleansing of the ten lepers, only one of whom, a Samaritan, returns to thank Jesus, Lk 17:15–16.
4. Rieger, ed., *Theology from the Belly of the Whale*, 16–17.
5. Unless otherwise specified, all biblical quotations are to the New Revised Standard Version (NRSV).
6. Goizueta, in *Opting for the Margins*, 144.
7. Rieger, *Remember the Poor*, 193. Rieger, *God and the Excluded*, 178.
8. Rieger, *God and the Excluded*, 5–7.
9. Ibid., 7.
10. Young, *Feminist Theology/Christian Theology*, 15.
11. Suchocki, "In Search of Justice," 149.
12. Petrella, Susin, and Althaus-Reid, ed., *Reclaiming Liberation Theology*, 185.
13. This process is sometimes referred to as *inculturation*, which Pope John Paul II described as "the incarnation of the Gospel in native cultures and also the introduction of these cultures into the life of the Church." John Paul II, *Slavorum Apostoli*.
14. Heup Young Kim, *Christ and the Tao*, 126.
15. Jung Young Lee, *The Trinity in Asian Perspective*.
16. Choi Man Ja, "Feminine Images of God in Traditional Religion," 80–89.
17. Representative works by these scholars include Ariarajah, *The Bible and People of Other Faiths*; De Silva, *The Problem of the Self in Buddhism and Christianity*; Panikkar, *The Cosmotheandric Experience: Emerging Religious Consciousness*; Pieris, *An Asian Theology of Liberation*; Thangaraj, *The Crucified Guru: An Experiment in Cross-cultural Christology*.
18. Hopkins, *Shoes That Fit Our Feet*, 16–20.
19. Ada María Isasi-Díaz, in *Mujerista Theology: A Theology for the Twenty-first Century*, refers to Latinas' *cotidiano* as theological source, which includes the *orixás* and the deities of Amerindian religions (66–67). Similarly, Kwok Pui-lan, in chapter 3 of *Introducing Asian Feminist Theology*, discusses Asian religions as sources and resources for Asian feminist theology.
20. Waters, *Globalization*, 5. It should be noted, however, that globalization is a contested concept, as Ivan Strenski notes in "The Religion in Globalization," 631.
21. Cf. Strenski, 646–47, especially the quote from Paul Krugman.
22. Cf. Waters, 44.
23. McLaren, *Che Guevara, Paulo Freire, and the Pedagogy of Revolution*, 38.
24. Kwok Pui-lan, in Rieger, *Opting for the Margins*, 85.
25. Palanca, "Religion and Economic Development," 66.
26. I am speaking here of the Christian situation formed by the self-identity of Christians themselves, not what Muslims, Buddhists, and others consider "Christian." This is because my overall concern is with Christian self-critique.
27. I choose this example because I am an Episcopalian; however, the reader should be able to apply the example easily enough to other denominations.

28. Meredith B. McGuire speaks of religious groups as "communities of memory": "they hold in common important collective memories and exist through the continuity of those memories. . . . Thus, the religious group's shared experiences and rituals continually reproduce—and transmit to the next generation—the collective sense of 'who we are' and 'what it means to be one of us'" (*Religion*, 20).

29. Peter Berger notes the crucial role played by internalization of cultural meanings in the socialization process: "The individual not only learns the objectivated meanings but identifies with and is shaped by them. He draws them into himself and makes them *his* meanings. He becomes not only one who possesses these meanings, but one who represents and expresses them" (*The Sacred Canopy*, 15).

30. The 2004 *Book of Resolutions of the United Methodist Church* contains guidelines for interreligious relationships ("Called to Be Neighbors and Witnesses— Guidelines for Interreligious Relationships," 252–61). However, my Methodist students report that this resolution is only sporadically implemented in local congregations.

31. Cf. Alistair E. McGrath's discussion of the sources of theology, in *Christian Theology: An Introduction*, 151.

32. Christianity thus acts as what Gilles Deleuze calls a reactive force: whereas "Active forces affirm their difference" and create rather than compare, "Reactive forces are what they are only through their negation of active forces." May, *Gilles Deleuze*, 67.

33. Heyes, *Line Drawings*.

Chapter 2

1. See, for example, James Fredericks's arguments in *Faith among Faiths*, 167–68; or in Fredericks, *Buddhists and Christians*, 26.

2. For example, Fredericks refers to the need for "an openness to the *truths* of non-Christian religions," and speculates that "The aspects of the [Buddhist] Dharma that differ most starkly from the Gospels may constitute the most valuable *truths* Buddhists have to teach Christians." *Faith among Faiths*, 163, emphasis mine.

3. Rieger, *Remember the Poor*; Rieger, *God and the Excluded*.

4. Rieger, *God and the Excluded*, 130.

5. Lacan, *Ecrits*, 8.

6. Rieger, *Remember the Poor*, 24.

7. Rieger, *God and the Excluded*, 130.

8. Rieger, *Remember the Poor*, 27.

9. Rieger, *God and the Excluded*, 130.

10. Ibid., 3.

11. At first glance, Badiou might seem an unlikely choice, since he describes himself as an atheist. For instance, in his *Ethics* he takes it as axiomatic that there is no God (25). Despite that fact, he has written a particularly perceptive study of St. Paul, which portrays the apostle as a revolutionary bearer of a new universal truth— themes crucial to Badiou's philosophy and Christian theology alike.

12. For a (relatively) concise yet thorough overview of Badiou's philosophy, see Hallward, "Generic Sovereignty," 87–111.

13. I am speaking here of the Christian situation formed by the self-identity of Christians themselves, not what Muslims, Buddhists, and others consider "Christian." This is because my overall concern is with Christian theology and its encounter with religious others.

14. Badiou refers to this selection process as the "count for one" ("Truth," 121).

15. Although Badiou identifies three types of situations, only one, the *historical*, is pertinent to my consideration of Christian discourse. The other two, *natural* and *neutral* situations, are discussed in Badiou, *Being and Event*, 177; and in Feltham and Clemens, "An Introduction to Alain Badiou's Philosophy," 24–25. The historical situation differs from the other two in that it alone has at least one "evental site."

16. It should also be noted that Badiou makes a crucial distinction between *belonging* and *inclusion*. Peter Hallward describes the distinction thus: "Elements or members belong to a set; subsets or parts are included in it" (*Badiou*, 85). In other words, belonging is a function of the "count-for-one" that creates the situation, while inclusion is an action of the state (or governing order). Generally, I use the term *exclusion* as the opposite of Badiou's *belonging*; I use the term *marginalization* as the opposite of Badiou's *inclusion*.

17. Badiou writes: "At the heart of every situation, as the foundation of its being, there is a 'situated' void, around which is organized the plenitude . . . of the situation in question" (*Ethics*, 68). Peter Hallward puts it this way: "Every situation . . . has its ways of authorizing and qualifying its members as legitimate members of the situation: the void of such a situation includes whatever can only be presented, in the situation, as utterly unqualified or unauthorized. It is precisely these unqualified or indiscernible capacities that make up the very being of the situation." Hallward, "Introduction," 8.

18. Badiou, *Being and Event*, 77.

19. For what I term the "governing order," Badiou uses the term *state* (which evokes its mission to maintain a static order within the situation). As Hallward puts it, the state "ensures that the potentially anarchic organisation of social combinations remains structured in such a way as to preserve the governing interests of the situation. The state keeps things in their place" ("Generic Sovereignty," 92). Since "state" can be confused with a political entity, I elect to depart from Badiou's terminology here.

20. Badiou, *Infinite Thought*, 61. Badiou also speaks of truth as "subtracted" from what is known. As Hallward notes, Badiou uses the term *soustraction* to mean "that truth *is* properly immediate, and so is *revealed* (comes to be) through the elimination of the mediate. It means that the living reality of human experience is what remains after the whole realm of the 'cultural' has been 'deposed' (though not eliminated)" (Hallward, "Generic Sovereignty," 97). This does not mean that Badiou understands truth to be transcendent in a metaphysical sense. Quite the contrary: he holds that truth is purely immanent within—in fact, a subset of—a given situation ("Truth," 121); I take him to mean something similar to the null set's immanence within any given set.

21. Badiou, *Ethics*, 70.

22. Ibid., 41.
23. Badiou's notion of the evental site is a bit difficult to describe. Peter Hallward calls it "one of the most important and most slippery aspects of Badiou's philosophy of truth" (*Badiou*, 117). It is clear, however, that Badiou closely associates the evental site with the void; in fact, its locus is the "edge" of the void, which is also the boundary of the situation. Hallward, "Introduction," 9.
24. Panikkar, *The Intrareligious Dialogue*, 48.
25. Fredericks, *Faith among Faiths*, 9.
26. Of course, not all forms of encounter are transformative. For example, as noted earlier, the European colonial project put European Christians into encounter with religious others on a global scale; however, as Kitagawa notes, Europeans generally assumed that religious others must conform to the European Christian synthesis: no change in Christian categories was deemed necessary. Such encounters merely reassert the boundaries of the Christian situation.
27. Badiou, *Saint Paul*, 14.
28. Cf. ibid., 40–43, 56–57.
29. Rieger, ed., *Theology from the Belly of the Whale*, 16–17.
30. Rieger, *God and the Excluded*, 51.

Chapter 3

1. Barth, *Protestant Theology in the Nineteenth Century*, 411.
2. Clements, *Friedrich Schleiermacher*, 36.
3. In *The Christian Faith*, he notes the novelty of applying the term "religion" to Christianity (Schleiermacher, *The Christian Faith*, 31). I have also consulted Schleiermacher's German text in *Der Christliche Glaube nach den Grundsätzen der Evangelischen Kirche im zusammenhange Dargestellt*, vol. 1.
4. Marina, "Schleiermacher on the Outpourings of the Inner Fire," 125–45.
5. Reynolds, "Reconsidering Schleiermacher and the Problem of Religious Diversity," 153. Reynolds credits the concept of dialectical pluralism to Anselm Min.
6. Ibid., 177.
7. Ibid., 174.
8. Richard Crouter notes that, while the relationship between these two works is a matter of some controversy among Schleiermacher scholars, "Schleiermacher never renounced the early book," which shares numerous elements in common with *The Christian Faith*. In Friedrich Schleiermacher, *On Religion*, 2.
9. As Thomas H. Curran writes, "We may say of Schleiermacher's *Glaubenslehre* that it theorizes upon or reflects upon the concrete expressions of actual Christian faith for the benefit of the government of (in this case) the Protestant German Church" (*Doctrine and Speculation in Schleiermacher's Glaubenslehre*, 52).
10. Schleiermacher, *The Christian Faith*, 42.
11. Schleiermacher, *On Religion*, 95. It is true that Schleiermacher also insists on the social character of religion. Indeed, Clements suggests that Schleiermacher's "view of religion is . . . fundamentally communal," since he "continually sees the human

self in relation to other selves in the actual world of space and time," and since "The feeling of absolute dependence can only be communicated and cultivated by human fellowship" (*Friedrich Schleiermacher*, 38). Nonetheless, the fact remains that Schleiermacher's stress is on the foundational piety (*Frömmigkeit*), which is fundamentally interior. The relationship between the interior or individual and the social dimensions is perhaps most clearly stated in Schleiermacher, *On Religion*, where he writes: "Once there is religion, it must necessarily also be social. That not only lies in human nature but also is preeminently in the nature of religion" (163). The progression is telling: *once* there is religion, it must *then* be social. Perhaps Schleiermacher means this to be a logical rather than a temporal priority, but either way, the priority of the interior is clear.

12. Schleiermacher, *The Christian Faith*, 18–19.
13. Ibid., 61.
14. Ibid., 21, 23.
15. Ibid., 25.
16. Ibid., 5.
17. Ibid., 29.
18. Ibid., 8–9. Schleiermacher echoes this in *On Religion*: Religion's essence "is neither thinking nor acting, but intuition and feeling" (102). What, precisely, Schleiermacher means by *Gefühl* is not easy to untangle. Louis Roy contends that *Gefühl* for Schleiermacher is "prereflective consciousness," and thus "transcends affectivity" ("Consciousness according to Schleiermacher," 217–19). I remain unconvinced. Schleiermacher's care in distinguishing *Gefühl* from Knowing suggests that he intends a state of consciousness that, whatever else it is, is not *cognitive*. Furthermore, I take his use of terms such as "pious emotions" (*fromme Erregungen*) and "religious affections" (*frommen Gemütszustände*) as clarifying his sense of *Gefühl*, not leading us astray, as Roy contends.
19. Schleiermacher, *The Christian Faith*, 22. On the feeling of absolute dependence, ibid., 26, 133. On piety, ibid., 171.
20. Ibid., 132.
21. Ibid., 34 (italics removed).
22. Ibid., 55.
23. Ibid.
24. See ibid., 31, 32.
25. Ibid., 35, 34 (italics removed). In this and similar cases, I prefer the use of the inclusive "human" for the translators' "man."
26. Ibid., 34, 35.
27. Ibid., 34–35.
28. Ibid., 37.
29. Ibid. Elsewhere, Schleiermacher speaks of "the partly one-sided and partly perverted mode" of God-consciousness in Judaism. Ibid., 319.
30. Ibid., 37.
31. Ibid., 38.
32. Schleiermacher, *On Religion*, 222.

33. Ibid.
34. Schleiermacher, *The Christian Faith*, 536.
35. Ibid., 53.
36. Ibid., 33.
37. Ibid., 54–55, also 355.
38. Ibid., 55, 56, 57. Schleiermacher claims that Judaism and Islam do not have redemption as "their main business," but treat it instead as a "derivative element." Ibid., 57.
39. Ibid., 63, 575.
40. Ibid., 477.
41. Ibid., 575.
42. Ibid., 425 (italics removed).
43. Ibid., 388.
44. Ibid., 527.
45. Ibid., 60 (italics removed), 61.
46. Ibid., 61, 380ff.
47. Ibid., 62.
48. Ibid., 729.
49. Ibid., 527.
50. Ibid., 478.
51. Ibid., 531.
52. Ibid., 107.
53. Ibid., 89.
54. Ibid., 43, 44.
55. On Philo, see ibid., 151. Schleiermacher's philosophical debt to the Jewish philosopher Spinoza is well known. However, this debt seems not to have translated into an interest in Judaism itself.
56. Ibid., 13, 26.
57. Crouter, in Schleiermacher, *On Religion*, 88n23.
58. Duke and Fiorenza, in Schleiermacher, *On the* Glaubenslehre, 6.
59. Schleiermacher, *The Christian Faith*, 76 (italics removed).
60. For the Dogmatics section of the *Glaubenslehre*, Schleiermacher is explicit in that he supports his doctrinal propositions with appeals to "the confessional documents of the Evangelical Church" or "in default of these, to the New Testament Scriptures" (ibid., 112, italics removed). On occasion he also cites pre-Reformation figures such as Augustine of Hippo and Anselm of Canterbury (e.g., ibid., 152–53).
61. Although at the time of writing the *Glaubenslehre* Schleiermacher was not officially aligned with Pietism, he characterized himself privately as a Moravian "of a higher order." See Clements, *Friedrich Schleiermacher*, 16.
62. Stoeffler, *German Pietism During the Eighteenth Century*, 144.
63. Rieger, *God and the Excluded*, 34.
64. Ibid., 35. For comparison, see also Jean-Paul Sartre's comments on the bourgeoisie's self-image as "universal class," in "A Plea for Intellectuals," 236.

65. Rieger, *Remember the Poor*, 26. Rieger explores Schleiermacher's own ties to colonialism in *Christ and Empire*, ch. 5.
66. Barth, "Concluding Unscientific Postscript on Schleiermacher," 80.
67. Clarke, *Deep Citizenship*, 11.
68. Ibid., 10.
69. Ibid., 14.
70. Ibid., 13.
71. Reynolds, "Reconsidering Schleiermacher," 177, 174.
72. Schleiermacher, *The Christian Faith*, 33.
73. Reynolds, "Reconsidering Schleiermacher," 176.
74. Schleiermacher, *The Christian Faith*, 33, 45.
75. Langer, "Jewish Understandings of the Religious Other," 271.
76. Ibid., 260–61.
77. Cf. Livingston, *Anatomy of the Sacred*, 307–8.
78. Easwaran, trans., *The Bhagavad Gita*, 162.
79. Easwaran comments: "Like a person walking around the same object, the Gita takes more than one point of view. Whenever Krishna describes one of the traditional paths to God he looks at it from the inside, extolling its virtues over the others. For the time being, that is *the* path." *The Bhagavad Gita*, 32.
80. Jayatilleke, "Extracts from 'The Buddhist Attitude to Other Religions,'" in Griffiths, ed., *Christianity Through Non-Christian Eyes*, 143.
81. Rieger, *Remember the Poor*, 24.
82. Schleiermacher, *The Christian Faith*, 37.
83. On the unicity of God, the Qur'an offers copious examples such as "Your God is one God! there is no god but He" (sura 2:163); "Say: He, Allah, is One. Allah is He on Whom all depend. He begets not, nor is He begotten. And none is like Him" (sura 112). On the punishment of idolaters, see, for example, sura 9:5: "Slay the idolaters wherever you find them, and take them captives and besiege them and lie in wait for them in every ambush."
84. Schleiermacher, *The Christian Faith*, 132.
85. *Holy Qur'an*, sura 1:2, 5–7.
86. Waines, *An Introduction to Islam*, 25.
87. The Qur'an describes Allah as the One "Who accepts repentance from His servants and pardons the evil deeds and He knows what you do; And He answers those who believe and do good deeds, and gives them more out of His grace; and (as for) the unbelievers, they shall have a severe punishment" (*Holy Qur'an*, sura 42:25–6).
88. This is even more striking given the well-known fact that he counted among his most intimate friends the Jewish couple Marcus and Henrietta Herz. See Clements, *Friedrich Schleiermacher*, 19–21.
89. Schleiermacher, *The Christian Faith*, 37.
90. Quoted in de Lange, *An Introduction to Judaism*, 34.
91. Ibid., 35.
92. Rieger, *God and the Excluded*, 36.
93. Ibid., 139.

94. See Schleiermacher, *The Christian Faith*, 575.

95. Ibid., 735, 729.

96. Ibid., 467, 536–37.

97. Fredericks, *Faith among Faiths*, 20. Fredericks cites Paul's Areopagus speech in Acts 17, as well as 1 Tim 2:4 and Rom 2:6–7.

98. Schleiermacher, *The Christian Faith*, 727. Although he does not use the qualifier "only" in his proposition 166, it is clear from the following discussion that he intends it. To those who argue that restriction of divine love to "the channel of redemption" is "unduly exclusive," Schleiermacher replies that "apart from redemption . . . divine love must always remain a matter of doubt." Ibid., 728.

99. Ibid., 729.

100. Ibid.

101. See ibid., 558–60, 720–22.

102. Ibid., 450. On civil authorities, see ibid., 470–73. On the separation of Church and world, see ibid., 582–85.

103. *The Book of Common Prayer and Administration of the Sacraments and Other Rites and Ceremonies of the Church* (New York: Oxford University Press, 1990), 304–5.

104. Hooker, *The Folger Library Edition of the Works of Richard Hooker*, vol. 2, 45.

105. Underhill, *The Essentials of Mysticism and Other Essays*, 101–3.

106. Rieger makes a similar point: "The focus on the self has the potential of opening theology more fully to all humanity. . . . All humanity is included since, at least in principle, everybody has access to some form of religious consciousness" (*God and the Excluded*, 33).

107. Schleiermacher, *The Christian Faith*, 260.

108. Ibid., 688.

109. Ibid., 676 (italics removed), 696.

110. Ibid., 678.

111. Ibid., 107.

112. For a recent analysis of covert religious belief in global capitalism, see Strenski, "The Religion in Globalization," 631–52.

Chapter 4

1. As is well known, Barth struggled with Schleiermacher and his legacy throughout his career. See, for example, his 1968 "Concluding Unscientific Postscript on Schleiermacher," in Barth, *Theologian of Freedom*, 66–90.

2. For a survey of the development of Barth's thought about religions, see Lai, "Barth's Theology of Religion," 248–49.

3. Barth, *Church Dogmatics*, I/2:281.

4. Knitter, *Introducing Theologies of Religions*, 26. For a survey of other scholars who see Barth as an exclusivist, see Harrison, "Karl Barth and the Nonchristian Religions," 209.

5. Di Noia, "Religion and the Religions," 244.

6. Ibid., 254–55.

7. Harrison, 208.

8. Ibid., 220, 223.

9. While I am mindful of the charge of a biographical fallacy here, Barth himself spoke of the role his personal experience played in his theology. See, for example, his "Concluding Unscientific Postscript on Schleiermacher," 70–75.

10. Barth, *Die Kirchliche Dogmatik*, I/2:377.

11. Busch, *The Great Passion*, 18–19. See also Barth, "Jesus Christ and the Movement for Social Justice," 33–34, 36.

12. Busch, 19.

13. Ibid., 19–20.

14. Rieger, *God and the Excluded*, 46.

15. Cf. Barth, *Church Dogmatics*, I/2:294.

16. These are my categories, not Barth's.

17. Barth, *Church Dogmatics*, I/2:1.

18. Barth is no biblicist. In *Church Dogmatics*, I/2, he writes: "It is really not laid upon us to take everything in the Bible as true *in globo*, but it is laid upon us to listen to its testimony when we actually hear it" (I/2:65). Barth's attitude toward Scripture will be discussed later in this chapter.

19. See, e.g., ibid., IV/3:96.

20. For example, he speaks of God's commission (to proclaim God's Word) as coming upon us "absolutely from without" (ibid., I/1:90). See also ibid., I/1:119–20.

21. Ibid., I/2:301.

22. Ibid., I/2:61.

23. Ibid., I/1:27–28.

24. Ibid., I/2:307.

25. Ibid., I/2:281–82.

26. Ibid., I/2:302.

27. Ibid., I/2:315.

28. Ibid., I/2:303.

29. Ibid., I/2:327.

30. Di Noia, 249–50. The 1956 English edition of *Church Dogmatics* I/2 translates *Unglaube* as "unbelief" (299).

31. Barth, *Church Dogmatics*, I/2:325.

32. Di Noia, 250.

33. Barth, *Church Dogmatics*, I/2:301.

34. Ibid., I/2:324.

35. Ibid.

36. Barth, *Die Kirchliche Dogmatik*, I/2:377.

37. Barth, *Church Dogmatics*, I/2:282.

38. Ibid., I/2:354.

39. The title in German of CD I/2, section 17 is "*Gottes Offenbarung als Aufhebung der Religion*" (Barth, *Die Kirchliche Dogmatik*, 304). This is rendered in the 1956 English translation as "The Revelation of God as the *Abolition* of Religion" (Barth, *Church Dogmatics*, I/2:280). Emphasis mine. As Di Noia argues, "abolition" is a misleading

translation of *Aufhebung*, which is better rendered "sublation" (245–46). Although Barth speaks of revelation "displacing" religion (*Church Dogmatics*, I/2:303), the displacement Barth has in mind is clearly a dialectical one.

40. Di Noia, 245, 248.
41. Barth, *Church Dogmatics*, I/2:282.
42. Di Noia, 251.
43. Barth, *Church Dogmatics*, I/2:350, 325.
44. Ibid., I/2:356.
45. Ibid., I/2:353–54. See also I/2:344–45 and IV/3:91.
46. Ibid., I/2:333.
47. It should be noted that Barth does mention the possibility that Pure Land Buddhism might develop toward "almost complete equality with Christian Protestantism." However, his subsequent comments indicate that it would still be unequal to Christianity, because it lacks "the name of Jesus Christ" (ibid., I/2:343).
48. Ibid., I/2:344, 343.
49. Buckley, "Christian Community, Baptism, and Lord's Supper," 202, 206.
50. Busch, 29. James J. Buckley notes that while Barth's early theology (e.g., his *Römerbrief*) was critical of the Church, by the time of the Göttingen Dogmatics (1921–22), he came to see the Church as the locus of authority in theology (Buckley, 200).
51. Barth, *Church Dogmatics*, I/2:344.
52. Ibid., I/2:358, 348.
53. Ibid., I/2:346.
54. See ibid., I/2:345.
55. Ibid., I/2:221.
56. Ibid., I/2:211.
57. "The Christian religion is simply the earthly-historical life of the Church and the children of God. As such we must think of it as an annexe to the human nature of Jesus Christ." Ibid., I/2:348.
58. Ibid., I/2:359.
59. Ibid., I/2:214.
60. Ibid.
61. Ibid., IV/3:88, 90.
62. Ibid., IV/3:88.
63. Ibid., I/2:342. Barth's term "Yodoism" comes from *Yodo-Shu* (*Jōdo-shū*), the school of Hōnen, and *Yodo-Shin-Shu* (*Jōdo-shin-shū*), the school of Shinran. *Jōdo* is Japanese for "Pure Land." The German edition uses "Jodo," while the English translation uses "Yodo."
64. Ibid., I/2:341.
65. Ibid., I/2:342.
66. Ibid., I/2:343.
67. Ibid.
68. Ibid., IV/3:101, 110.
69. Ibid., IV/3:101.
70. Harrison, 223.

71. Barth, *Church Dogmatics*, IV/3:124.
72. Ibid., IV/3:86, 88.
73. Ibid., IV/3:89–90.
74. Ibid., IV/3:100–1.
75. Ibid., IV/3:102. It is noteworthy that Barth criticizes not only Catholics, but also Protestants, including the Reformers, for succumbing to this tendency.
76. Ibid., IV/3:96–97, 110–11.
77. Ibid., IV/3:107.
78. Ibid.
79. Ibid., IV/3:108.
80. Ibid., I/2:14. He writes that "the aim of theology is to understand the revelation attested *in the Bible*" (ibid., I/2:7, emphasis mine). Although this passage is embedded in a conditional clause, it is clear from the following discussion that the conditional is in fact an assertion.
81. Ibid., I/1, section 4. George Hunsinger comments on this threefold form: "Jesus Christ is viewed by Barth as the truth of the gospel. This truth takes secondary form in the written testimony of the scripture, and tertiary form, so to speak, in the verbal testimony of the church. Neither form of testimony occurs in such a way that the truth of Jesus Christ is simply a semantic feature of those sentences by which this testimony is expressed" (*How to Read Karl Barth*, 171).
82. Hunsinger, *How to Read Karl Barth*, 171.
83. Barth, *Church Dogmatics*, I/2:280.
84. Ibid.
85. Barth, *Evangelical Theology*, 26.
86. Harrison, 215.
87. Fredericks, *Faith among Faiths*, 21.
88. Barth, *Church Dogmatics*, I/2:284–91.
89. Ibid., I/2:300, 302–3, 303–7.
90. Ibid., IV/3:90.
91. Cf. Lai, 257.
92. Barth bases this claim on the "clear" New Testament witness that humans have no knowledge of God except through Jesus Christ (see *Church Dogmatics*, I/2:301, 303–7).
93. Rieger, *Remember the Poor*, 30.
94. See Rieger, *God and the Excluded*, 140–46.
95. See Barth, *Church Dogmatics*, I/1:43, 113.
96. Ibid., I/1:113–14, 115.
97. Ibid., I/1:254, 257.
98. Ibid., I/1:256.
99. Ibid., I/2:314.
100. Ibid., I/1:60.
101. Bracher, *Lacan, Discourse, and Social Change*, 25.
102. Rieger speaks of the discourse of the Master as presenting "the illusion of being whole, undivided, self-identical" (*God and the Excluded*, 143, 142).
103. Ibid., 66–67.

104. Ibid., 145.
105. Ibid.
106. See ibid., 62.
107. See Barth, *Church Dogmatics*, IV/3:90–91.
108. His discussion of Pure Land Buddhism, while commendable for the reasons stated earlier, only serves to reinforce this assessment. In his study of Pure Land teacher Shinran, Alfred Bloom suggests that Barth's final dismissal of Shinran's teachings is due to "the lack of a sufficiently full presentation of [his] thought" (*Shinran's Gospel of Pure Grace*, vii). Discussing Bloom's critique, Waldrop notes that Barth's assessment of Pure Land is based on outdated information ("Karl Barth and Pure Land Buddhism," 588).
109. Harrison, 215.
110. Barth, *Church Dogmatics*, I/2:302.
111. See Flood, *An Introduction to Hinduism*, 11, 36.
112. Waldrop, 582.
113. Ibid., 583.
114. Barth, *Church Dogmatics*, I/2:325–26.
115. Waldrop, 594.
116. Ibid.
117. Barth, *Church Dogmatics*, I/2:342.
118. Quoted in Min, *The Solidarity of Others in a Divided World*, 8.
119. Rieger, *Christ and Empire*, 204.

Chapter 5

1. Lindbeck, *The Nature of Doctrine*, 15.
2. Surin, "'Many Religions and the One True Faith,'" 187. David Tracy argues that *The Nature of Doctrine* is in fact two books, one concerned with a "rule-theory" of doctrine (equivalent to Surin's second task), the other setting out a new "cultural-linguistic" paradigm for religion ("Lindbeck's New Program for Theology," 460). Lindbeck characterizes his theory as "non-theological" in Lindbeck, *The Nature of Doctrine*, 46.
3. Lindbeck writes that this model "emphasizes the cognitive aspects of religion and stresses the ways in which church doctrines function as informative propositions or truth claims about objective realities" (*The Nature of Doctrine*, 16). Lindbeck associates this model chiefly with premodern thought and gives it only cursory examination.
4. Ibid. It should be noted that Lindbeck also posits a combination of these two models, "favored especially by ecumenically inclined Roman Catholics" such as Karl Rahner and Bernard Lonergan (ibid.). However, he does not make much of this third approach.
5. Ibid., 34. As will be discussed below, Lindbeck does not altogether reject the notion that Christianity, and presumably other religions as well, makes first-order statements referring to a divine reality that transcends those statements. Nonetheless, his attention focuses on the dynamics and relations internal to a given religion.
6. Ibid., 37, 34.

7. Ibid., 37–38.

8. Ibid., 18.

9. Ibid., 30, 33.

10. Ibid., 62. Religion "is first of all a comprehensive interpretive medium or categorial framework within which one has certain kinds of experiences and makes certain kinds of affirmations." Ibid., 80.

11. Ibid., 83. At one point, however, Lindbeck attempts to nuance his otherwise unilateral account of the religion-experience relation. He claims that their relation is "dialectical" or "reciprocal" rather than unilateral: "Patterns of experience alien to a given religion can profoundly influence it" (ibid., 33). Lindbeck gives an example: "The warrior passions of barbarian Teutons and Japanese occasioned great changes in originally pacifistic Christianity and Buddhism." Yet it is difficult to reconcile this claim with Lindbeck's claim that "religions are producers of experience," or that religion "shapes the entirety of life and thought." This sliding between determinative and dialectical is confusing, to say the least. Furthermore, the dialectical aspect gets short shrift in Lindbeck's treatment, as Stephen Stell observes ("Hermeneutics in Theology and the Theology of Hermeneutics," 681.) Whatever Lindbeck's own commitment to a dialectical understanding of religion and experience, his project pivots on the notion that religion shapes (or determines) experience, not vice versa.

12. Lindbeck appeals to "anthropological, sociological, and philosophical literature" about religion, and mentions specifically Ludwig Wittgenstein, Peter Berger, and Clifford Geertz (*The Nature of Doctrine*, 17, 20). Lindbeck cites Proudfoot at ibid., 29n31. The Kantian element surfaces explicitly only once in *The Nature of Doctrine*: "A religion can be viewed as a kind of cultural and/or linguistic framework or medium that shapes the entirety of life and thought. It functions somewhat like a Kantian *a priori*, although in this case the *a priori* is a set of acquired skills that could be different" (ibid., 33). As C. John Sommerville notes, "The school of thinkers to which Lindbeck appeals argues that there is no uninterpreted experience and that anything that counts as an experience goes beyond an immediate intuition" ("Is Religion A Language Game?" 596).

13. Lindbeck, *The Nature of Doctrine*, 35.

14. Ibid., 18. See also ibid., 80. On Lindbeck's use of the term "doctrine," see Wood, Review of *The Nature of Doctrine*, 235.

15. Lindbeck, *The Nature of Doctrine*, 79. It should be noted that Lindbeck recognizes at least some of the problems inherent to this approach. He notes the difficulties involved in determining who is a competent practitioner in the diverse Christian context, given the fact that membership in a Christian community does not guarantee competence: "Most Christians through most of Christian history have spoken their own official tongue very poorly" (ibid., 99–100). Lindbeck's solution is to identify religious competence with those who are "flexibly devout" (the characteristics of which he identifies at ibid., 100). However, I believe that other problems remain. For one thing, who decides what is "flexible" and what is simply heterodox or heretical? Also, there is a troubling circularity to this: only

the religiously competent are qualified to determine who is religiously competent. Unfortunately, these issues lie beyond the scope of this work.

16. Ibid., 40.
17. Ibid., 48–49. It should be noted that Lindbeck slides from conditional language ("may be incommensurable") to assertorial language ("are incommensurable").
18. Ibid., 49.
19. Lindbeck, "The Gospel's Uniqueness," 226.
20. Lindbeck, *The Nature of Doctrine*, 49, emphasis mine.
21. Bruce D. Marshall, private communication, 7 February 2006.
22. Ibid.
23. Lindbeck, *The Nature of Doctrine*, 114.
24. Marshall, "Absorbing the World," 73.
25. The definition is Kathryn Tanner's, quoted in Marshall, "Absorbing the World," 72–73.
26. Ibid., 73–74.
27. Ibid., 74.
28. Marshall explains that while alien discourse "may not become necessary to its identity ('internal' in the strictest sense), it nonetheless has a legitimate and traceable location within the community's comprehensive vision of the world (and so is at least beneficial for the community to hold true)." Ibid.
29. Lindbeck, *The Nature of Doctrine*, 118.
30. Lindbeck, quoted in Marshall, "Absorbing the World," 80.
31. Lindbeck, quoted in Marshall, "Absorbing the World," 77.
32. Marshall, "Absorbing the World," 74.
33. Ibid., 76–77.
34. Ibid., 78. Lindbeck writes that "the reasonableness of a religion is largely a function of its assimilative powers, of its ability to provide an intelligible interpretation in its own terms of the varied situations and realities adherents encounter" (*The Nature of Doctrine*, 131).
35. Marshall continues: "Consequently, although one can apply the test of assimilative power to many different religions and worldviews, one cannot use this value to decide between alternative religions and their respective criteria of truth in the way in which one can, within a religion, apply its criteria to decide between competing truth claims" ("Absorbing the World," 82).
36. Ibid., 81.
37. Ibid., 76–77.
38. Sommerville, 597.
39. Lindbeck, *The Nature of Doctrine*, 62.
40. Nor, for that matter, does he explain why a given term should be called "religious" rather than, say, "cultural" or "political" or "scientific."
41. Lindbeck, *The Nature of Doctrine*, 49.
42. Marshall, "Absorbing the World," 73.
43. Knitter, *Introducing Theologies of Religions*, 183.
44. Lindbeck, *The Nature of Doctrine*, 80.

45. Ibid., 83.
46. Ibid., 65.
47. Ibid., 51.
48. The phrase "in the last instance" alludes to Louis Althusser's comment on Friedrich Engels's notion that society is determined by the economy "in the last instance": "The lonely hour of the 'last instance' never comes" (Althusser, *For Marx*, 113). "Coherentist" refers to the coherence theories of truth, which generally hold that truth is a function of the coherence of a statement or belief with other statements or beliefs in a system; this is opposed to (among other theories) a correspondence theory of truth, which holds that the truth of a statement or belief depends on how well it reflects the world.
49. In fact, Lindbeck also speaks of "categorial truth" and "intrasystematic truth." As Marshall notes, Lindbeck has acknowledged that this terminology confuses the issue ("Absorbing the World," 98n5). Following Marshall's lead, then, I will use the terms "categorial adequacy" and "intrasystematic coherence."
50. Lindbeck, *The Nature of Doctrine*, 48.
51. Marshall, "Absorbing the World," 71–72.
52. Lindbeck, *The Nature of Doctrine*, 48.
53. Marshall, "Absorbing the World," 72.
54. Lindbeck, *The Nature of Doctrine*, 64. Lindbeck gives an example and comment: "The crusader's battle cry '*Christus est Dominus*,' for example, is false when used to authorize cleaving the skull of the infidel (even though the same words in other contexts may be a true utterance). When thus employed, it contradicts the Christian understanding of Lordship as embodying, for example, suffering servanthood." Ibid.
55. Ibid.
56. Lindbeck, quoted in Marshall, "Absorbing the World," 80; Lindbeck, *The Nature of Doctrine*, 118.
57. Rieger, *God and the Excluded*, 149, 148.
58. That is, the terms of other religions are "subtracted from presentation" in the situation of a given religion. Feltham and Clemens, "An Introduction," 15.
59. Lindbeck, "The Gospel's Uniqueness," 229.
60. Lindbeck, *The Nature of Doctrine*, 32, 33.
61. Ibid., 18–19.
62. Ibid., 84.
63. Ibid., 34.
64. This presumably includes not only religious others (e.g., Hindus, Buddhists) but also what we might call "nonreligious" others, those who interpret experience and world according to other frameworks (e.g., Darwinian evolution, Marxism-Leninism). However, I will focus on religious others.
65. Fredericks, "A Universal Religious Experience?" 81.
66. Thus Lindbeck's statement that "It need not be the religion that is primarily reinterpreted as world views change, but rather the reverse: changing world views may be reinterpreted by one and same [*sic*] religion" (*The Nature of Doctrine*, 82).

67. Lindbeck, "Unbelievers and the 'Sola Christi,'" 78.
68. Ibid., 78–79.
69. Lindbeck, *The Nature of Doctrine*, 61.
70. Ibid., 61–62.
71. Ibid.
72. Ibid., 40.
73. He acknowledges his unfamiliarity with Islam in Lindbeck, "The Gospel's Uniqueness," 249.
74. Rudolf Otto's *Mysticism East and West* is cited at *The Nature of Doctrine*, 70n9; E. E. Evans-Pritchard's *Nuer Religion* at 136n3 and 135n2; Clifford Geertz's *Interpretation of Cultures* at 27n13, 43n16, 45n24, and 71n19; and Peter Berger's *The Sacred Canopy* at 27n10 and 28n23.
75. Lindbeck, "Unbelievers and the 'Sola Christi,'" 78.
76. Ibid., 80.
77. Ibid., 83.
78. Ibid.
79. Lindbeck, "Response to Michael Wyschogrod's 'Letter to a Friend,'" 205; Lindbeck, "Confession and Community," 495.
80. Lindbeck, "Confession and Community," 495.
81. Ibid., 493, 495.
82. Lindbeck, "The Gospel's Uniqueness," 248, 246.
83. Ibid., 249.
84. Rieger, *God and the Excluded*, 147.
85. Lindbeck, *The Nature of Doctrine*, 65.
86. Ibid., 114.
87. Thiemann, "Response to George Lindbeck," 378.
88. Along these lines, see for comparison David Tracy's conclusion that the cultural-linguistic approach is "a methodologically sophisticated version of Barthian confessionalism," with "occasional 'ad hoc' apologetic skirmishes" ("Lindbeck's New Program for Theology," 465, 469–70). Lindbeck, Tracy argues, "wants theology to be done purely from 'within' the confessing community" (ibid., 465–66).
89. Abhishiktānanda, *Saccidānanda*, 5.
90. Paul Knitter cites another positive point, Lindbeck's intent "to preserve, honor, and protect the real differences between the faiths. . . . [and] to make sure that [each religion's] identity and integrity are not violated by another religion" (182–83).
91. This is Rieger's term for what Lacan calls the "discourse of the university" (*God and the Excluded*, 146).
92. Ibid., 148.
93. Ibid., 150.
94. Indeed, Lindbeck at times seems to fear what lies beyond; for instance, he warns of the ever-present "*danger* . . . that . . . extrabiblical materials inserted into the biblical universe will themselves become the basic framework of interpretation" (*The Nature of Doctrine*, 118, emphasis mine).
95. Ibid., 62.

96. Cf. ibid., 100.
97. Marshall, "Absorbing the World," 76–77.
98. Marshall, private communication.
99. Cf. James L. Fredericks's critique in "A Universal Religious Experience," 81. For his part, Lindbeck acknowledges that "Those for whom conversation is the key to solving interreligious problems are likely to be disappointed" by his approach ("The Gospel's Uniqueness," 229).
100. Knitter, 224–25.
101. Amaladoss, "Interreligious Dialogue," 2.
102. Ibid.

Chapter 6

1. Gutiérrez, *A Theology of Liberation*, 174.
2. Gutiérrez, *Las Casas: In Search of the Poor of Jesus Christ*.
3. Simon Strong writes: "Peruvian society is still racist to its very core. For all the intermarriage, the economic scale from riches to rags can be correlated directly with skin color; the whites are the richest and the Indians are the poorest. . . . Dark skin is seen by the whites as ugly and worthless: National beauty contests exclude overly dark girls almost by definition. . . . The Indians are perceived to be an inferior race, the Achilles heel of the nation. . . . Indians' relationships with whites in Peru are on an almost exclusively servile footing. They and the poorer mestizos are forced to work for a pittance in order to survive because of chronic unemployment and underemployment" (*Shining Path*, 51–52).
4. Ferm, *Profiles in Liberation*, 155.
5. Levine and Mainwaring, "Religion and Popular Protest in Latin America," 206, 203.
6. For a survey and sociological study of guerrilla movements in Latin America, see Wickham-Crowley, "Winners, Losers, and Also-Rans," 132–81.
7. Although Washington usually justified this involvement on the basis of defense against communist "aggression," the underlying reason often was predominantly economic—to preserve U.S. access to cheap raw materials and U.S. dominance of Latin American markets.
8. Gutiérrez, "Search for Identity," 63.
9. Cadorette, *From the Heart of the People*, 103.
10. Gutiérrez, *A Theology of Liberation*, 11.
11. Ibid., xiv. In his 1991 work, *The God of Life*, Gutiérrez puts this point in slightly different terms, noting that Latin America is "the only continent in which the majority are at the same time Christian and poor" (48).
12. Gutiérrez, *A Theology of Liberation*, 12.
13. Ibid., xxi.
14. Ibid., 115.
15. Ibid., 12.
16. Ibid., 9.

17. Ibid., 81. Elsewhere, however, he equates theological reflection with "the understanding of the faith," present at least in "rough outline" in all Christians (3). He also states that "Theology must be critical reflection on humankind, on basic human principles" (9).
18. Ibid., 174.
19. Ibid., 10.
20. Nickoloff, in Gustavo Gutiérrez, *Essential Writings*, 6–7.
21. Gutiérrez, *A Theology of Liberation*, 9.
22. Ibid., 9–10.
23. Ibid., 34.
24. Ibid., 40–41.
25. Ibid., 147, 143.
26. Ibid., 96–97.
27. Ibid., 143.
28. The Vatican's Congregation for the Doctrine of the Faith sought to portray Gutiérrez as a Marxist. The Congregation's charges are contained in a 1983 document, "Ten Observations on the Theology of Gustavo Gutiérrez." This document, which more closely resembles slander than theological critique, accuses him of having an "uncritical acceptance of a Marxist interpretation," of reducing the Christian message to "the Marxist conception of history, structured around class struggle," and of reducing God to history. For a discussion and refutation of these absurd charges, see Brown, *Gustavo Gutiérrez*, 136–41. For his part, Gutiérrez briefly discusses the influence of Marxist thought on Christian theology at Gutiérrez, *A Theology of Liberation*, 8.
29. Gutiérrez, *A Theology of Liberation*, 85.
30. Ibid., 103.
31. Ibid., 86.
32. Ibid., 85.
33. Ibid.
34. Ibid., 104.
35. Christopher L. Chiappari puts Gutiérrez's connection of salvation and liberation this way: "Worldly liberation is a necessary but not sufficient condition for the realization of the Kingdom of God" ("Toward a Maya Theology of Liberation," 51).
36. Gutiérrez, *A Theology of Liberation*, 97. Gutiérrez depicts salvation history as a threefold process: creation; political liberation, understood as human self-creation; and re-creation and complete fulfillment (ibid., 86–90).
37. Ibid., 104. See also Chiappari, 51.
38. Gutiérrez, *A Theology of Liberation*, 84.
39. Ibid., 170–71.
40. Ibid., 171.
41. Berryman, *Liberation Theology*, 109.
42. Gutiérrez, *Las Casas*, 263.
43. Under the *encomienda* ("entrustment") system, Spanish settlers in the conquered lands were entrusted with Indians, on the pretext of evangelizing them; in fact the Indians so "entrusted" served as slaves to work the fields and the mines. Though

Las Casas himself had been an *encomendero* in Cuba, he gave up his position in order to work against the system. See Gutiérrez, *Las Casas*, 46–53.

44. Smith, "*Las Casas* as Theological Counteroffensive," 69.
45. Smith reaches a similar conclusion: "Gutiérrez allows the historical figure of Bartolomé de Las Casas to stand for and speak the truth that, really, he wants to and is also speaking. Las Casas has enunciated already what for Gutiérrez is the truth" (71). This is not to say that Las Casas serves as a mere mouthpiece for Gutiérrez, or that Gutiérrez skews his depiction of Las Casas so as to turn him into one. Gutiérrez supports his depiction with copious documentation from Las Casas' own writings, and he works to make clear the context (both theological and historical) in which Las Casas operated and the differences between Las Casas' context and Gutiérrez's own. See also Gutiérrez's comments on Las Casas in Gutiérrez, *The Density of the Present*, 107–8.
46. In *A Theology of Liberation*, Gutiérrez draws upon, for instance, Karl Marx (19), Che Guevara (56, 138), José Carlos Mariátegui (56), and Ernst Bloch (123–24). Gutiérrez's rationale for the use of the social sciences as theological sources can be found in his "Theology and the Social Sciences," in Gutiérrez, *Essential Writings*, 42–49.
47. Gutiérrez, *A Theology of Liberation*, xiv.
48. Gutiérrez, *Las Casas*, 226.
49. Ibid., 234.
50. Ibid., 261.
51. Gutiérrez, *A Theology of Liberation*, 144.
52. Ibid., 143–44.
53. Ibid., 45.
54. Ibid., 147.
55. Fredericks, *Faith among Faiths*, 73.
56. Gutiérrez, *A Theology of Liberation*, 46.
57. Ibid., 84.
58. Ibid., 109.
59. Ibid.
60. Heribert Mühlen, quoted in Gutiérrez, *A Theology of Liberation*, 112.
61. Gutiérrez, *Las Casas*, 254.
62. Ibid., 261.
63. Gutiérrez, *A Theology of Liberation*, xxxiv. Emphasis mine.
64. Ibid., 116.
65. Cleary and Steigenga, "Resurgent Voices," 5, 7.
66. Gutiérrez seems to recognize the deficiency in his introduction to the revised version of *A Theology of Liberation*, where he acknowledges the need for dialogue with "the various cultures to be found in Latin America." He cites Felipe Guamán Poma de Ayala, César Vallejo, José Carlos Mariátegui, and José María Arguedas, among others, as "Peruvians who . . . have been able to express, as few others have, the soul of the nation, its Amerindians and mestizos." He adds, "But, I repeat, this is an area in which far more remains to be done than has so far been accomplished" (xxxv).
67. Ibid., xxi.

68. Gutiérrez, *The God of Life*, 40.
69. Ibid., 2.
70. Gutiérrez, *A Theology of Liberation*, 86–87.
71. Gutiérrez, *The God of Life*, 67.
72. See Brown, 136–41.
73. Gutiérrez, *The God of Life*, 26.
74. Gutiérrez, *A Theology of Liberation*, 106.
75. Ibid., 109. In *The God of Life*, Gutiérrez writes that "Galatians 2:8 . . . makes it clear that due to the graciousness and holiness of God all are called to salvation. The call of Paul to evangelize the gentiles brings out the universality of the proclamation of Jesus Christ. If limitations are placed on this universalism, the message is distorted and mutilated, and an attempt is made to set up barriers to the inspiration of the Spirit" (31).
76. Heribert Mühlen, quoted in Gutiérrez, *A Theology of Liberation*, 112.
77. Gutiérrez, *The God of Life*, 27.
78. Ibid., 29.
79. Ibid.
80. Gutiérrez, *A Theology of Liberation*, 110; Gutiérrez, *The God of Life*, 47. Gutiérrez also expresses this point in terms of the presence or absence of God: "The God of Biblical revelation is known through interhuman justice. When justice does not exist, God is not known; God is absent" (*A Theology of Liberation*, 111). "When and where God's reign and demand that we 'do what is right and just' are denied, God is not present" (*The God of Life*, 69).
81. Gutiérrez, *The God of Life*, 49.
82. Ibid., 48.
83. Ibid., 56.
84. Gutiérrez, *A Theology of Liberation*, 21, 20.
85. Ibid., 106, 104.
86. Cleary, "New Voice in Religion and Politics in Bolivia and Peru," 45.
87. Barth, "Concluding Unscientific Postscript on Schleiermacher," 80.
88. Albó, "The Aymara Religious Experience," 159–61.
89. Ibid., 126.
90. Gutiérrez, *The God of Life*, 27.
91. Gutiérrez, *A Theology of Liberation*, 87.
92. Ibid., 97.
93. Ibid., 43.
94. Abe, "Buddhist *Nirvana*," 20.
95. Ibid., 21.
96. Ibid.
97. Ibid., 22.
98. Rieger, *God and the Excluded*, 153. Lacan's term is "discourse of the analyst." Rieger's alternative designation is based on the fact that the analyst's task in Lacanian psychoanalysis is "to relate to that which is repressed and marginalized" (ibid.).
99. Ibid., 155.

100. Ibid., 156.
101. Gutiérrez, *The God of Life*, 48.
102. Brown, 136–41.
103. Rieger, *God and the Excluded*, 158.
104. Ibid.
105. See the editors' introduction to Rostas and Droogers, eds., *The Popular Use of Popular Religion in Latin America*, 1–16.
106. Cleary and Steigenga, "Resurgent Voices," 5, 7.
107. Bourque, "The Power to Use and the Power to Change," 179–91.
108. Judd, "The Indigenous Theology Movement in Latin America," 215.
109. Chiappari, 60.
110. Cleary, 45.
111. Chiappari, 61. I take it that Chiappari's "they should be allowed to practice" is ironic.
112. Ibid.
113. Gutiérrez, *A Theology of Liberation*, xiv.
114. Of course, others have taken up this question since *A Theology of Liberation* was initially published in 1971. There has arisen a veritable cottage industry of liberation theologies both from Christians outside Latin America and from non-Christians. Since this literature is vast, I cannot give a full bibliography here. Some important representatives include: S. J. Samartha, ed., *Living Faiths*; Emmanuel Martey, *African Theology: Inculturation and Liberation*; Jung Young Lee, ed., *An Emerging Theology in World Perspective: Commentary on Korean Minjung Theology*; Choan-Seng Song, *Third-Eye Theology: Theology in Formation in Asian Settings*; Michael Amaladoss, *Making All Things New: Dialogue, Pluralism, and Evangelization in Asia*; and Raimon Panikkar, *The Cosmotheandric Experience: Emerging Religious Consciousness*.
115. See, for example, the essays in Cohn-Sherbok, ed., *World Religions and Human Liberation*, where liberation is presented from Jewish, Muslim, Hindu, Buddhist, and African perspectives.
116. Thomas, "Liberation for Life," 150. The liberation theologian Jon Sobrino recognizes the support interreligious dialogue can offer to a Christian theology of liberation. Reflecting on his own encounter with the religions of Asia, he writes that "in every religion there is an important seed of liberation. . . . By liberation I understand that which frees the poor from the proximity of death and encourages them to live" ("Eastern Religions and Liberation: Reflections on an Encounter," 114).

Conclusion

1. Gutiérrez, *A Theology of Liberation*, 81.
2. Wood, *Vision and Discernment*, 21, 39–40.
3. Ibid., 24.
4. Gutiérrez, *A Theology of Liberation*, 45.
5. Ibid., 147.
6. Fredericks, *Faith among Faiths*, 170–71.

7. In the interest of full disclosure, I should note that much of my own public work to date has been in the area of Buddhist–Christian comparative theology. See Brockman, "The Challenge of Yogācāra to David Tracy's Epistemology," 1–22; and Brockman, "An All-Pervading Self."

8. See, for example: Fredericks, *Faith among Faiths;* Fredericks, *Buddhists and Christians;* Clooney, *Hindu God, Christian God;* Keenan, *The Meaning of Christ.*

9. Fredericks, *Faith among Faiths*, 167–68.

10. Fredericks, *Buddhists and Christians*, 26.

11. Clooney does remark on the marginalizing tendencies in some Hindu and Christian theologies he compares in *Hindu God, Christian God.* See, for example, his discussions of Karl Barth and Kumārila, 166 and 168; and of Sudarśana and von Balthasar, 168. However, Clooney's investigation focuses not on the dynamics of power and repression, but on theological reasoning regarding the existence and identity of God, divine embodiment, and the role of revelation. See Clooney, *Hindu God, Christian God*, 12–13.

12. Clooney's *Hindu God, Christian God* recognizes the existence of such discursive structures. However, he speaks of them in terms of patterns of theological reasoning, rather than in terms of dynamics of power and repression.

13. Goizueta, "Knowing the God of the Poor," 144.

14. Young, *Feminist Theology/Christian Theology*, 19–20.

15. Tracy, *Blessed Rage for Order*, 46.

16. Mk 16:9 (the so-called "longer ending," probably not original to the gospel); Jn 20:14–18.

17. Catherine Keller notes that "in the idea . . . of three persons who share one essence, each person distinct in identity and functions yet inseparable from the others, the basis of an alternative metaphysic symbolically suggests itself: a metaphysic of internally related individuals, pointing toward the radically social and interdependent character of all individuality." Keller, *From a Broken Web*, 166. Catherine Mowry LaCugna explores similar implications in *God for Us: The Trinity and Christian Life.*

18. Barth, "The Humanity of God," 46–66. For an exploration of logical and other problems raised by the concept of God incarnate, see Hick, *The Metaphor of God Incarnate*, especially 47–88. While I do not share Hick's negative assessment of the Chalcedonian formulation, I believe that he raises important issues that neither christology nor theological anthropology can afford to ignore.

19. See Habito, *Experiencing Buddhism*, 47–51. I should note that my own experience in Zen meditation also leads me to believe that *anattā* is in some sense true. For my own thoughts on this, see Brockman, "Encountering 'the Event' as Event."

20. Some PhD programs are already moving in a similar direction. Boston University, for instance, requires its PhD students to have training in two religious traditions. See the Boston University Web site: http://www.bu.edu/religion/graduate/index.html.

21. Possible examples might include the *varna/jati* (caste) system, teachings about the preferability of male children, and the tradition of *sati* (widow suicide).

22. Examples include Mitter, *Dharma's Daughters*, and works in the recent tradition of engaged Buddhism.

23. Of course, the World Wide Web is no panacea. Internet access is drastically limited, especially among those socially and economically marginalized others we wish to reach. The proliferation and rapid obsolescence of computer technology has created environmental problems that remain unresolved. And there is the problem of cultural imperialism that inevitably accompanies the diffusion of Western technology —the phenomenon of "McDonaldization." However, scholars and theologians should be able to make the technology work for good, to promote intercultural and interreligious awareness.
24. Fredericks, *Faith among Faiths*, 112.
25. Gutiérrez, *A Theology of Liberation*, 137, 138.
26. Panikkar, *Christophany*.
27. Ibid., 11, 12.
28. Ibid., 12.
29. Ibid., 13.
30. Ibid., 31–35.
31. Ibid., 5.
32. Ibid., 174–75.
33. She now labels herself a "salimist" theologian, from the Korean word "salim," meaning "making things alive." Union Theological Seminary faculty page for Chung Hyun Kyung. URL: http://www.utsnyc.edu/Page.aspx?pid=355. Accessed 18 June 2010.
34. Chung, *Struggle to Be the Sun Again*.
35. Chung, "'Han-pu-ri,'" 52–62. See also Chung, "Seeking the Religious Roots of Pluralism," 399–402.
36. Chung, "Seeking the Religious Roots," 402.
37. Chung, interview, 14. For an examination of responses to Chung's "syncretism," see Kim, "Spirit and 'Spirits' at the Canberra Assembly of the World Council of Churches, 1991," 349–65. Panikkar makes a similar observation about christology in *Christophany*, 4.
38. Chung, "Seeking the Religious Roots," 401; Poethig, "Riffing about the Rim," 53–60.
39. Chung, "Seeking the Religious Roots," 400–1.
40. Habito, "Buddhist? Christian? Both? Neither?" 51–3. For additional perspectives on MRB, see Cornille, "Double Religious Belonging," 43–49; and Carlson, "Responses," 77–83.
41. Recently I was handed a pamphlet from the North American Mission Board of the Southern Baptist Convention. On the cover is a single question: "Do you *know for certain* that you have ETERNAL LIFE and that you will go to Heaven when you die?" (emphasis mine). While the stress on certitude addresses a deep human desire for security, it too often translates to a "holier than thou" attitude toward those who are different (God does not hear the prayers of Jewish persons, etc.).

Appendix

1. I also recommend the very accessible discussions of Badiou's philosophy in Feltham and Clemens, "An introduction to Alain Badiou's philosophy"; and Hallward,

"Generic Sovereignty," 87–111. Readers interested in exploring Badiou's philosophy in greater depth can consult Hallward, *Badiou: A Subject to Truth* and Feltham, *Alain Badiou: Live Theory.*

2. Readers interested in a more detailed discussion of Badiou's trajectory might consult Barker, *Alain Badiou*, 1–12.

3. The influence of Lacan and Althusser carries through into Badiou's mature philosophy. His notion of truth resembles Lacan's Real; his notion of the event resembles Althusser's epistemological break.

4. Badiou, *Theory of the Subject.* Chapter 1 of *Théorie de la Contradiction* has appeared in English in "An Essential Philosophical Thesis," 669–77.

5. However, Badiou never made a complete and decisive break from Maoism. Rather than an "ex-Maoist," he is probably best considered a "post-Maoist": he explored Maoist thought, took what he found useful, and moved beyond it. The continuing influence of Mao on Badiou's thought can be seen, for instance, in "Beyond Formalisation," 116–21. Bruno Bosteels comments on Badiou's continuing debt to Maoism in "Logics of Antagonism," 93–107.

6. Badiou, *Being and Event.*

7. Jason Barker calls it "Badiou's defiant riposte to the postmodern condition" (*Alain Badiou*, 4).

8. Barker, 4, emphasis in the original.

9. Ibid. For an in-depth examination of the mathematical foundations of Badiou's thought, see Hallward, *Badiou*, 49–106.

10. Badiou, *Ethics*; Badiou, *Saint Paul.*

11. Badiou, *Logics of Worlds.*

12. As Hallward notes, Badiou's distinction between consistency and inconsistency "remain[s] one of the most confusing in all of Badiou's work for first-time readers" (*Badiou*, 90). Hallward explains the distinction this way: while "pure or inconsistent multiplicity is the very being of being," "consistency is the attribute of *a* coherent presentation of such inconsistent multiplicity as *a* multiplicity, that is, as a coherent collecting of a multiplicity into a unity, or one" (ibid.).

13. Badiou, *Ethics*, 25.

14. Badiou, *Manifesto for Philosophy*, 36. Of the three types of situations Badiou identifies, only the historical is pertinent to my argument in this book. The other two, natural and neutral situations, are discussed in Feltham and Clemens, 24–25. The historical situation differs from the other two in that it has at least one "evental site."

15. Badiou, "Truth," 121.

16. Feltham and Clemens, 11.

17. Ibid., 9–10.

18. Just as in set theory there is no "universal set," so for Badiou there is no universal situation. As I mentioned in Chapter 3, Badiou distinguishes between *belonging* and *inclusion*. Hallward describes the distinction thusly: "Elements or members belong to a set; subsets or parts are included in it" (*Badiou*, 85). In other words, belonging is a function of the "count-for-one" that creates the situation, while inclusion is an action of the state (or governing order). Generally speaking, I use

the term *exclusion* as the opposite of Badiou's *belonging*; I use the term *marginaliza-tion* as the opposite of Badiou's *inclusion*.

19. Feltham and Clemens, 15.
20. Hallward, "Introduction," 8. As Hallward points out, Badiou makes a further dis-tinction between the void and the "edge" of the void. The void is uncountable. The edge of the void, on the other hand, "is occupied by that foundational element which, as far as the situation is concerned, contains nothing other than the void." For example, in the numerical situation of positive integers, the void is zero, whereas the edge of the void is 1, that number that "contains" nothing but zero. Ibid.
21. For instance, let m equal the set of all males, and f equal the set of all females. The intersection of m and f is the null set ($m \cap f = \varnothing$). Yet $\varnothing$ is also a member of both sets, m and f.
22. Badiou, *Ethics*, 68. Hallward links the void to Badiou's ontological pluralism: "Inconsistent multiplicity is the very being of being and the sole ground of a truth. . . . Every situation . . . includes a link to this ontological ground, namely that which, considered according to the criteria whereby the situation counts its elements, remains uncountable . . . . Whereas inconsistent multiplicity, as the 'stuff' counted by any situation, is itself effectively meta-situational, this nothing or *void* is always void *for* a situation. The void is inconsistent multiplicity 'accord-ing to a situation'" ("Introduction," 8).
23. Badiou, *Being and Event*, 77. Elsewhere, Badiou also notes that there is only one void for any given situation: "There are not 'several' voids, there is only one void; rather than signifying the presentation of the one, this signifies the unicity of the unpresentable such as marked within presentation" (*Being and Event*, 69).
24. Feltham and Clemens, 15–16.
25. Hallward, "Generic Sovereignty," 92.
26. Ibid.
27. Ibid.
28. Hallward, "Introduction," 9. "In a national [situation], for example, whose elements include the population *counted as* nationals, the state is what organises its parts as taxpayers, voters, social security recipients, criminals, and so on" (ibid., 92).
29. Badiou, "Truth," 123.
30. See Badiou, *Ethics*, 142n2.
31. Badiou, *Infinite Thought*, 47.
32. Ibid., 54, 48–49.
33. Ibid., 48–49, 52.
34. Hallward, *Badiou*, 159.
35. Ibid., 154.
36. Ibid.
37. Although he acknowledges that different people within a given situation will have different access to its knowledge, Badiou holds that within any given situation "there is always an encyclopaedia of knowledge which is the same for everybody [in that situation]"; Badiou sees this encyclopaedia of knowledge as ultimately

identical to the Marxist concept of a dominant ideological *dispositif* (apparatus) (*Infinite Thought*, 171).

38. Ibid., 62.

39. Hallward, "Introduction," 9.

40. Badiou, *Infinite Thought*, 61. Badiou also speaks of truth as "subtracted" from what is known. As Hallward notes, Badiou uses the term *soustraction* to mean "that truth *is* properly immediate, and so is *revealed* (comes to be) through the elimination of the mediate. It means that the living reality of human experience is what remains after the whole realm of the 'cultural' has been 'deposed' (though not eliminated)" ("Generic Sovereignty," 97).

41. Badiou, "Truth," 121.

42. Ibid., 124.

43. Hallward, *Badiou*, 155. Hallward notes that Badiou conceives the human subject "as the bearer of a truth that exceeds him [*sic*]" (ibid., 180).

44. Badiou, *Ethics*, 70.

45. Ibid., 41–42.

46. Ibid., 67.

47. Ibid., 69.

48. The evental site is not easily explained. Hallward calls the role it plays "one of the most important and most slippery aspects of Badiou's philosophy of truth" (*Badiou*, 117).

49. Hallward, "Introduction," 9.

50. Badiou, *Ethics*, 41.

51. Ibid.

52. Ibid., 43.

53. Hallward, *Badiou*, 141.

54. Badiou, *Saint Paul*, 81.

55. Hallward, *Think Again*, 2–3.

Bibliography

Abe, Masao. "Buddhist *Nirvana*: Its Significance in Contemporary Thought and Life." In Samartha, *Living Faiths and Ultimate Goals*, 12–22.

Abhishiktananda. *Saccidānanda: A Christian Approach to Advaitic Experience*. Delhi: ISPCK, 1984.

Albó, Xavier. "The Aymara Religious Experience." In *The Indian Face of God in Latin America*, edited by Manuel M. Marzal, Eugenio Maurer, Xavier Albó, and Bartomeu Melià, translated by Penelope R. Hall, 119–67. Maryknoll, NY: Orbis Books, 1996.

Althusser, Louis. *For Marx*. Translated by Ben Brewster. New York: Verso, 1996.

Amaladoss, Michael. "Interreligious Dialogue: A View from Asia." *International Bulletin of Missionary Research* 19, no. 1 (1995): 2–5.

———. *Making All Things New: Dialogue, Pluralism, and Evangelization in Asia*. Maryknoll, NY: Orbis Books, 1990.

Ariarajah, Wesley. *The Bible and People of Other Faiths*. Geneva: World Council of Churches, 1985.

Badiou, Alain. *Being and Event*. Translated by Oliver Feltham. New York: Continuum, 2005.

———. "Beyond Formalisation: An Interview." Translated by Bruno Bosteels and Alberto Toscano. *Angelaki* 8, no. 2 (August 2003): 116–21.

———. "An Essential Philosophical Thesis: 'It Is Right to Rebel against the Reactionaries.'" Translated by Alberto Toscano. *Polygraph* 13, no. 3 (2005): 669–77.

———. *Ethics: An Essay on the Understanding of Evil*. Translated by Peter Hallward. New York: Verso, 2002.

———. *Infinite Thought: Truth and the Return to Philosophy*. Translated and edited by Oliver Feltham and Justin Clemens. New York: Continuum, 2003.

———. *Logics of Worlds*. Translated by Alberto Toscano. New York: Continuum, 2009.

———. *Manifesto for Philosophy*. Translated and edited by Norman Madarasz. Albany, NY: State University of New York Press, 1999.

———. *Saint Paul: The Foundation of Universalism*. Translated by Ray Brassier. Stanford, CA: Stanford University Press, 2003.

———. *Theory of the Subject*. Translated by Bruno Bosteels. New York: Continuum, 2009.

———. "Truth: Forcing and the Unnameable." In Alain Badiou, *Theoretical Writings*, edited and translated by Ray Brassier and Alberto Toscano, 120–33. New York: Continuum, 2004.

Barker, Jason. *Alain Badiou: An Introduction*. Sterling, VA: Pluto Press, 2002.

Barth, Karl. *Church Dogmatics*. 2nd ed. Translated by G. W. Bromiley. Edited by G. W. Bromiley and T. F. Torrance. New York: T&T Clark International, 2004.

———. "Concluding Unscientific Postscript on Schleiermacher." In Barth, *Theologian of Freedom*, 66–90.

———. *Evangelical Theology: An Introduction*. Translated by Grover Foley. New York: Holt, Rinehart and Winston, 1963.

———. "Jesus Christ and the Movement for Social Justice." In Hunsinger, *Karl Barth and Radical Politics*, 19–45.

———. *Die Kirchliche Dogmatik*. I/2. Vierte Auflage. Zollikon-Zürich: Evangelischer Verlag, A.G., 1948.

———. *Protestant Theology in the Nineteenth Century: Its Background and History*. New ed. Translated by Brian Cozens and John Bowden. 1959. Grand Rapids, MI: William B. Eerdmans, 2001.

———. *Theologian of Freedom*. Edited by Clifford Green. Minneapolis: Augsburg Fortress, 1991.

Berger, Peter L. *The Sacred Canopy: Elements of a Sociological Theory of Religion*. New York: Anchor Books, 1990.

Berryman, Phillip. *Liberation Theology*. New York: Pantheon Books, 1987.

Bloom, Alfred. *Shinran's Gospel of Pure Grace*. Ann Arbor, MI: Association for Asian Studies, 1965.

The Book of Common Prayer and Administration of the Sacraments and Other Rites and Ceremonies of the Church. New York: Oxford University Press, 1990.

Bosteels, Bruno. "Logics of Antagonism: In the Margins of Alain Badiou's 'The Flux and the Party.'" *Polygraph* 15/16 (2004): 93–107.

Bourque, Nicole. "The Power to Use and the Power to Change: Saints' Cults in a Quichua Village in the Central Ecuadorian Highlands." In Rostas and Droogers, *The Popular Use*, 179–91.

Bowman, John. *The Samaritan Problem: Studies in the Relationships of Samaritanism, Judaism, and Early Christianity*. Translated by Alfred M. Johnson, Jr. Pittsburgh: Pickwick Press, 1975.

Bracher, Mark. *Lacan, Discourse, and Social Change: A Psychoanalytic Cultural Criticism*. Ithaca, NY: Cornell University Press, 1993.

Brockman, David R. "An All-Pervading Self: The Challenge of the Tathāgatagarbha Tradition to Christian Theological Anthropology." Unpublished presentation to the Philosophy of Religion section, Southwest Regional meeting of the American Academy of Religion, March 2004.

———. "The Challenge of Yogācāra to David Tracy's Epistemology." *Koinonia* XV (2003): 1–22.

———. "Encountering 'The Event' as Event: Transforming Christian Theological Reflection about Religious Others." In *Event and Decision: Ontology and Politics in Badiou, Deleuze, and Whitehead*, edited by Roland Faber and Henry Krips, 279–301. Newcastle on Tyne, UK: Cambridge Scholars Publishing, forthcoming.

———. "Thinking Theologically about Religious Others." In *The Gospel among the Religions: Theology, Ministry, and Spirituality in a Global Context*, edited by David R. Brockman and Ruben L. F. Habito. Maryknoll, NY: Orbis Books, 2010.

Brown, Robert McAfee. *Gustavo Gutiérrez: An Introduction to Liberation Theology*. Maryknoll, NY: Orbis Books, 1990.

Buckley, James J. "Christian Community, Baptism, and Lord's Supper." In Webster, *The Cambridge Companion to Karl Barth*, 195–211.

Busch, Eberhard. *The Great Passion: An Introduction to Karl Barth's Theology*. Translated by Geoffrey W. Bromiley. Edited by Darrell L. Guder and Judith J. Guder. Grand Rapids, MI: William B. Eerdmans Publishing Company, 2004.

Cadorette, Curt. *From the Heart of the People: The Theology of Gustavo Gutiérrez*. Oak Park, IL: Meyer-Stone Books, 1988.

Carlson, Jeffrey Daniel. "Responses." *Buddhist-Christian Studies* 23 (2003): 77–83.

Chiappari, Christopher L. "Toward a Maya Theology of Liberation: The Reformulation of a 'Traditional' Religion in the Global Context." *Journal for the Scientific Study of Religion* 41, no. 1 (2002): 47–67.

Choan-Seng Song. *Third-Eye Theology: Theology in Formation in Asian Settings*. Rev. ed. Maryknoll, NY: Orbis Books, 1979.

Choi Man Ja. "Feminine Images of God in Traditional Religion." In *Frontiers in Asian Christian Theology: Emerging Trends*, edited by R. S. Sugirtharajah, 80–89. Maryknoll, NY: Orbis Books, 1994.

Chung Hyun Kyung. "'Han-pu-ri': Doing Theology from Korean Women's Perspective." In *Frontiers in Asian Christian Theology: Emerging Trends*, edited by R. S. Sugirtharajah, 52–62. Maryknoll, NY: Orbis Books, 1994.

———. Interview. *Zion's Herald*, 177, no. 5 (September/October 2003): 14–16.

———. "Seeking the Religious Roots of Pluralism." *Journal of Ecumenical Studies* 34, no. 3 (Summer 1997): 399–402.

———. *Struggle to Be the Sun Again: Introducing Asian Women's Theology*. Maryknoll, NY: Orbis Books, 1990.

Clarke, Paul Barry. *Deep Citizenship*. Chicago: Pluto Press, 1996.

Cleary, Edward L. "New Voice in Religion and Politics in Bolivia and Peru." In Cleary and Steigenga, *Resurgent Voices*, 43–64.

Cleary, Edward L., and Timothy J. Steigenga. "Resurgent Voices: Indians, Politics, and Religion in Latin America." In Cleary and Steigenga, *Resurgent Voices*, 1–24.

———, ed. *Resurgent Voices: Indians, Politics, and Religion in Latin America*. Piscataway, NJ: Rutgers University Press, 2004.

Clements, Keith. *Friedrich Schleiermacher: Pioneer of Modern Theology*. San Francisco: Collins, 1987.

Clooney, Francis X. *Hindu God, Christian God: How Reason Helps Break Down the Boundaries between Religions*. New York: Oxford University Press, 2001.

Cohn-Sherbok, Dan. *The Crucified Jew: Twenty Centuries of Christian Anti-Semitism*. Grand Rapids, MI: William B. Eerdmans, 1997.

———, ed. *World Religions and Human Relations*. Maryknoll, NY: Orbis Books, 1992.

Cornille, Catherine. "Double Religious Belonging: Aspects and Questions." *Buddhist-Christian Studies* 23 (2003): 43–49.

Cracknell, Kenneth. *In Good and Generous Faith: Christian Responses to Religious Pluralism*. Peterborough, UK: Epworth, 2005.

Craddock, Fred B. *Luke*. Interpretation series. Louisville, KY: John Knox Press, 1990.

Crosby, Alfred W. *Ecological Imperialism: The Biological Expansion of Europe, 900–1900*. New York: Cambridge University Press, 1986.

Crossan, John Dominic. *Jesus: A Revolutionary Biography*. New York: HarperCollins Publishers, 1994.

Crouter, Richard. "Introduction." In Schliermacher, *On Religion*, xi–xxxix.

Curran, Thomas H. *Doctrine and Speculation in Schleiermacher's Glaubenslehre*. New York: Walter de Gruyter, 1994.

de Lange, Nicholas. *An Introduction to Judaism*. New York: Cambridge University Press, 2000.

De Silva, Lynn A. *The Problem of the Self in Buddhism and Christianity*. New York: Barnes & Noble, 1979.

Di Noia, Joseph. "Religion and the Religions." In Webster, *Cambridge Companion to Karl Barth*, 243–57.

Duke, James, and Francis Fiorenza. "Translators' Introduction." In Schleiermacher, On the Glaubenslehre, 1–32.

Easwaran, Eknath, trans. *The Bhagavad Gita*. Tomales, CA: Nilgiri Press, 1985.

Eck, Diana L. *A New Religious America: How a "Christian Country" Has Become the World's Most Religiously Diverse Nation*. San Francisco: HarperSanFrancisco, 2001.

Eckstein, Susan, ed. *Power and Popular Protest: Latin American Social Movements*. Berkeley: University of California Press, 1989.

Feltham, Oliver. *Alain Badiou: Live Theory*. New York: Continuum, 2008.

Feltham, Oliver, and Justin Clemens. "An Introduction to Alain Badiou's Philosophy." In Badiou, *Infinite Thought*, 1–38.

Ferm, Deane William. *Profiles in Liberation: 36 Portraits of Third World Theologians*. Mystic, CT: Twenty-Third Publications, 1988.

Flood, Gavin. *An Introduction to Hinduism*. New York: Cambridge University Press, 1996.

Foucault, Michel. *The Archaeology of Knowledge and the Discourse on Language*. Translated by A. M. Sheridan Smith. New York: Pantheon Books, 1972.

Fredericks, James L. *Buddhists and Christians: From Comparative Theology to Solidarity*. Maryknoll, NY: Orbis Books, 2004.

———. *Faith among Faiths: Christian Theology and Non-Christian Religions*. Mahwah, NJ: Paulist Press, 1999.

———. "A Universal Religious Experience? Comparative Theology as an Alternative to a Theology of Religions." *Horizons* 22, no. 1 (1995): 67–87.

Goizueta, Roberto S. "Knowing the God of the Poor: The Preferential Option for the Poor." In Rieger, *Opting for the Margins*, 143–56.

Griffiths, Paul J., ed. *Christianity Through Non-Christian Eyes*. Maryknoll, NY: Orbis Books, 1990.

Gutiérrez, Gustavo. *The Density of the Present: Selected Writings.* Maryknoll, NY: Orbis Books, 1999.

———. *Essential Writings.* Edited by James B. Nickoloff. Maryknoll, NY: Orbis Books, 1996.

———. *The God of Life.* Translated by Matthew J. O'Connell. Maryknoll, NY: Orbis Books, 1991.

———. *Las Casas: In Search of the Poor of Jesus Christ.* Translated by Robert R. Barr. Maryknoll, NY: Orbis Books, 1993.

———. "Search for Identity." Translated by Fred Murphy. *Latin American Perspectives* 19, no. 3 (Summer 1992): 61–66.

———. *A Theology of Liberation: History, Politics, and Salvation.* Rev. ed. Translated by Sister Caridad Inda and John Eagleson. Maryknoll, NY: Orbis Books, 1988.

Habito, Ruben L. F. "Buddhist? Christian? Both? Neither?" *Buddhist-Christian Studies* 23 (2003): 51–53.

———. *Experiencing Buddhism: Ways of Wisdom and Compassion.* Maryknoll, NY: Orbis Books, 2005.

———. "Maria Kannon Zen: Explorations in Buddhist-Christian Practice." *Buddhist-Christian Studies* 14 (1994): 145–56.

Hallward, Peter. *Badiou: A Subject to Truth.* Minneapolis: University of Minnesota Press, 2003.

———. "Generic Sovereignty: The Philosophy of Alain Badiou." *Angelaki* 3, no. 3 (1998): 87–111.

———. "Introduction: Consequences of Abstraction." In Hallward, *Think Again,* 1–20.

———, ed. *Think Again: Alain Badiou and the Future of Philosophy.* New York: Continuum, 2004.

Harrison, Peter. "Karl Barth and the Nonchristian Religions." *Journal of Ecumenical Studies* 23, no. 2 (Spring 1986): 207–24.

Heup Young Kim. *Christ and the Tao.* Hong Kong: Christian Conference of Asia, 2003.

Heyes, Cressida J. *Line Drawings: Defining Women Through Feminist Practice.* Ithaca, NY: Cornell University Press, 2000.

Hick, John. *The Metaphor of God Incarnate: Christology in a Pluralistic Age.* Louisville, KY: Westminster/John Knox Press, 1993.

Holy Qur'an. Translated by M. H. Shakir. Elmhurst, NY: Tahrike Tarsile Qur'an, Inc., 1985.

Hooker, Richard. *The Folger Library Edition of the Works of Richard Hooker.* Vol. 2 (*Laws*, book V), edited by W. Speed Hill. Cambridge, MA: Belknap Press of Harvard University Press, 1977.

Hopkins, Dwight N. *Shoes That Fit Our Feet: Sources for a Constructive Black Theology.* Maryknoll, NY: Orbis Books, 1993.

Hunsinger, George. *How to Read Karl Barth: The Shape of His Theology.* New York: Oxford University Press, 1991.

———, ed. *Karl Barth and Radical Politics.* Philadelphia: Westminster Press, 1976.

Isasi-Díaz, Ada María. *Mujerista Theology: A Theology for the Twenty-first Century.* Maryknoll, NY: Orbis Books, 1996.

Jayatilleke, K. N. "Extracts from 'The Buddhist Attitude to Other Religions.'" In Griffiths, ed., *Christianity Through Non-Christian Eyes*, 141–52.

John Paul II. *Slavorum Apostoli* (June 2, 1985). http://www.vatican.va/holy_father/john_paul_ii/encyclicals/documents/hf_jp-ii_enc_19850602_slavorum-apostoli_en.html (accessed June 30, 2008).

Judd, Stephen P. "The Indigenous Theology Movement in Latin America: Encounters of Memory, Resistance, and Hope at the Crossroads." In Cleary and Steigenga, *Resurgent Voices*, 210–30.

Jung Young Lee, ed., *An Emerging Theology in World Perspective: Commentary on Korean Minjung Theology*. Mystic, CT: Twenty-Third Publications, 1988.

Keenan, John P. *The Meaning of Christ: A Mahāyāna Christology*. Maryknoll, NY: Orbis Books, 1989.

Keller, Catherine. *From a Broken Web: Separation, Sexism, and Self.* Boston: Beacon Press, 1986.

Kim, Kirsteen. "Spirit and 'Spirits' at the Canberra Assembly of the World Council of Churches, 1991." *Missiology: An International Review* 32, no. 3 (July 2004): 349–65.

Knitter, Paul F. *Introducing Theologies of Religions.* Maryknoll, NY: Orbis Books, 2002.

———. *One Earth Many Religions: Multifaith Dialogue and Global Responsibility.* Maryknoll, NY: Orbis Books, 1995.

Kwok Pui-lan. *Introducing Asian Feminist Theology.* Cleveland: Pilgrim Press, 2000.

Lacan, Jacques. *Ecrits: A Selection.* Translated by Bruce Fink. New York: W.W. Norton, 2002.

LaCugna, Catherine Mowry. *God for Us: The Trinity and Christian Life.* San Francisco: HarperSanFrancisco, 1991.

Lai Pan-chiu. "Barth's Theology of Religion and the Asian Context of Religious Pluralism." *Asia Journal of Theology* 15, no. 2 (October 2001): 247–67.

Langer, Ruth. "Jewish Understandings of the Religious Other." *Theological Studies* 64, no. 2 (June 2003): 255–77.

Lee, Jung Young. *The Trinity in Asian Perspective.* Nashville: Abingdon Press, 1996.

Lee, Jung Young, ed. *An Emerging Theology in World Perspective: Commentary on Korean Minjung Theology.* Mystic, CT: Twenty-Third Publications, 1988.

Levine, Daniel H., and Scott Mainwaring. "Religion and Popular Protest in Latin America: Contrasting Experiences." In Eckstein, *Power and Popular Protest*, 203–40.

Lindbeck, George A. *The Church in a Postliberal Age.* Edited by James J. Buckley. Grand Rapids, MI: William B. Eerdmans Publishing Company, 2002.

———. "Confession and Community: An Israel-like View of the Church." *The Christian Century* 107, no. 16 (May 9, 1990): 492–96.

———. "The Gospel's Uniqueness: Election and Untranslatability." In Lindbeck, *The Church in a Postliberal Age*, 223–52.

———. *The Nature of Doctrine: Religion and Theology in a Postliberal Age.* Philadelphia: Westminster Press, 1984.

———. "Response to Michael Wyschogrod's 'Letter to a Friend.'" *Modern Theology* 11, no. 2 (April 1995): 205–10.

———. "Unbelievers and the '*Sola Christi.*'" In Lindbeck, *The Church in a Postliberal Age*, 77–87.

Livingston, James C. *Anatomy of the Sacred: An Introduction to Religion*. 5th ed. Upper Saddle River, NJ: Pearson Education, 2005.

Lochhead, David. *The Dialogical Imperative: A Christian Reflection on Interfaith Encounter*. Maryknoll, NY: Orbis Books, 1988.

Marina, Jacqueline. "Schleiermacher on the Outpourings of the Inner Fire: Experiential Expressivism and Religious Pluralism." *Religious Studies* 40, no. 2 (June 2004): 129–43.

Marshall, Bruce D. "Absorbing the World: Christianity and the Universe of Truths." In *Theology and Dialogue: Essays in Conversation with George Lindbeck*, edited by Bruce D. Marshall, 69–103. Notre Dame, IN: University of Notre Dame Press, 1990.

———. Private communication. February 7, 2006.

Martey, Emmanuel. *African Theology: Inculturation and Liberation*. Maryknoll, NY: Orbis Books, 1993.

May, Todd. *Gilles Deleuze: An Introduction*. New York: Cambridge University Press, 2005.

McGrath, Alister E. *Christian Theology: An Introduction*. Cambridge, MA: Blackwell, 1994.

McGuire, Meredith B. *Religion: The Social Context*, 5th ed. Belmont, CA: Wadsworth Thomson Learning, 2002.

McLaren, Peter. *Che Guevara, Paulo Freire, and the Pedagogy of Revolution*. Lanham, MD: Rowman & Littlefield, 2000.

Min, Anselm Kyongsuk. *The Solidarity of Others in a Divided World: A Postmodern Theology after Postmodernism*. New York: T&T Clark, 2004.

Mitter, Sara. *Dharma's Daughters: Contemporary Indian Women and Hindu Culture*. New Brunswick, NJ: Rutgers University Press, 1991.

Nicholas of Cusa. *De Pace Fidei and Cribratio Alkorani*. 2nd ed. Translated by Jasper Hopkins. Minneapolis: Arthur J. Banning Press, 1994. http://cla.umn.edu/sites/jhopkins/CAI-12-2000.pdf (accessed July 23, 2007).

Nickoloff, James B. "Introduction." In Gutiérrez, *Essential Writings*, 1–22.

Olson, Charles. "COLE'S ISLAND." In *Selected Poems*, edited by Robert Creeley. Berkeley: University of California Press, 1993.

Palanca, Ellen H. "Religion and Economic Development." In *God and Global Justice*, edited by Frederick Ferré and Rita H. Mataragnon, 65–83. New York: Paragon House, 1985.

Panikkar, Raimundo. *Christophany: The Fullness of Man*. Translated by Alfred DiLascia. Maryknoll, NY: Orbis Books, 2004.

———. *The Cosmotheandric Experience: Emerging Religious Consciousness*. Maryknoll, NY: Orbis Books, 1993.

———. *The Intrareligious Dialogue*. Rev. ed. New York: Paulist Press, 1999.

Petrella, Ivan, Luiz Carlos Susin, and Marcella Althaus-Reid, ed. *Reclaiming Liberation Theology: Another Possible World*. New York: SCM Press, 2007.

Pieris, Aloysius. *An Asian Theology of Liberation*. Maryknoll, NY: Orbis Books, 1988.

Poethig, Kathryn. "Riffing about the Rim: Breakfast with Chung Hyun Kyung." *Journal of Women and Religion* 13 (1995): 53–60.

Race, Alan. *Christians and Religious Pluralism: Patterns in the Christian Theology of Religions.* Maryknoll, NY: Orbis Books, 1983.

Reynolds, Thomas. "Reconsidering Schleiermacher and the Problem of Religious Diversity: Toward a Dialectical Pluralism." *Journal of the American Academy of Religion* 73, no. 1 (March 2005): 151–81.

Rieger, Joerg. *Christ and Empire: From Paul to Postcolonial Times.* Minneapolis: Fortress Press, 2007.

———. *God and the Excluded: Visions and Blindspots in Contemporary Theology.* Minneapolis: Fortress Press, 2001.

———, ed. *Opting for the Margins: Postmodernity and Liberation in Christian Theology.* New York: Oxford University Press, 2003.

———. *Remember the Poor: The Challenge to Theology in the Twenty-First Century.* Harrisburg, PA: Trinity Press International, 1998.

———, ed. *Theology from the Belly of the Whale: A Frederick Herzog Reader.* Harrisburg, PA: Trinity Press International, 1999.

Rostas, Susanna, and André Droogers, ed. *The Popular Use of Popular Religion in Latin America.* Amsterdam: CEDLA, 1993.

Roy, Louis. "Consciousness according to Schleiermacher." *The Journal of Religion* 77, no. 2 (April 1997): 217–32.

Samartha, S. J., ed. *Living Faiths and Ultimate Goals: Salvation and World Religions.* Maryknoll, NY: Orbis Books, 1974.

Sartre, Jean-Paul. "A Plea for Intellectuals." In *Between Existentialism and Marxism: Sartre on Philosophy, Politics, Psychology, and the Arts,* translated by John Mathews, 228–85. New York: Pantheon Books, 1974.

Schleiermacher, Friedrich. *The Christian Faith.* Edited by H. R. Macintosh and J. S. Stewart. Edinburgh: T&T Clark, 1999.

———. *Der Christliche Glaube nach den Grundsätzen der Evangelischen Kirche im zusammenhange Dargestellt.* Vol. 1. Berlin: Walter de Gruyter, 1960.

———. *On the* Glaubenslehre: *Two Letters to Dr. Lücke.* Translated by James Duke and Francis Fiorenza. Atlanta: Scholars Press, 1981.

———. *On Religion: Speeches to Its Cultured Despisers.* Translated by Richard Crouter. New York: Cambridge University Press, 1988.

Smith, Christian. "*Las Casas* as Theological Counteroffensive: An Interpretation of Gustavo Gutiérrez's *Las Casas: In Search of the Poor of Jesus Christ.*" *Journal for the Scientific Study of Religion* 41, no. 1 (2002): 69–73.

Sobrino, Jon. "Eastern Religions and Liberation: Reflections on an Encounter." In Cohn-Sherbok, *World Religions,* 113–26.

Sommerville, C. John. "Is Religion A Language Game? A Real World Critique of the Cultural-Linguistic Theory." *Theology Today* 51, no. 4: 594–99.

Song, Choan-Seng. *Third-Eye Theology: Theology in Formation in Asian Settings.* Rev. ed. Maryknoll, NY: Orbis Books, 1979.

Stell, Stephen L. "Hermeneutics in Theology and the Theology of Hermeneutics: Beyond Lindbeck and Tracy." *Journal of the American Academy of Religions* 51, no. 4 (Winter 1993): 679–703.

Stoeffler, F. Ernst. *German Pietism During the Eighteenth Century.* Leiden: E. J. Brill, 1973.

Strenski, Ivan. "The Religion in Globalization." *Journal of the AAR* 72, no. 3 (September 2004): 631–52.

Strong, Simon. *Shining Path: Terror and Revolution in Peru.* New York: Times Books, 1992.

Suchocki, Marjorie Hewitt. "In Search of Justice: Religious Pluralism from a Feminist Perspective." In *The Myth of Christian Uniqueness*, edited by John Hick and Paul F. Knitter, 149–61. Maryknoll, NY: Orbis Books, 1987.

Surin, Kenneth. "'Many Religions and the One True Faith': An Examination of Lindbeck's Chapter Three." *Modern Theology* 4, no. 2 (January 1988): 187–209.

Thangaraj, M. Thomas. *The Crucified Guru: An Experiment in Cross-cultural Christology.* Nashville: Abingdon Press, 1994.

Thiemann, Ronald. "Response to George Lindbeck." *Theology Today* 43, no. 3 (October 1986): 377–82.

Thomas, Norman E. "Liberation for Life: A Hindu Liberation Philosophy." *Missiology: An International Review* 16, no. 2 (April 1988): 149–62.

Tracy, David. *Blessed Rage for Order: The New Pluralism in Theology.* Minneapolis: Seabury Press, 1975.

———. "Lindbeck's New Program for Theology: A Reflection." *The Thomist* 49, no. 3 (July 1985): 460–72.

Underhill, Evelyn. *The Essentials of Mysticism and Other Essays.* New York: AMS Press, 1976.

Union Theological Seminary faculty page for Chung Hyun Kyung. URL: http://www.utsnyc.edu/Page.aspx?pid=355. Accessed June 18, 2010.

Waines, David. *An Introduction to Islam.* New York: Cambridge University Press, 1995.

Waldrop, Charles T. "Karl Barth and Pure Land Buddhism." *Journal of Ecumenical Studies* 2, no. 4 (Fall 1987): 574–97.

Waters, Malcolm. *Globalization.* 2nd ed. New York: Routledge, 2001.

Webster, John, ed. *The Cambridge Companion to Karl Barth.* New York: Cambridge University Press, 2000.

Wickham-Crowley, Timothy P. "Winners, Losers, and Also-Rans: Toward a Comparative Sociology of Latin American Guerrilla Movements." In Eckstein, *Power and Popular Protest*, 132–81.

Wood, Charles M. Review of *The Nature of Doctrine. Religious Studies Review* 11, no. 3 (July 1985): 235–40.

———. *Vision and Discernment: An Orientation in Theological Study.* Atlanta: Scholars Press, 1985.

Young, Pamela Dickey. *Feminist Theology/Christian Theology: In Search of Method.* Minneapolis: Augsburg Fortress, 1990.

Index

CPSIA information can be obtained at www.ICGtesting.com
Printed in the USA
BVOW040521220212

283489BV00002B/6/P